Eastern North America's

WILDFLOWERS

Louis C. Linn

A Sunrise Book

E. P. DUTTON   NEW YORK

Dedicated to the Glory of God
and the memory of my husband

Text prepared by Ruth Hearn Linn under the direct supervision of Dr. Frederick G. Meyer, Supervisory Botanist In-Charge of the Herbarium, U.S. National Arboretum, Washington, D.C.

Library of Congress Cataloging in Publication Data

Linn, Louis C.
  Eastern North America's wildflowers.

  "A Sunrise book."
  Includes index.
  1. Wildflowers—United States—Identification.
  I. Title.
  QK115.L56   582′.13′0973   77-4314

ISBN: 0-87690-262-X

Published simultaneously in Canada by Clarke, Irwin & Company Limited, Toronto and Vancouver

10 9 8 7 6 5 4 3 2 1

First Edition

Printed in Hong Kong

Acknowledgments

-»»

This book could never have come into existence without the devoted and continuous supervision, help, and encouragement of Dr. Frederick G Meyer, Director of the Herbarium of the National Arboretum. More than twenty-five years after Louis Linn's death, I took his work to Dr. Meyer. The paintings, Dr. Meyer told me, were as timely as when they were done. And while a number of field guides existed with beautiful color photographs, there was not yet in the United States a field book of painted flowers in which every detail was in focus.

Dr. Meyer sent me first to Dr. John Churchill, who had prepared an herbarium for the University of Michigan. He too was enthusiastic, and patiently and painstakingly researched each plant and updated the taxonomy. For months, he devoted a day of each weekend to the project.

Dr. Meyer then set himself the task of supervising a script. He made the library of the National Arboretum available to me, and after thirteen months, three writings, and numerous trips to the herbarium, a text has slowly evolved. He has read, corrected, and reread it, mostly home at nights. His patience, work, unflagging interest, and faith in the project have made it possible.

Dr. William Steere, President Emeritus and Senior Scientist at the Botanical Garden in New York, after seeing the paintings and learning that Dr. Meyer was supervising the text, volunteered to write individual letters to Garden Club presidents, conservation groups, and, later, publishers in support of the publication of the book. This he faithfully did, and the approval of the work by such an outstanding authority in the field has gained it the endorsement of such groups.

I am grateful for the support and enthusiasm of Mrs. George P. Bissell, Jr., President of the Garden Club of America, and

Mrs. Vernon L. Conner, President of the National Council of State Garden Clubs. They either reviewed the work themselves or had competent board members review it, and endorsed it to their respective executive committees. Each wrote that the field guide was unanimously endorsed.

It also has the approval of the National Wildlife Federation and the Audubon Naturalist Society.

Dr. Stanwyn G. Shetler, President of the Audubon Naturalist Society of the Central Atlantic States, and Associate Curator at the Department of Botany at the Smithsonian Institution, had a special showing of the paintings in the institution's botanical department for the benefit of his colleagues and some members of his board of directors. He has continued to be helpful and encouraging and to offer moral and tangible support (in the form of letters to publishers) in his capacity as president of the Audubon Naturalist Society.

Also without the competent, cheerful, and interested help and constant cooperation of Jackie Schafer, who typed the whole manuscript, I would have been lost.

No acknowledgment should fail to record my great indebtedness to the authorities in print in the field: Fernald's eighth edition of *Gray's Manual of Botany,* Gleason's revised *Britton and Brown Illustrated Flora,* and Lawrence's *Taxonomy of Vascular Plants.* All scientific names and data about leaves and flowers were checked with these authorities.

Contents

─────────────────────────────────────

⋙⋙⋙⋙⋙⋙⋙⋙⋙⋙⋙⋙⋙⋙⋙⋙⋙⋙⋙⋙⋙⋙⋙⋙⋙⋙⋙⋙⋙⋙⋙

Foreword

As a field guide, *Eastern North America's Wildflowers* supplies
a much-needed aid to identification of our most common wildflowers. It was the aim of the late Louis C. Linn, who was an
artist, to produce a wildflower guide in the medium of watercolors; his sudden death more than a quarter of a century ago
delayed its publication until now. These wildflower paintings
have achieved the highest degree of structural accuracy and
fidelity of color that is possible in the medium of watercolors.
All the paintings were done on location, and they convey the
spirit and vitality of the living flowers. Ruth Linn's decision to
publish the paintings at this time is a tribute to her late husband. Mrs. Linn's text is written in simple, nontechnical lan-
guage, and the descriptions of the plants are concise and to the
point. A short glossary has been provided to define special terms
that must be used in describing flowers, and line drawings of
leaf and flower types and parts are intended to explain the terms
visually. Descriptions of the flower families are included to
show the book's user that individual plants, like humans,
belong to families and that kinship among plants is an attribute
everywhere present in nature. Plants are grouped into families
by virtue of their common close relationships.

The object of the book is to enable easy recognition of 372
of the common and rarer wildflowers found in various parts of
the eastern United States. This is a small proportion of the
perhaps 6000 species of flowering plants that occur in the area
covered by this guide. We hope that your acquaintance with
these 372 will stimulate a further interest in wildflowers and
in their conservation, because many kinds have become increas-
ingly rare in recent years.

Frederick G. Meyer

Introduction

Louis Linn's purpose in painting wildflowers was twofold: to preserve them and to enrich the life of the beholder. He wanted to alert people to the existence of wildflowers so they would not carelessly step on some small half-hidden bloom, pass by some marvel of creation with an unseeing eye, or gather great armfuls of gorgeous color that would be wilted in the next half hour. He wanted to share with others the thrill of recognizing wildflowers by name; he wanted to help them see and wonder at the intricate beauty of even a weed.

As a nine-year-old riding one day with his father in a horse-drawn buggy, Louis Linn's eyes were filled with the blue of the tall weeds growing thickly by the road. What were they? Home again, later in the day, he searched around the farm and found similar flowers, but they were faded and dying. Why were the flowers so beautiful by the road and so ugly and dying at home?

The next morning he was surprised to see all the chicory plants full of bright new blue flowers. And so he learned that each bloom lasts only for a morning. A lifetime of interest was awakened in him.

Louis Linn had no degree in botany, but always painted. He attended evening classes at the Corcoran Art Gallery in Washington, D.C., while in high school; then studied two years full time at the Academy of Fine Arts in Philadelphia. Still later he painted with the Art Student's League in New York. He designed textiles and furniture and wrote and illustrated stories about nature. When he came home from the First World War, he decided to devote himself to painting. He lived in a beautiful natural setting, 5 acres on the Potomac River near Washington, a wildflower haven with woods, rich open ground, and river banks. There he encouraged and cherished a succession of wildflowers from Spring-Beauties to the latest-blooming fall asters.

Botanists from the universities around Washington encouraged him to paint the wildflowers. He never went out without a sketch pad and watercolor box, and usually sketched and painted a flower from two positions. The flower was never picked. Once a plant was located and in bud, he would wait for it to reach full maturity. Sometimes the weather would turn warmer, and on the next visit the flower would be past its prime, or a thunder storm would have scattered it. Then a new plant had to be found. He made numerous trips to Maine, Long Island, western New York State, the pine barrens of New Jersey, the mountains of Maryland and Virginia and the Southern Appalachians, the bogs of the Carolinas and northern Florida. In this way the paintings accumulated over a period of thirteen years.

Louis Linn purposely limited the number of watercolors in the book because he wanted the flowers to be shown life-size. Some are bountiful in the southern states and rarer in more northern ones, or the reverse. Some are demanding as to habitat and can survive in only a few areas. A few are in danger of extinction. Although the flowers are found primarily in the eastern United States, many of the plants occur as far west as eastern Kansas and north to Canada.

The plants are arranged chronologically according to season: spring, summer, and autumn. The first are those that bloom earliest in the spring. Of course, some flowers, such as the Common Dandelion, start blooming in early spring and continue through the summer, even straggling into late fall. In general, each flower is placed according to its main blooming season, but this may vary depending on altitude, latitude, and other factors.

How to Use This Book to Identify Wildflowers

Those of you who are mainly interested in identifying wildflowers should first enjoy the book's life-size illustrations and have the thrill of recognizing some flowers with which you are already familiar. For these and others you will probably want to go on to read their descriptions in the text. This way you will have some idea of the kinds of information the book can supply before going into the field.

At first glance you may feel it is unnecessary or too technical to give the Latin as well as the common name. In the Arrowheads, for example, some authors have selected characteristics of the plant to help individualize the common name (such as broad-leaved) but the Latin name assures its identity all over the world.

In the descriptions, each plant's height is given. Height varies somewhat depending on soil, weather, etc., yet it immediately separates those plants which are ground covers, low-growing plants, and tall ones.

Of greatest importance in identification is habit. It includes:

1. General overall appearance (for example, a single stem, many stems from the base, much branched, etc.)
2. The size and shape of the leaves and their position on the stem
3. The characteristics of the stem itself (examples: smooth, hairy, square, etc.)
4. The parts, the color, and form of the flower

Some botanical words have been used to describe leaves and flowers as they save whole sentences of description. These words are defined in the glossary, pages 268–271. On pages 266–267 are line drawings of types of leaves and flowers. And, of course, most of the wildflowers' individual characteristics may be seen immediately in the paintings.

The habitat tells where the plant may be found, its range of territory, and its entire blooming season.

The Color Key to Identification, which precedes the paintings, is another tool, although a somewhat arbitrary one as colors are variable. The key is also grouped by seasons. If, on a walk, you see a white flower in the spring, you need to search only among those paintings listed under *white spring* flowers.

While you may find many flowers which are not illustrated here, the book does include examples from seventy flower families. Descriptions of these families are grouped together on pages 251–265 giving the characteristics on which they are based. By referring to these you may have the satisfaction of classifying the flower you see in the proper family even if that particular flower is not included in the illustrations.

Most of all, I urge you to treasure the loveliness of flowers that grow in the wild. When they have ceased to bloom, you will still have their unfading images at hand in Louis Linn's water-color paintings.

Ruth Hearn Linn

Color Key to Identification

-»»

The arrangement of flowers in color groups has to be somewhat arbitrary because:

1. Flowers are rarely a pure color. Some flowers are multi-colored—tinged, streaked, spotted—or definitely bi-colored.
2. Individual species of plants may vary in color depending on the quality and acidity (or lack of it) of the soil, the amount of sunshine received, and other environmental factors.
3. Color is subjective—all eyes do not see colors alike.

The color groups are:

1. White (cream-colored, slightly greenish, or tinged with other colors)
2. Greenish to yellowish
3. Pale to golden yellow
4. Orange to red
5. Pink to red
6. Pink to lavender
7. Lavender to blue
8. Purplish
9. Brownish

Those starred are cross referenced and listed in two or more appropriate groups.

The color key does not apply to members of the Composite Family, such as asters, goldenrod, sunflowers, and their relatives. Individual identification depends on other than flower characteristics. See index for page references.

White (cream-colored, slightly greenish,
or tinged with other colors)

Spring
Harbinger-of-spring
Common Chickweed
*Trailing Arbutus (pink-red)
Spring Cress
Garlic Mustard
Bloodroot
Dogs'-tooth Violet
Dutchman's-breeches
Squirrel-corn
Twinleaf
Pussytoes
Early Saxifrage
Rue-anemone
Wood Anemone
Cut-leaved Toothwort
Crinkleroot
Shepherd's Purse
Rock Cress
Small Bitter Cress
Johnny-jump-up
Pale violet
Pennywort
*Pyxie-moss (pink-red)
Rock Cress
Wild Strawberry
Blackberry
Star Chickweed
Field Chickweed
Mouse-ear Chickweed
May-apple
Wild Stonecrop
*Wild Comfrey (lavender-
    blue)
Field Daisy
*Foxglove Beardtongue
    (lavender)
False Spikenard
Starry False Solomon's-seal
Star-of-Bethlehem
Water Arum
Indian Physic

Summer
*Cancer-root (pink-lavender)
*Water-willow

White Clover
Daisy Fleabane
Yarrow
Waterleaf
Goat's-beard
Black Cohosh
Tall Meadow-rue
Thimbleweed
White Avens
Starry Campion
Japanese Honeysuckle
Spotted Wintergreen
Pipsissewa
Indian Pipe
*Moth Mullen (yellow)
Lizard's-tail
Partridge-berry
*Large Houstonia (purplish)
Rough Bedstraw
White Wild Licorice
Queen Anne's Lace
*Horse Nettle (purplish)
Grass-of-Parnassus
Seneca Snakeroot
Common Mallow
*Hedge Bindweed (pink-red)
Dropseed
Pearly Everlasting
White-topped Aster
Dog-fennel
Enchanter's Nightshade
Wintergreen
*Pokeberry (greenish)
White Sweet Clover
*Hemp-nettle
    (pink-lavender)
Thimbleweed
Virgin's-bower
Culver's-root
Flowering Spurge
Water-parsnip
New Jersey Tea
*Fog-fruit (pink, blue)
Evening Lychnis

Water-plantain
Arrowhead
Water-lily
Rattlesnake-plantain
Nodding Ladies'-tresses
Spring Ladies'-tresses
Devil's-bit
Round-leaved Sundew
Venus's-flytrap
Biennial Gaura
Crimson-eye Rose-mallow
White Woodland Aster
White Snakeroot
Boneset
Fireweed
Round-leaved Pyrola
White Vervain
*Wild Mint (lavender,
   purplish)
Catnip
Black Nightshade

Sand Vine
Wild or Prickly Cucumber

Autumn
Jumpseed
Turtlehead
*Mock Pennyroyal (lavender-
   blue)
Mountain-mint or Basil
Perilla
Small White Aster
White Aster
*Smooth Aster (lavender-
   blue)
*Heart-leaved Aster
   (lavender-blue)
White Heath Aster
Silver-rod
Catfoot or Cudweed
Rattlesnake-root
Live-forever
Climbing False Buckwheat

Greenish to Yellowish

Spring
Golden Saxifrage
Blue Cohosh
Jack-in-the-pulpit
Skunk Cabbage
Solomon's-seal
Indian Cucumber
Puttyroot
Dragon Arum

Summer
Curly Dock
*Wood-betony (purplish)
*Pokeberry (white)

Autumn
Closed Gentian
*Lady's-thumb (pink-red)
*Common Smartweed (pink-
   red)
*Halberd-leaved Tearthumb
   (pink-red)

Pale to Golden Yellow

Spring
Dog's-tooth Violet
Golden Corydalis
Golden Ragwort
Common Dandelion
Swamp Buttercup

Small-flowered Crowfoot
Winter Cress
Smooth Yellow Violet
Trumpets
Early Meadow Parsnip
Cinquefoil

Tall Buttercup
Celandine
Yellow Wood-sorrel
Rattlesnake-weed
Dwarf Dandelion
Golden Star
Bellwort
Yellow Lady's-slipper
Small Yellow Lady's-slipper
Cynthia

Summer
Common Sundrops
Fringed Loosestrife
Moneywort
Yellow Clover
Low Hop Clover
Black-eyed Susan
Tickseed
Gold-eyed Grass
Common St. Johnswort
Golden St. Johnswort
St. Andrew's Cross
Spotted St. Johnswort
Yellow Meadow Lily
Great Mullein
*Moth Mullein (white)
*Butter-and-eggs (orange)
Smooth False Foxglove
*Yellow Milkwort (orange)
Four-leaved Loosestrife
Swamp Candle
Common Dodder
Whorled Rosinweed
Sharp-leaved Goldenrod
Tansy
Black Mustard
Wild Indigo
Yellow Melilot
Partridge-pea
Rattlebox
Pencil Flower

*American Germander
  (pink-lavender)
Common or Tall Buttercup
*Jewelweed (orange-red)
Pale Jewelweed
Water-stargrass
Yellow Pond-lily
Evening Primrose
Seedbox
Jerusalem Artichoke
Sneezeweed
Tall Coneflower
Tall Tickseed
Tall Sunflower
Rosinweed
Leafcup
Tickseed-sunflower
Thin-leaved Coneflower
Yellow Ironweed
Crown-beard
Early Goldenrod
Hawkweed
Wild Sensitive-plant
Wild Senna
Virginia Ground-cherry
Agrimony
Norway Cinquefoil

Autumn
Yellow False Foxglove
Richweed
Golden-aster
Larger Bur-marigold
Spanish Needles
Beggar-ticks
Slender Goldenrod
Blue-stemmed Goldenrod
Stout Goldenrod
Spreading Goldenrod
Coneflower
Elecampane
Smaller Bur-marigold

Orange to Red

Spring
*Columbine (pink-red)

Summer
Trumpet-vine

Day-lily
*Butter-and-eggs (yellow)
Sheep Sorrel
*Yellow Milkwort (yellow)
Butterfly-weed
Common or Scarlet
    Pimpernel

*Jewelweed (yellow)
Blackberry-lily

Autumn
None

Pink to Red

Spring
*Liverleaf (lavender-blue)
*Trailing Arbutus (white)
Spring-beauty
*Columbine (orange-red)
Downy Phlox
*Ground Phlox (purplish)
*Pyxie-moss (white)
Wild Pink
Wild Geranium
Pink Wood-sorrel
Pink Lady's-slipper
Showy Lady's-slipper
Daisy Fleabane

Swamp Milkweed
*Hedge Bindweed (white)
Mountain Phlox
Pink Wild Bean
*Fog-fruit (blue)
Wood Lily
Meadow-beauties
Musk Mallow
Tick-trefoil
*Ground Nut or Wild Bean
    (brownish)
Spreading Dogbane
Cardinal Lobelia
Rose-gentian

Summer
Pasture Rose
Sweetbriar Rose
Leather-flower
Bouncing Bet
Deptford Pink
Rose Pogonia
Grass-pink

Autumn
Prince's Feather
*Lady's-thumb (greenish)
Common Smartweed
    (greenish)
*Halberd-leaved Tearthumb
    (greenish)
Hardhack

Pink to Lavender

Spring
Shooting-star
Wild Valerian
*Foxglove Beardtongue
    (white)
Showy Orchis
Rosebud Orchid
*Cancer-root (white)
Wild Geranium

Summer
Rabbit's-foot Clover
Common Milkweed

Joe-Pye-weed
Butterfly Pea
Tick-trefoil
*False Dragonhead
    (purplish)
*American Germander
    (yellow)
Basil
Wild Bergamot
Rough Hedge-nettle
*Hemp-nettle (white)
*Monkey-flower (purplish)
*Fog-fruit (white, blue)

Nodding Wild Onion
Marsh Mallow
Elephant's-foot
Wild or Hog-peanut
*Giant Hyssop (purplish)
Buttonweed
Dittany

Autumn
*Slender-leaved Gerardia
(purplish)
*Purple Gerardia (purplish)
Climbing Hempweed
*Smaller Burdock (purplish)

Lavender to Blue

Spring
*Liverleaf (pink-red)
Virginia Bluebell
Grape-hyacinth
Bluets
*Wild Comfrey (white)
Robin's Plantain
Common Speedwell
Lyre-leaved Sage
Blue Flag
Miami-mist
Small-flowered Phacelia

Summer
Blue False Indigo
Wood-vetch
Chicory
Tall Bellflower
Venus's Looking-glass
Blue-eyed Grass
Hairy Ruellia
Narrow-leaved Vervain
Blue Lupine
Morning-glory
Mistflower
False Pimpernel

*Fog-fruit (pink-red, white)
Tall Blue Lettuce
Blue Vervain
*Wild Mint (white, purplish)
Bluecurls
Virginia Dayflower
Asiatic Dayflower
Jimsonweed
Great Lobelia
Pale-spiked Lobelia
Indian-tobacco

Autumn
*Mock Pennyroyal (white)
*New England Aster
(purplish)
Wavy-leaved Aster
*Spreading Aster (purplish)
Bristle-leaved Aster
*Smooth Aster (white)
Crooked-stemmed Aster
*Large-flowered Aster
(purplish)
*Heart-leaved Aster (white)
Bushy Aster

Purplish

Spring
Henbit
*Purple Trillium (brownish)
Ground-ivy
Red Dead-nettle
Birdfoot Violet
Purple Violet

Wood Violet
*Ground Phlox (pink-red)
*Wild Ginger (brownish)
Larkspur
Flowering Raspberry
Spiderwort
Hairy Beardtongue

Hairy Skullcap
Large Skullcap
Large Twayblade
Viper's Bugloss
Passionflower

Summer
*Water-willow (white)
Common Vetch
*Large Houstonia (white)
*Horse Nettle (white)
*Wood-betony (greenish)
Large Purple Fringed Orchis
Lopseed
Ironweed
Pale Purple Coneflower
*False Dragonhead
  (pink-lavender)
Selfheal
*Monkey-flower (pink-
  lavender)
Corn-cockle
Pickerelweed
Teasel

Common or Bull Thistle
Pasture Thistle
Blazing Star
Nodding Pogonia
Bush-clover
*Wild Mint (white, blue)
*Giant Hyssop (pink-
  lavender
Swamp Loosestrife
Clammy Cuphea

Autumn
*Slender-leaved Gerardia
  (pink-lavender)
Purple Gerardia
*New England Aster
  (lavender-blue)
*Spreading Aster (lavender-
  blue)
*Large-flowered Aster
  (lavender-blue)
*Smaller Burdock (pink-
  lavender)

Brownish

Spring
*Purple Trillium (purplish)
*Wild Ginger (purplish)
*Large Twayblade
  (purplish)

Summer
False Beechdrops

Narrowleaf Plantain
*Ground Nut or Wild Bean
  (pink-red)

Autumn
None

Descriptions of Flowers*

>>>->>>

HARBINGER-OF-SPRING (*Érigenìa bulbòsa*)   PLATE p. 87
  PARSLEY FAMILY (Umbellíferae)
Height: 3 to 6 inches.
Habit: A small, delicate, low plant with leaves just developing
when in bloom, later maturing into finely divided, narrow,
toothless segments. The umbel of tiny flowers, with white petals
and purple stamens, gives a speckled effect; thus, another name:
Pepper and Salt.
Habitat: Rich, damp soil; roadsides and woods. Western New
York to Alabama; west to Minnesota and Arkansas. February to
May. One of our earliest spring flowers, although not very
showy.

GOLDEN SAXIFRAGE (*Chrysosplènium americànum*)
  SAXIFRAGE FAMILY (Saxifragàceae)   PLATE p. 87
Height: 3 to 7 inches.
Habit: A small, branched perennial with erect, short-hairy stems
and opposite, roundish, finely scalloped, short, stalked leaves.
The small, inconspicuous, purplish green flowers, in the upper
leaf axils, have four or five sepals, four to ten stamens, and
orange anthers.
Habitat: Wet places, running brooks, mud. Maine to Georgia;
west to Ohio, Indiana, Iowa, Michigan, and Minnesota. March
to June.

COMMON CHICKWEED (*Stellària mèdia*)   PLATE p. 87
  PINK FAMILY (Caryophyllàceae)

---

* The accents on the Latin names are an aid to pronunciation. The acute accent
(´) indicates a short vowel sound; the grave accent (`) indicates a long vowel
sound.

Height: 2 to 12 inches.

Habit: A weak-stemmed, low, matting and spreading plant with small, ovate, bright green leaves, ¾ to 1 inch long, progressively shorter-stalked upward to sessile. The small, starlike, white flowers have five petals, each deeply cut, and five sepals longer than the petals.

Habitat: Lawns, dooryards, damp ground. Throughout the United States. March to July. One of our commonest weeds. An immigrant from Europe.

LIVERLEAF (*Hepática americàna*)   PLATE p. 88
CROWFOOT OR BUTTERCUP FAMILY (Ranunculàceae)

Height: 2 to 3 inches.

Habit: A low, clumping perennial, with long-stalked, thick, leathery leaves, each having three rounded lobes. Leaves are mottled with brown blotches, having persisted over the winter. New leaves appear after the flowers. The delicate, fragrant, blue, purple, or almost white flowers are borne singly on hairy stalks. The buds are soft and woolly.

Habitat: Rich woods. Nova Scotia to northern Florida; west to Minnesota and Missouri. March to May. *H. acutiloba* differs in having pointed leaf lobes. It is found in the same range.

TRAILING ARBUTUS (*Epigaèa rèpens*)   PLATE p. 88
HEATH FAMILY (Ericàceae)

Height: 1 to 2 inches.

Habit: A very leafy, prostrate, shrubby evergreen with rough, leathery, oval leaves. The matting, rusty, bristly shoots spread 6 to 12 inches. Small, spicy-fragrant, pink or white tubular flowers with five equal lobes are in small clusters in the leaf axils.

Habitat: Acid, peaty to rocky woodlands. Maine to Florida; west to Kentucky, Wisconsin, and Minnesota. March to May. The state flower of Massachusetts, where it is known as Mayflower. Very difficult to transplant into gardens.

BLUE COHOSH or PAPOOSE ROOT (*Caulophýllum thalictroìdes*)   PLATE p. 89
BARBERRY FAMILY (Berberidàceae)

Height: 1 to 4 feet.

Habit: A tall, stout plant with a simple, unbranched stem and a long-stalked, large, compound leaf, with lobed leaflets completely separated along the midrib. It is topped by a loose cluster of small, greenish yellow flowers with six pointed sepals and six tiny hood-shaped petals. Later, dark blue berries are produced.

Habitat: Rich, damp woodlands. Maine to South Carolina and

Alabama; west to Missouri, Nebraska, and South Dakota. April to June.

SPRING CRESS or BITTER CRESS (*Cardámine bulbòsa*)
MUSTARD FAMILY (Crucíferae)   PLATE p. 89
Height: 1 to 2 feet.
Habit: A smooth, erect, slender perennial with one to a few stems, unbranched or branched above. Basal leaves are roundish and long-stalked; stem leaves are ovate to lance-shaped, toothed, and shorter-stalked upward to sessile. The plant is topped by a cluster of short, stalked, white flowers, each with four petals.
Habitat: Bottomlands, meadows, wet woods. Quebec to Florida; west to Michigan, Wisconsin, Minnesota, Kansas, and Texas. March to June. A very abundant plant.

GARLIC MUSTARD (*Alliària officinàlis*)   PLATE p. 89
MUSTARD FAMILY (Crucíferae)
Height: 1 to 2 feet.
Habit: A tall, erect, stout-stemmed biennial, simple or little-branched, with an unmistakable odor of garlic when crushed. The lower leaves are wider than long. Stem leaves are almost triangular and coarsely scalloped, indented at the base, and stalked. The plant is topped by a cluster of small, white flowers with four petals, each wider at the tip than the base.
Habitat: Open fields and woods. Quebec to Virginia; west to Kentucky and Kansas. April to June. A European immigrant, widely naturalized in the United States. The Latin name is derived from *allium* ("onion") because of its odor.

SCOURING RUSH or HORSETAIL (*Equisètum hyemàle*)
HORSETAIL FAMILY (Equisetàceae)   PLATE p. 90
Height: 1 to 4 feet.
Habit: A leafless, nonflowering, unbranched, erect plant with jointed, rough, hollow stems. It may be solitary or numerous. Sheathes are at the joints or toothed ridges. It has no true flowers, but reproduces by spores in a conelike structure at the top of the stem.
Habitat: Low ground, poor meadows, damp open woods. Throughout the United States, and often abundant, as it grows from creeping rhizomes. The Horsetail Family has only one modern genus, a remnant of an ancient plant group, much more prominent in earlier geological times.

HORSETAIL (*Equisètum arvénse*)   PLATE p. 90
HORSETAIL FAMILY (Equisetàceae)
Height: 1 to 2 feet.
Habit: A leafless, nonflowering plant with a sterile green stem, tufted at the joints, and a fertile, pinkish tan stem with felted-

toothed bands at the nodes. It is topped by a spore-bearing cone. *Habitat:* Low ground, stream banks, damp open woods. Throughout the United States. See note on preceding Horsetail. In olden times these plants were used for scouring, thus the name Scouring Rush.

HENBIT (*Làmium amplexicaùle*)   PLATE p. 90
    MINT FAMILY (Labiàtae)
Height: 6 to 10 inches.
Habit: An annual with several smooth, leafy stems from the base, spreading, sometimes reclining. The basal leaves are deeply scalloped and long-stalked, becoming progressively shorter-stalked, and the upper ones sessile and clasping or whorled. Small, purplish flowers in a whorl (often six to ten) are in axils of the upper leaves.
Habitat: Wastelands, lawns, fields, roadsides. Throughout the United States; commoner southward. March to November. One of our commonest weeds. An immigrant from Eurasia and North Africa.

VIRGINIA BLUEBELLS (*Merténsia virgínica*)   PLATE p. 91
    BORAGE OR FORGET-ME-NOT FAMILY (Boraginàceae)
Height: 1 to 2 feet.
Habit: A very smooth, succulent, erect, light green, leafy perennial. The basal leaves are elliptic or ovate, up to 6 inches long, and long-stalked; middle and upper leaves are progressively shorter-stalked to sessile. The funnel-shaped corollas, pink in bud, opening to light blue, nod in a loose one-sided cyme.
Habitat: Rich soil, moist semishade, river banks. Southern Ontario to Georgia; west to Kansas and Minnesota. March to May. Plants may be solitary or carpet the ground.

BLOODROOT (*Sanguinària canadénsis*)   PLATE p. 91
    POPPY FAMILY (Papaveràceae)
Height: 3 to 10 inches.
Habit: A low perennial from a thick, red rootstalk. The long-stalked, deeply three-lobed leaf is up to 4 inches wide, dark green above, blue green beneath. The naked scape is topped by a handsome white flower with eight to twelve glistening white petals, orange anthers, and a ring of stamens in the center. The flowers close in the evening.
Habitat: Dry, rocky slopes; borders of rich woods; shady roadsides. Quebec to Florida and Alabama; west to Illinois, Kansas, and Oklahoma. March to May.

DOG'S-TOOTH VIOLET or TROUT LILY (*Erythrònium*
    americànum and *Erythrònium álbidum*)   PLATE p. 92
    LILY FAMILY (Liliàceae)
Height: 4 to 8 inches.

Habit: Two glossy, smooth, ovate leaves sheathe the base of the naked scape. The leaves of *E. álbidum* are rarely mottled, but those of *E. americànum* are commonly mottled with dark purple. The scape is topped by a single nodding flower, dull white in *E. álbidum* and yellow in *E. americànum.*
Habitat: Rich woods, bottomlands, meadows. Nova Scotia to Georgia; west to Kentucky, Missouri, and Oklahoma. Late March to June.

GRAPE-HYACINTH (*Muscàri racemòsum*)   PLATE p. 92
LILY FAMILY (Liliàceae)
Height: 5 to 10 inches.
Habit: A plant from a bulb, with a tuft of narrow, channeled leaves at the base. The small, deep blue, bell-shaped flowers are crowded in a raceme at the top of the naked scape. They have a musky odor.
Habitat: Fields, roadsides, lawns, fallow ground. Massachusetts to Georgia and Mississippi; west to Michigan. April and May. Introduced from Europe. Often occurs in sheets of blue in Maryland and Virginia.

PURPLE TRILLIUM (*Tríllium séssile*)   PLATE p. 92
LILY FAMILY (Liliàceae)
Height: 4 to 12 inches.
Habit: A low perennial with a stout, simple stem having at the top a whorl of three broad, oval, sessile leaves mottled with purplish brown. A single maroon and yellow green flower is at the center of the whorl, with three spreading sepals and three erect petals. It is aromatic. Common also are the white trillium and the painted trillium.
Habitat: Open woods. Western New York to Georgia and Arkansas; west to Missouri. April to early June. Often abundant.

DUTCHMAN'S-BREECHES (*Dicéntra cucullària*)
POPPY FAMILY (Papaveràceae)   PLATE p. 93
Height: 6 to 12 inches.
Habit: A low perennial from a granular scaly bulb, with thin, finely dissected, fernlike, long-stalked leaves. The nodding white flowers have two divergent inflated spurs at the base resembling upside-down breeches. They are in few-flowered racemes on naked scapes.
Habitat: Woods; moist, shady ledges. Quebec to Florida and Alabama; west to Arkansas, Kansas, Oregon, and Washington. April to early June.

SQUIRREL-CORN (*Dicéntra canadénsis*)   PLATE p. 93
POPPY FAMILY (Papaveràceae)
Height: 2 to 12 inches.

Habit: The leaves closely resemble those of Dutchman's-breeches (see preceding) , but this plant grows from underground shoots having separate cornlike grains. The white flowers are heart-shaped, with a blunt, rounded base, but (like those of Dutchman's-breeches) are inflated and nod from a naked scape.
Habitat: Rich woods. Quebec to North Carolina; west to Tennessee and Missouri. April and May.

GOLDEN CORYDALIS (*Corýdalis flàvula*)   PLATE p. 93
POPPY FAMILY (Papaveràceae)
Height: 6 to 12 inches.
Habit: A slender, low, branching biennial with long-stalked lower leaves, progressively shorter-stalked upward; blades all finely dissected. The plant is topped by a raceme of pale yellow, tubular flowers, with a stubby spur at the base.
Habitat: Moist woodlands, slopes, open woods. Connecticut to North Carolina; west to Oklahoma, Kansas, and Nebraska. March to May.

TWINLEAF (*Jeffersònia diphýlla*)   PLATE p. 94
BARBERRY FAMILY (Berberidàceae)
Height: 8 to 16 inches.
Habit: A low, smooth, erect perennial with long-stalked, deeply two-parted leaves, the outer margins widest and toothed. Single white flowers, with eight flat petals and eight stamens, are on long naked scapes. The flowers are very ephemeral.
Habitat: Woods. New York to Maryland and Alabama; west to Wisconsin and Iowa. April and May. Named in honor of Thomas Jefferson, third president of the United States.

SPRING-BEAUTY (*Claytònia virgínica*)   PLATE p. 94
PURSLANE FAMILY (Portulàcaceae)
Height: 6 to 12 inches.
Habit: A small, delicate perennial with two long, narrow leaves about the middle of the stem. It is topped by a loose umbel of five to nineteen pink (sometimes white) flowers with deeper pink veins.
Habitat: Open, moist woods; fields; thickets. Quebec to Georgia and Alabama; west to Minnesota and Texas. March to May. *C. caroliniana,* a closely related species, has wider, spatulate leaves; often found with *C virginica.* Named for John Clayton, an early Virginia botanist.

GOLDEN RAGWORT (*Senécio aùreus*)   PLATE p. 95
COMPOSITE FAMILY (Compósitae)
Height: 1 to 3 feet.
Habit: An erect perennial with a basal tuft of long-stalked, roundish to spatulate leaves and finely cut stem leaves becoming

sessile upward. It is topped by an umbel of yellow flower heads with eight to twelve rays.
Habitat: Meadows, swamps, moist woodlands. Maryland to Florida; west to Arkansas, Kentucky, and Missouri. April and May.

COMMON DANDELION *(Taráxacum officinàle)* PLATE p. 95
COMPOSITE FAMILY (Compósitae)
Height: 6 to 12 inches.
Habit: A low perennial with a rosette of coarsely cut and variously indented leaves and heads of orange yellow flowers on long, naked, milky scapes. These later produce fluffy balls of seed attached to pappi that drift in the wind.
Habitat: Lawns, grasslands. Everywhere throughout the United States. March to December. A naturalized weed from Europe. The leaves may be eaten for spring greens.

PUSSYTOES *(Antennària neodiòica)*   PLATE p. 95
COMPOSITE FAMILY (Compósitae)
Height: 3 to 9 inches.
Habit: A very woolly perennial with a rosette of basal leaves, narrowly to broadly obovate, smooth above, gray-hairy beneath. At the top of the flowering stem are small, flat, whitish flower heads surrounded by dry, papery bracts. Male and female flowers are on different plants.
Habitat: Poor, dry ground; rocky barrens; pastures. Newfoundland to Virginia; west to Indiana and Minnesota. May to July. Plants form loose to dense mats spreading 2 to 8 feet.

GROUND-IVY *(Glechòma hederàcea)*   PLATE p. 96
MINT FAMILY (Labiàtae)
Height: 6 to 16 inches
Habit: A trailing and spreading plant, forming a dense intertwining ground cover. The ovate to roundish leaves have scalloped margins and slender stalks. Small bluish purple flowers, the tube flaring into a lobed upper lip and a three-lobed lower lip, are in the leaf axils.
Habitat: Roadsides, woods, yards. Throughout the area. April to July. A naturalized plant from Europe.

RED DEAD-NETTLE *(Làmium purpùreum)* PLATE p. 96
MINT FAMILY (Labiàtae)
Height: 6 to 12 inches.
Habit: A low annual having heart-shaped leaves with scalloped margins; the lower ones long-stalked, the uppermost crowded and reddish. There are three to six small reddish purplish flowers, in a whorl, among the uppermost leaves.
Habitat: Roadsides, waste places. Newfoundland to South Carolina; west to Ohio, Indiana, Illinois, and Missouri. April to

October. A naturalized weed from Europe. See Henbit (*L. amplexicaùle*) for another species.

EARLY SAXIFRAGE (*Saxifraga virginiénsis*)   **PLATE p. 96**
   SAXIFRAGE FAMILY (Saxigragàceae)
Height: 6 to 8 inches.
Habit: A low plant with a basal rosette of wedge-shaped, broadly toothed leaves. The sticky-hairy stem is topped by clusters of small white flowers with five petals and ten yellow stamens.
Habitat: Rock ledges and slopes. Quebec to Georgia; west to Tennessee, Missouri, and Oklahoma. April to June.

COLUMBINE (*Aquilègia canadénsis*)   **PLATE p. 97**
   CROWFOOT OR BUTTERCUP FAMILY (Ranunculàceae)
Height: 1 to 2 feet.
Habit: An erect perennial with several stems from the base. The leaves are divided and redivided into threes; leaflets are broadly ovate. Each of the large, showy, nodding, scarlet and yellow flowers has five spurs and many yellow projecting stamens.
Habitat: Rocky, dry, wooded soil. Quebec to Georgia; west to Tennessee and Wisconsin. April to July.

SWAMP BUTTERCUP (*Ranùnculus septentrionàlis*)
   CROWFOOT OR BUTTERCUP FAMILY (Ranunculàceae)
Height: 12 to 16 inches.   **PLATE p. 97**
Habit: A perennial with one to a few hollow stems and coarse trailing or prostrate branches. The leaves are divided into three leaflets with toothed margins. Flower stems are erect and bear a single glossy, golden yellow flower with five petals and numerous stamens.
Habitat: Stream banks, woods, meadows, bottomlands. Quebec to Maryland; west to Kentucky, Arkansas, and Texas. April to July.

SMALL-FLOWERED CROWFOOT (*Ranùnculus abortìvus*)
   CROWFOOT OR BUTTERCUP FAMILY (Ranunculàceae)
Height: 1 to 2 feet.   **PLATE p. 97**
Habit: A tall, slender, erect, very smooth, branched perennial with round to ovate, scalloped basal leaves and stem leaves divided into blunt segments. The stem is topped by tiny, inconspicuous, yellow flowers with five spreading, pointed petals.
Habitat: Woodlands, open ground. Maine to Florida; west to Oklahoma and Colorado. March to August.

RUE-ANEMONE (*Anemonélla thalictroìdes*)   **PLATE p. 98**
   CROWFOOT OR BUTTERCUP FAMILY (Ranunculàceae)
Height: 6 to 12 inches.
Habit: A smooth, delicate, black-stemmed perennial with three-

lobed, long-stalked, basal leaves and two or three opposite or whorled, slightly notched stem leaves under the flowers. Flowers are white or rarely pinkish, with five spreading, petallike sepals. *Habitat:* Open woods. Maine to Florida and Alabama; west to Mississippi, Oklahoma, and Minnesota. April to June.

WOOD ANEMONE or WIND FLOWER (*Anemòne
    quinquefòlia*)   PLATE p. 98
    CROWFOOT OR BUTTERCUP FAMILY (Ranunculàceae)
Height: 9 to 12 inches.
Habit: A delicate plant with long-stalked basal leaves divided into three leaflets, variously toothed and cut. About midway, the stem has a whorl of three short-stalked leaves, palmately divided and variously incised. Stem is topped by a single, small, white (or tinged with pink) flower with five petallike sepals. *Habitat:* Open woods, thickets, clearings. Quebec to North Carolina and mountains of Georgia and Kentucky; west to New York and locally in Ohio. April to June. One of our earliest wind flowers.

WINTER CRESS or YELLOW ROCKET (*Barbarèa
    vulgàris*)   PLATE p. 98
    MUSTARD FAMILY (Crucíferae)
Height: 1 to 3 feet.
Habit: A smooth biennial with erect, leafy stems, branching above. The bright green basal leaves are pinnately lobed, the terminal lobe largest and rounded. Stem leaves are progressively shorter-stalked to sessile and clasping, with fewer lobes. Compact racemes have very small, bright golden yellow flowers, later producing elongated, erect seedpods. *Habitat:* Fields, roadsides, wasteland. Newfoundland to Virginia; west to Kentucky and Kansas. April to August. Introduced from Europe.

CUT-LEAVED TOOTHWORT (*Dentària laciniàta*)
    MUSTARD FAMILY (Crucíferae)   PLATE p. 99
Height: 8 to 19 inches.
Habit: A low, woodland perennial with sparingly woolly stem and three (rarely two) slashed stem leaves, deeply and coarsely toothed, whorled on the stem at intervals. The stem is topped by white flowers tinged with pink, each having four petals. The basal leaves develop after the flowers. *Habitat:* Moist woods, borders of thickets. Quebec to Florida; west to Louisiana, Alabama, and Kansas. March to May.

CRINKLEROOT (*Dentària diphýlla*)   PLATE p. 99
    MUSTARD FAMILY (Crucíferae)
Height: 6 to 18 inches.

Habit: A low perennial with long-stemmed, three-lobed, toothed basal leaves and two similar opposite stem leaves. A cluster of white to slightly pinkish flowers with four petals in a cross tops the stem. The long, wrinkled root is edible.
Habitat: Borders of low, moist woods. Quebec to South Carolina; west to Kentucky and Michigan. Mid-April to early June.

SHEPHERD'S PURSE (*Capsélla búrsa-pastòris*)   PLATE p. 99
   MUSTARD FAMILY (Crucíferae)
Height: 6 to 18 inches.
Habit: A wiry, erect stem arises from a rosette of toothed and variously cut basal leaves. The stem leaves are small, lance-shaped, clasping, and alternate. The stem is topped by an elongating raceme of tiny, white, stalked flowers, later producing small seeds in the shape of tiny purses.
Habitat: Roadsides, cultivated ground. Throughout our range and beyond. March to December. Naturalized from Europe.

ROCK CRESS (*Arabis lyràta*)   PLATE p. 99
   MUSTARD FAMILY (Crucíferae)
Height: 1 to 2 feet.
Habit: A biennial or perennial with a cluster of hairy, toothed, oblanceolate to spatulate basal leaves and one to several delicate stems with scattered spatulate to linear leaves, pinnately cleft, the terminal lobe largest. The branches are topped by small racemes of white flowers with four petals, later producing erect seedpods, ½ to 1½ inches long.
Habitat: Ledges, cliffs, sand. Ontario to northern Georgia; west to Tennessee, Missouri, and Minnesota. April and May.

SMALL BITTER CRESS (*Cardámine pensylvánica*)
   MUSTARD FAMILY (Crucíferae)   PLATE p. 99
Height: 1 to 2 feet.
Habit: An erect biennial with a basal rosette of pinnately, deeply cleft or divided leaves, with one to six rounded leaflets. Stem leaves are narrower and smaller, ⅓ to ¾ inch long. The stems are topped by small, white, four-petaled flowers, less than ¼ inch across, followed by erect seedpods, ⅘ to 1 inch long.
Habitat: Low, moist ground; in springs. Canada to Florida; west to Arkansas, Texas, and Oregon. March to August. Our commonest species, a bitter-tasting herb; a substitute for watercress.

JOHNNY-JUMP-UP (*Vìola rafinésquii*)   PLATE p. 100
   VIOLET FAMILY (Violàceae)
Height: 3 to 8 inches.
Habit: A slender, low annual with leafy stems, branched or unbranched from the base. The basal leaves are long-stalked with

scalloped margins; stem leaves are small and very narrow. Stems
are topped by bluish white flowers up to ⅜ inch long.
Habitat: Open woodlands, fields. New York to Georgia. April
and May. A naturalized plant. Often carpets fallow fields like
snow.

PALE VIOLET (*Vìola striàta*)   PLATE p. 100
  VIOLET FAMILY (Violàceae)
Height: 6 to 12 inches.
Habit: A large, vigorous perennial with clumps of leafy stems
on long, sturdy stalks; basal leaves rounded; stem leaves heart-
shaped. Stems are topped by white to cream-colored flowers, the
lower petal with purple lines and lateral petals bearded.
Habitat: Moist woods and fields. Western New England; south
along the Alleghenies to Georgia; west to Missouri and Minnesota. April and May.

BIRDFOOT VIOLET (*Vìola pedàta*)   PLATE p. 100
  VIOLET FAMILY (Violàceae)
Height: 4 to 10 inches.
Habit: Our largest-flowered violet. The three to five cleft, palmate leaves are often again divided into nine segments and are
tufted from the rootstalk. The flowers are in two principal
colors: var. *pedata* is bicolored with two upper dark petals and
three lower lilac purple petals; var. *lineariloba* is uniformly
lilac purple. Both have large orange stamens.
Habitat: Dry fields, open woods. Variety *pedàta* is most plentiful from Pennsylvania to North Carolina. Variety *lineariloba*
is more widely distributed from Massachusetts to Florida; west
to Texas, Kansas, and Minnesota. Late March to early June.
Plants with white flowers occur rarely.

SMOOTH YELLOW VIOLET (*Vìola pensylvánica*)
  VIOLET FAMILY (Violàceae)   PLATE p. 100
Height: 4 to 9 inches.
Habit: A smooth, erect perennial with leafy stems, leaves deeply
indented at the base and elongated heart-shaped; basal leaves
are smaller and more kidney-shaped. The bright yellow flowers
have brownish purple veins near the base.
Habitat: Damp woods and bottomlands. Nova Scotia to Georgia
and Alabama; west to Arkansas, Oklahoma, and Minnesota.
April and May.

PURPLE VIOLET or COMMON VIOLET (*Vìola
    papilionàcea*)   PLATE p. 101
  VIOLET FAMILY (Violàceae)
Height: 3 to 10 inches.
Habit: The leaves and flowers grow from a rhizome. The long-

stalked, tufted leaves are heart-shaped. The rich violet-colored petals are white-centered.
Habitat: Low grounds, grassy banks, meadows. Massachusetts to Georgia; west to Kentucky, Arkansas, and Oklahoma. April to June. Our commonest violet in the northeastern United States; often invades gardens. The plant produces seedpods without flowers throughout the summer.

WOOD VIOLET (*Vìola palmàta*) PLATE p. 101
VIOLET FAMILY (Violàceae)
Height: 4 to 8 inches.
Habit: A smooth to fine-hairy plant having erect, heart- to kidney-shaped, deeply divided leaves, with five to eleven lobes, the terminal lobe largest. The flowers are a bright light violet, rarely white.
Habitat: Dry ground, woodlands. Maine to Georgia; west to Arkansas, Nebraska, and Minnesota. April and May.

PENNYWORT (*Obolària virgínica*) PLATE p. 101
GENTIAN FAMILY (Gentianàceae)
Height: 5 to 9 inches.
Habit: A low, smooth, purplish green perennial with a thick, stiff stem and opposite, very small, oval leaves, ½ inch long. Dull white or purplish, tubular flowers with four pointed lips are solitary or in groups of threes in the leaf axils.
Habitat: Moist woodlands and gulleys. New Jersey to Florida; west to Texas and Illinois. March to May.

BLUETS or QUAKER-LADIES (*Houstònia caerùlea*)
MADDER FAMILY (Rubiàceae) PLATE p. 101
Height: 4 to 6 inches.
Habit: A small, smooth, slender perennial with a basal tuft of light green, spatulate leaves ⅓ to ½ inch long, and stalked. Stem leaves are opposite, much smaller and narrower. Each stem is topped by a tiny, lavender blue, tubular flower, ¼ to ½ inch across, with four lobes and a yellowish "eye."
Habitat: Moist, grassy places; sandy soil. Maine to Georgia and Alabama; west to Michigan. April to July. They form lovely colonies.

DOWNY PHLOX (*Phlóx pilòsa*) PLATE p. 102
PHLOX FAMILY (Polemoniàceae)
Height: 8 to 30 inches.
Habit: A perennial with erect or ascending downy stems and mostly opposite, small, linear leaves, 1½ to 2 inches long. The clustered pink to rose, rarely white, tubular flowers open widely with five equal lobes, wider at the tip than the base.
Habitat: Dry open woods, sand hills, open meadows. Connecti-

cut to Florida; west to Michigan, Missouri, and Kansas. May and June.

GROUND PHLOX or MOSS-PINK (*Phlóx subulàta*)
PHLOX FAMILY (Polemoniàceae)   PLATE p. 102
Height: 3 to 6 inches.
Habit: A prostrate, very leafy, freely branching perennial forming broad, dense mats. Leaves are stalkless and needlelike, ½ to ¾ inch long. The flowers make a carpet of color, rose purple or pink with a darker "eye," varying to white. The small, tubular flowers have five deeply notched, flared lobes.
Habitat: Rocky ledges and sandy soil. Maine to North Carolina; west to Tennessee and Michigan. April to July.

PYXIE-MOSS (*Pyxidanthèra barbulàta*)   PLATE p. 102
DIAPENSIA FAMILY (Diapensiàceae)
Height: 2 to 3 inches.
Habit: A handsome, creeping, much-branched, matting plant with woody stems and alternate, awl-pointed leaves, less than ½ inch long. The numerous small, sessile, white or rose-colored, tubular flowers have five widely spreading lobes. They appear as if clustered.
Habitat: Pine barrens, crannies of rocks. New Jersey, southeastern Virginia to South Carolina. April and May.

JACK-IN-THE-PULPIT (*Arisaèma triphýllum*) PLATE p. 103
ARUM FAMILY (Aràceae)
Height: 6 to 24 inches.
Habit: A perennial from a thickened, tuberlike corm, having a single scape and two opposite, long-stalked leaves, divided into three large, ovate leaflets with prominent veining. The tiny flowers are at the base of the club-shaped spadix (the "Jack"). This is surrounded by the spathe (the "pulpit"), which is green or striped purplish brown. A cluster of fleshy scarlet berries is produced in autumn.
Habitat: Moist woods, peat bogs, and swamps. Quebec to Florida and Louisiana; west to Kansas. April to June.

SKUNK CABBAGE (*Symplocárpus foètidus*)   PLATE p. 103
ARUM FAMILY (Aràceae)
Height: Leaves, 1 to 3 feet; flower, 3 to 6 inches.
Habit: The purple-tinged or striped and spotted spathe almost encloses the thick rounded spadix which bears the tiny flowers, each having four sepals, four stamens, and a pistil. The leaves are absent at blooming time; later they are very large, ovate, and veiny, 1 to 3 feet long, cabbagelike. The flower has a foul-smelling, skunklike odor.
Habitat: Wet meadows, swampy woods, thickets. Quebec to

Georgia; west to Tennessee, Ohio, Indiana, and Illinois. February to May. One of our earliest blooming plants.

SHOOTING-STAR *(Dodecátheon meàdia)*   PLATE p. 104
 PRIMROSE FAMILY (Primulàceae)
Height: 8 to 18 inches.
Habit: A low, smooth perennial with a basal rosette of elliptic to lance-shaped leaves, tapering to the stalk, the veins marked with red. Nodding flowers are in an umbel at the top of a naked scape. The five pink to magenta or lavender petals are recurved, exposing the yellow, conelike anthers.
Habitat: Moist hillsides, thin woods, meadows. Pennsylvania to Georgia; west to Arkansas, Texas, and Wisconsin. April to June. The bright anthers and sharply recurved petals suggest a shooting star.

WILD GINGER *(Ásarum canadénse)*   PLATE p. 104
 BIRTHWORT FAMILY (Aristolochiàceae)
Height: 6 to 12 inches.
Habit: A low, creeping, leafy plant with a tiny, bell-shaped, purplish brown flower in the leaf axils. The three calyx lobes are sharp-pointed and cleft to the ovary. Large, heart-shaped leaves, 3 inches or more across, have soft-hairy stalks, 7 or 8 inches long.
Habitat: Rich, moist woods. Quebec to North Carolina and Alabama; west to Arkansas, Kentucky, Kansas, and Illinois. April and May. More common northward. It is not true ginger.

TRUMPETS *(Sarracénia flàva)*   PLATE p. 105
 PITCHER-PLANT FAMILY (Sarraceniàceae)
Height: 1 to 2 feet.
Habit: A plant of bogs and wetlands, with hollow, stiff, erect leaves, 1 to 2 feet long, narrow at the base, with an open, trumpet-shaped mouth and a pointed hood. Translucent spots near the top let light penetrate to the upper part of the "pitcher." A large, showy, bright yellow, solitary flower, 3 to 4 inches across, nods on a naked scape. A large umbrellalike style covers the numerous stamens.
Habitat: Low, swampy ground; sand bogs; wet pinelands. Southeastern Virginia to Florida and Alabama. The modified leaves collect water and trap insects, which enter, drown, and are digested by the plant.

ROCK CRESS *(Árabis laevigàta)*   PLATE p. 106
 MUSTARD FAMILY (Crucíferae)
Height: 2 to 3 feet.
Habit: A tall, smooth, erect, simple or branching biennial. The first year (autumn) it has a rosette of spatulate leaves. In spring

it puts up a sturdy, leafy stem with clasping, narrowly lance shaped to linear, ascending, toothed, and pointed leaves. The stem is topped by a loose raceme of small, nodding, whitish flowers, which later produce horizontal or downward-arching pods up to 4 inches long.
Habitat: Wooded hillsides, ledges. Quebec to Georgia and Alabama; west to Arkansas, Oklahoma, Minnesota, and Colorado. Late March to July.

EARLY MEADOW PARSNIP or GOLDEN ALEXANDERS
    (*Zízia aùrea*)   PLATE p. 106
    PARSLEY FAMILY (Umbellíferae)
Height: 1 to 3 feet.
Habit: A tall, smooth, leafy perennial, the leaves long-stalked at the base, divided into three short-stalked leaflets, lance-shaped and sharp-toothed. Small, bright yellow flowers are in an umbel, with six to twenty umbellets, without bracts.
Habitat: Roadsides and damp meadows. Pennsylvania to Georgia and Alabama; west to Arkansas, Missouri, Oklahoma, and Texas. April to June.

LARKSPUR (*Delphínium tricórne*)   PLATE p. 107
    CROWFOOT or BUTTERCUP FAMILY (Ranunculàceae)
Height: 2 to 3 feet.
Habit: A tall, unbranched perennial, with compound leaves, palmately divided nearly to the base and variously lobed. The few flowers, violet variegated with white, are 1 to 1¼ inches across. Each has five petallike sepals, one prolonged into a spur at the base, and four small irregular petals, two continued backward into the spur, the other two with short claws.
Habitat: Woods and rich meadows. Pennsylvania to Georgia and Alabama; west to Arkansas and Oklahoma. April and May. The name *tricorne* refers to the three-horned seedpod. The paintings in this book show two color variants of this plant.

WILD STRAWBERRY (*Fragària virginiàna*)   PLATE p. 108
    ROSE FAMILY (Rosàceae)
Height: 3 to 6 inches.
Habit: A perennial with runners and numerous compound, long-stalked leaves, from the base, divided into three ovate, sharply toothed, hairy leaflets. The small white flowers, rising above the leaflets, have five rounded white petals, five green pointed calyx lobes, and many orange yellow stamens. Later, they produce small, edible, nearly globular red fruits, nodding on slender stalks.
Habitat: Fields, edges of woods. Canada to Georgia and Alabama; west to Oklahoma. April to July. This species, crossed

with the wild strawberry of Chile (*F. chiloensis*), produced the cultivated strawberry.

BLACKBERRY (*Rubus* species)   PLATE p. 108
  ROSE FAMILY (Rosaceae)
Height: 2 to 5 feet.
Habit: Shrubs, often forming extensive colonies of many prickly canes, erect or high-arching. They have alternate, compound leaves with three to seven leaflets, smooth or hairy. The raceme or panicle consists of showy white flowers with five petals and numerous stamens. Later, purplish black, plump, juicy, edible fruit is produced.
Habitat: Dry clearings, thickets, waste ground. Flowering May and June; fruiting July to September.

CINQUEFOIL (*Potentilla canadénsis*)   PLATE p. 109
  ROSE FAMILY (Rosàceae)
Height: 6 to 12 inches.
Habit: A low, prostrate perennial, spreading by runners. The alternate, compound leaves have three to five silky-hairy, wedge-shaped or narrowly triangular leaflets, coarsely and deeply toothed, the middle leaflet largest, ¾ to 1½ inches long. The long-stalked, solitary flowers have deep yellow to cream-colored petals, rounded and notched.
Habitat: Dry, open soil. Maine to South Carolina and Alabama; west to Ohio and Missouri. March to June.

FLOWERING RASPBERRY or THIMBLEBERRY
  (*Rùbus odoràtus*)   PLATE p. 109
  ROSE FAMILY (Rosàceae)
Height: 3 to 6 feet.
Habit: A coarse, erect, bristly shrub (not prickly) with large, alternate leaves, 3 to 3½ inches across, three- to five-lobed, the middle one longest, smooth above, velvety beneath, irregularly toothed and lobed. The showy, rose purple, fragrant flowers, with five rounded petals, are 1 to 1¾ inches across. The plant blooms all summer and produces dry, insipid fruits.
Habitat: Thickets, borders of woods. Quebec to Georgia and Tennessee; west to Michigan. June to September.

STAR CHICKWEED (*Stellària pùbera*)   PLATE p. 110
  PINK FAMILY (Caryophyllàceae)
Height: 6 to 12 inches.
Habit: An erect, densely tufted perennial with few to many slender, four-angled stems. It has opposite, elliptic to oblong leaves, 1 to 3 inches long. The white star-shaped flowers, in leafy cymes, have five deeply notched, pointed petals, ¼ inch long, shorter sepals, and ten stamens.

Habitat: Rich woods, shaded rocky slopes. New Jersey to Florida and Alabama; west to Illinois. March to May.

FIELD CHICKWEED (*Cerástium arvénse*)   PLATE p. 110
PINK FAMILY (Caryophyllàceae)
Height: 1 to 2 feet.
Habit: A matted or tufted, downy but green, perennial, simple or freely branching. The leafy stems may be smooth, hairy, or sticky. It has small, opposite, linear to lance-shaped leaves, 1 to 3 inches long. The stems are topped by small white flowers with five deeply notched petals, $1/4$ to $1/2$ inch long.
Habitat: Sandy soil, poor ground. Throughout our area. April to August.

COMMON MOUSE-EAR CHICKWEED (*Cerástium* - near
   C. vulgàtum)   PLATE p. 110
PINK FAMILY (Caryophyllàceae)
Height: 4 to 20 inches.
Habit: A matting, spreading, sticky, hairy perennial with opposite leaves. The lower leaves are spatulate; the small stem leaves are ovate, lance-shaped, $1/8$ to $1/3$ inch long. The stem is topped by a loosely branched inflorescence of small white flowers with five narrow petals, deeply cleft, $1/8$ to $1/4$ inch long; it is followed by curved capsules, $1/4$ to $1/3$ inch long.
Habitat: Roadsides, fields, cultivated ground. Throughout our area. Early spring to late autumn. Naturalized from Europe. May be a troublesome weed.

WILD PINK (*Silène caroliniàna*)   PLATE p. 110
PINK FAMILY (Caryophyllàceae)
Height: 6 to 8 inches.
Habit: A tufted, open-branched perennial with sticky-hairy stems. It has a basal rosette of linear to lance-shaped and blunt-tipped leaves and two or three pairs of opposite, ovate, sessile stem leaves. The flowers are in clusters of five to thirteen; each is short-stalked with a five-toothed calyx, five pink, wedge-shaped, and notched petals, and ten stamens.
Habitat: Open fields; dry, sandy ground. New Hampshire to South Carolina and Alabama; west to Ohio and Missouri. April to early June.

WILD GERANIUM (*Gerànium maculàtum*)   PLATE p. 111
GERANIUM FAMILY (Geraniàceae)
Height: $1\frac{1}{2}$ to 2 feet.
Habit: A tall, erect, branching, hairy perennial with paired rough-hairy leaves palmately divided into three to five wedge-shaped segments, notched at the tips and long-stalked. The showy pink to rose purple flowers, $1\frac{1}{2}$ inches across, have five

spreading petals, many stamens, and a "crane's bill" in the center.
Habitat: Open woods and roadsides. Maine to Georgia; west to Tennessee and Arkansas. April to July.

SPIDERWORT (*Tradescántia virginiàna*)   PLATE p. 111
SPIDERWORT or DAYFLOWER FAMILY (Commelinàceae)
Height: 6 to 18 inches.
Habit: A coarse perennial with many succulent stems, tuftea from the base. Long, narrow, light green, linear leaves fold lengthwise, up to 1 foot long and 1/4 to 5/8 inch wide. Clusters of showy, rich, dark purple to purplish blue flowers with conspicuous golden anthers open one at a time. They bloom only in the morning.
Habitat: Rich, moist meadows and roadsides. Maryland to Georgia; west to Tennessee and Missouri. May to August.

TALL BUTTERCUP (*Ranùnculus ácris*)   PLATE p. 111
CROWFOOT or BUTTERCUP FAMILY (Ranunculàceae)
Height: 2 to 3 feet.
Habit: A tall, erect, much-branched, rather hairy perennial. The leaves are palmately divided into three to seven linear, toothed, hairy segments, forming a rosette with numerous lower stem leaves. The upper, nearly leafless branches are topped by long-stalked, lustrous, shining, golden yellow flowers, 1 inch across, lighter without. Each has five broad, overlapping petals and conspicuous stamens.
Habitat: Meadows, fields, roadsides. Canada to Virginia; west to Ohio, Kansas, and westward. May to August.

MAY-APPLE or MANDRAKE (*Podophýllum peltàtum*)
BARBERRY FAMILY (Berberidàceae)   PLATE p. 112
Height: 1 to 2 feet.
Habit: A common, handsome woodland perennial, easily recognized by its long-stalked, large, smooth, shiny, umbrella-like leaves, deeply cut into seven to nine lobes, and again notched. The leaves rise above the solitary, nodding, white, waxy flower, 1½ to 2 inches across, with six rounded petals and twelve to eighteen stamens. The flower is borne in the paired leaf axils. Later, it produces a large, yellowish, lemon-shaped fruit, edible when ripe (leaves and roots are poisonous).
Habitat: Moist, shady or open woods; low meadows. Rare in New England states, more common south to Florida and west to Texas and Minnesota. Flowering late April and May; fruiting in late summer.

WILD VALERIAN (*Valeriàna pauciflòra*)   PLATE p. 112
VALERIAN FAMILY (Valerianàceae)
Height: 2 to 3 feet.

Habit: A slender, unbranched perennial, with long runners from the base. The leaves are mostly basal, ovate to heart-shaped, simple or with a pair of leaflets; stem leaves are opposite, pinnately divided into three to seven segments, the terminal one largest and ovate. The long, slender, pinkish lavender, tubular flowers, ½ to ⅝ inch long, have tiny lobes and projecting stamens.
Habitat: Rich woods, river bottoms. Pennsylvania to Virginia; west to Kentucky and Illinois. May and June.

WILD STONECROP (*Sèdum ternàtum*)   PLATE p. 112
    ORPINE OR SEDUM FAMILY (Crassulàceae)
Height: 3 to 9 inches.
Habit: A fleshy, succulent perennial with creeping stems and a basal rosette of wedged-shaped leaves. The single, upright, short stem with a few small scattered leaves has two to four forked flowering branches. Tiny, crowded, white flowers have five sharp-pointed petals.
Habitat: Rocky ledges, cliffs, woods. New York to Georgia; west to Tennessee, Arkansas, and Michigan. May and June.

WILD COMFREY (*Cynoglóssum virginiànum*)   PLATE p. 113
    BORAGE OR FORGET-ME-NOT FAMILY (Boraginàceae)
Height: 1 to 2 feet.
Habit: An erect, unbranched perennial with a bristly, hairy stem and large, clasping, rough, ovate to lance-shaped leaves becoming smaller above. The small, pale violet to blue or white, tubular flowers, with five rounded lobes, are on a few long, naked stalks.
Habitat: Hillsides and open woodlands. Connecticut to Florida and Louisiana; west to Missouri, Oklahoma, Illinois, and Ohio. Late April to early June.

CELANDINE or SWALLOWWORT (*Chelidònium màjus*)
    POPPY FAMILY (Papaveràceae)   PLATE p. 113
Height: 2 to 3 feet.
Habit: A tall, erect, branched biennial with yellow juice. The leaves are pinnately divided, with five to nine segments, the terminal one largest and three-lobed; all are toothed. The stem is topped by a few small yellow flowers, ¾ inch across, with four petals, a prominent green style, and many stamens. Flowers are in a stalked umbel.
Habitat: Waste places, moist ground. Quebec to Georgia; west to Missouri and Iowa. April to September. Naturalized from Europe.

PINK WOOD-SORREL (*Óxalis violàcea*)   PLATE p. 113
    WOOD-SORREL FAMILY (Oxalidàceae)
Height: 3 to 9 inches.

Habit: A low, delicate, somewhat succulent woodland perennial with cloverlike leaves, equally divided into three heart-shaped leaflets, broadest and indented at the tips. The rose magenta flowers have five equal petals and ten stamens. The long-stalked umbel rises above the leaves.

Habitat: Rocky ground, shaded slopes, dry upland woods. Massachusetts to Florida; west to Texas and Minnesota. May and June.

YELLOW WOOD-SORREL (*Óxalis corniculàta*)
Wood-Sorrel Family (Oxalidàceae)   **Plate p. 113**
Height: 3 to 12 inches.

Habit: A delicate, low, creeping, leafy perennial with rather smooth stems that root at the nodes and long-stalked, cloverlike leaves with three equal leaflets indented at the tips. The small yellow flowers have five petals (twisted in bud) and ten stamens on a branched stalk.

Habitat: A common, weedy plant in fields, gardens, roadsides. Quebec to Georgia; west to North Dakota and Oklahoma. April to November.

RATTLESNAKE-WEED (*Hieràcium venòsum*)   **Plate p. 114**
Composite Family (Compósitae)
Height: 1 to 2 feet.

Habit: A tall, slender, smooth perennial with a basal rosette of red or purple-veined, obovate or oblong leaves, and one to six narrow stem leaves. Upper stem forks into two to seven slender stalks terminated by deep yellow to orange flower heads, $\frac{1}{2}$ to $\frac{3}{4}$ inch across, all ray flowers.

Habitat: Dry woods, wastelands. Maine to Florida; west to Louisiana and Michigan. May to October. Easily identified by the reddish leaf veins.

DWARF DANDELION (*Krígia virgínica*)   **Plate p. 114**
Composite Family (Compósitae)
Height: 2 to 12 inches.

Habit: A low, slender perennial, with narrow often pinnatifid leaves, all basal. The naked scapes are terminated by solitary flower heads, $1\frac{1}{2}$ to 2 inches across, of orange ray flowers.

Habitat: Meadows and roadsides. New Jersey to the Gulf States; west to Kansas. April to June. Resembles the common dandelion, but is less robust and has slenderer flowering scapes.

FIELD DAISY (*Leucanthemum vulgáre*)   **Plate p. 115**
Composite Family (Compósitae)
Height: 1 to 3 feet.

Habit: An erect perennial with numerous stems forked near the top. The lower leaves are long-stalked and spatulate; upper ones, progressively smaller and sessile; all deeply and distantly blunt-toothed. Stems are topped by flower heads, 1½ to 2 inches across, with perfect, yellow, disk flowers surrounded by fifteen to thirty spreading, white, pistillate rays, up to ¾ inch long. *Habitat:* Roadsides, fields, throughout our area, but mainly in the northern part. May to October. Our familiar large white daisy, one of our commonest wildflowers, long ago introduced from Europe. Often in extensive colonies and frequently transplanted into gardens.

GOLDENSTAR (*Chrysógonum virginiànum*)   PLATE p. 115
  COMPOSITE FAMILY (Compósitae)
Height: 6 to 24 inches.
Habit: A perennial with one to several sticky, rough-hairy, leafy stems. The opposite leaves are ovate to oblong and hairy beneath, 1 to 3½ inches long. One to a few flower heads, 1½ inches across, have yellow disks and a few deep golden rays. The flower stalks are leafy. The plant blooms even when very small. *Habitat:* Moist or dry woodlands. Southern Pennsylvania to Florida and Louisiana. April to June.

ROBIN'S PLANTAIN (*Erigeron pulchéllus*)   PLATE p. 115
  COMPOSITE FAMILY (Compósitae)
Height: 6 to 24 inches.
Habit: A slender biennial with runners. The basal leaves are obovate to spatulate, ¾ to 4¾ inches long, and shallowly toothed; the stem leaves are ovate to lance-shaped, progressively smaller upward. The stem is topped by long-stalked, showy flower heads, 1 to 1½ inches across, with yellow disks and fifty to one hundred threadlike lavender to whitish rays, ¼ to ⅓ inch long.
Habitat: Fields, open woods. Maine to Florida; west to Minnesota and Texas. April to July. The Latin name *pulchellus* means "beautiful," which describes the flower.

HAIRY BEARDTONGUE (*Penstémon hirsùtus*)
  FIGWORT OR SNAPDRAGON FAMILY (Scrophulariàceae)
Height: 2 to 4 feet.   PLATE p. 116
Habit: A tall, erect, fine-hairy perennial, mostly with lanceshaped, oblong, or elliptic basal leaves. Stem leaves are opposite, sessile and somewhat clasping the stem, and progressively smaller upward. The stem is topped by purplish tubular flowers, ⅘ to 1 inch long, with small white lobes.
Habitat: Rocky, open woods; fields. Quebec to Virginia; west to Tennessee, Wisconsin, and Oklahoma. May to July. One of our commonest species.

FOXGLOVE BEARDTONGUE (*Penstémon digitàlis*)
  FIGWORT OR SNAPDRAGON FAMILY (Scrophulariàceae)
Height: 2 to 5 feet.   PLATE p. 116

Habit: A tall, erect perennial with broadly oblanceolate, long-stalked basal leaves in a rosette. Upper stem leaves are partly clasping, lance-shaped, and sessile. The stem is topped by an open, many-flowered panicle; the white or faintly lavender-tinted or lined tubular flowers, 1 inch long, have inflated throats and five uneven lobes.
Habitat: Open woods, moist thickets, meadows. Maine to Virginia and Alabama; west to South Dakota and Texas. May to July.

COMMON SPEEDWELL or GYPSYWEED (*Verónica officinàlis*)   PLATE p. 116
FIGWORT OR SNAPDRAGON FAMILY (Scrophulariàceae)
Height: 4 to 40 inches.
Habit: A low, matted perennial with trailing, hairy stems and rather thick, obovate to wedge-oblong leaves. Short, erect branches rise above the leaves, topped by spikelike racemes, 1 to 2 inches long, of four-lobed tubular flowers, ¼ inch across, lavender to blue, lined with purple.
Habitat: Dry, open fields; open woodland. Newfoundland to North Carolina; west to Tennessee and Wisconsin. May to July.

LYRE-LEAVED SAGE (*Sálvia lyràta*)   PLATE p. 117
MINT FAMILY (Labiàtae)
Height: 1 to 2 feet.
Habit: A perennial with obovate or irregularly cleft, lyre-shaped leaves in a basal rosette. The erect, unbranched stem bears one or two pairs of coarsely notched and toothed leaves (rarely leafless) . The stem is topped by an interrupted spike of whorled, pale blue to violet, tubular flowers, ¾ to 1 inch long.
Habitat: Dry, sandy woodlands; clearings. Connecticut to Florida; west to Oklahoma and Texas. April to June. Often abundant where found. The lyre-shaped leaves are distinctive.

HAIRY SKULLCAP (*Scutellària ellíptica*)   PLATE p. 117
MINT FAMILY (Labiàtae)
Height: 6 to 24 inches.
Habit: A short-hairy perennial with several stems from the base and two to five pairs of stem leaves, heart-shaped to oblong-ovate, rather distantly spaced. Each stem is topped by a short, branched raceme of six to twenty tubular flowers, ¾ inch long, lips blue violet and tube paler.
Habitat: Dry woods, borders of fields, thickets. New York to Florida; west to Missouri and Texas. May to August.

LARGE SKULLCAP (*Scutellària integrifòlia*)   PLATE p. 117
MINT FAMILY (Labiàtae)
Height: 1 to 2 feet.
Habit: An erect perennial with one to several fine-downy stems

from the base and simple, often ascending branches. Leaves are in three to eight pairs; the lowest ones are stalked and toothed, ascending ones become successively narrower, smaller, untoothed, and sessile. The large, showy, lavender to purple, tubular flowers, 1 to 1¼ inches long, are in a terminal bracted raceme.
Habitat: Dry woods, borders of fields. Massachusetts to Florida; west to Tennessee, Ohio, Kentucky, and Missouri. May to July.

FALSE SPIKENARD (*Smilacìna racemòsa*)   PLATE p. 118
LILY FAMILY (Liliàceae)
Height: 1 to 3 feet.
Habit: An unbranched leafy perennial, upright or ascending, with alternate parallel-veined leaves, oblong to ovate, sessile or slightly stalked, 4 to 5 inches long, closely placed on the slightly zigzag stem. The numerous small, white flowers, with projecting stamens, are in a compound, many-flowered terminal panicle.
Habitat: Moist woods. Quebec to Virginia; west to Tennessee and Missouri. May to July. Flowers are followed in late summer by red berries speckled with purple.

SOLOMON'S-SEAL (*Polygónatum biflòrum*)   PLATE p. 118
LILY FAMILY (Liliàceae)
Height: 1 to 3 feet.
Habit: A slender, ascending, single-stemmed perennial with many large, alternate, lance-shaped to broadly ovate, bright green leaves, 1¼ to 4 inches long, with prominent parallel veins. Two small, greenish yellow, tubular flowers, on a short divided stalk, droop from each leaf axil. Later in the summer they produce small blue black berries.
Habitat: Wooded slopes, thickets. Southern Ontario to Florida; west to eastern Kansas and Nebraska. May and June.

BELLWORT (*Uvulària perfoliàta*)   PLATE p. 118
LILY FAMILY (Liliàceae)
Height: 4 to 24 inches.
Habit: An erect, leafy-stemmed perennial, forked above the middle, with large, alternate, oblong to ovate leaves, 1 to 4½ inches long, that seem to be pierced by the stem (perfoliate). A single bell-shaped, stalked flower nods from the forking leafy stem, with three petals and three sepals alike, varying in color from bright yellow to greenish yellow, with six short stamens and a pistil.
Habitat: Rich, moist woods; clearings. Massachusetts to Florida and Louisiana. Late April to early June.

INDIAN CUCUMBER (*Medèola virginiàna*)   PLATE p. 119
LILY FAMILY (Liliàceae)
Height: 1 to 3 feet.

Habit: A tall, slender, erect, unbranched perennial with a whorl of five to nine obovate to lance-shaped, parallel-veined leaves near the middle of the stem. An upper, smaller whorl of three leaves is just below the umbel of small, greenish yellow flowers hanging on long, threadlike stalks. The three sepals and three petals are alike and sharply recurved, showing the divided stigma resembling three brown threads.

Habitat: Damp, rich woods; mossy banks. Quebec to Florida, Alabama, and Louisiana. May and June. The underground fleshy stem is edible and tastes somewhat like cucumber.

STARRY FALSE SOLOMON'S-SEAL (*Smilacìna stellàta*)
  LILY FAMILY (Liliàceae)   PLATE p. 119
Height: 12 to 24 inches.
Habit: An erect to arching or slightly zigzag, leafy-stemmed perennial with alternate, spreading to strongly ascending leaves, 1¼ to 5 inches long, elliptic to oblong, and parallel-veined, sessile, or slightly clasping the stem. The raceme is terminal, with a few to several small white flowers, ¼ inch across.
Habitat: Thickets, meadows, edges of woods. Canada to New Jersey and West Virginia; west to Ohio, Indiana, Missouri, Kansas, New Mexico, and Arizona. May to early August.

STAR-OF-BETHLEHEM (*Ornithógalum umbellàtum*)
  LILY FAMILY (Liliàceae)   PLATE p. 119
Height: 6 to 12 inches.
Habit: A low, densely tufted perennial from a bulb, with numerous long, narrow, channeled, lustrous leaves, spreading and ascending. The white, spreading, six-pointed, starlike flowers, ¾ to 1½ inches across, are borne on naked scapes above the leaves.
Habitat: Fields, meadows, wastelands, roadsides, lawns. Canada to North Carolina; west to Mississippi, Missouri, and Kansas. April to June. Introduced from Europe.

SHOWY ORCHIS (*Órchis spectábilis*)   PLATE p. 120
  ORCHID FAMILY (Orchidàceae)
Height: 6 to 12 inches.
Habit: A low, erect perennial with two oblong-ovate, bright green, glossy leaves, 2¼ to 5 inches long. A few showy, waxy flowers, ¾ inch long, are in a bracted raceme. The pink or purple hood, of sepals and lateral petals, arches above the lower white lip.
Habitat: Rich woods. New Brunswick to Georgia; west to Arkansas and the Dakotas. May and June.

LARGE TWAYBLADE (*Líparis lilifòlia*)   PLATE p. 120
  ORCHID FAMILY (Orchidàceae)
Height: 6 to 10 inches.

Habit: A low perennial, with two large, ovate to elliptic basal leaves, distinctly parallel-veined, sheathing the stem. It has a loose raceme of inconspicuous flowers, sometimes nodding, the color of dead leaves. The narrow sepals are pale green; the dull, mauve purple flowers have threadlike lateral petals.
Habitat: Rich, damp thickets; forested slopes. Maine to Georgia; west to Missouri and Minnesota. May to early July. These inconspicuous plants are rare, and it is a thrill to find one.

ROSEBUD ORCHID (*Cleìstes divaricàta*)   PLATE p. 121
ORCHID FAMILY (Orchidàceae)
Height: 1 to 2 feet.
Habit: A low, erect perennial with a solitary, sheathing, sessile leaf, 1½ to 4½ inches long, just above the middle of the stem. The plant is topped by a single nodding flower with three narrow, brownish, spreading sepals, 1½ to 2½ inches long. The pink to white petals and lip form a slender tube, 1 to 1½ inches long.
Habitat: Acid, peaty soil; pine barrens; thickets. New Jersey to Florida; west to Kentucky and Texas. June and July. Mostly found on the coastal plain, but rare and local.

PUTTYROOT (*Apléctrum hyemàle*)   PLATE p. 121
ORCHID FAMILY (Orchidàceae)
Height: 1 to 2 feet.
Habit: A perennial with a solitary large, ovate, bluish green basal leaf, produced in late summer, that persists through the winter but withers and dies before the plant blooms in the spring. It then bears a loose raceme of eight to fifteen greenish, yellowish, or whitish flowers with purplish markings.
Habitat: Mucky, wet soil in wooded bottoms; peat bogs. Quebec to Georgia; west to Arkansas. May and June. Early settlers made a sticky paste from the bulblike roots for mending pottery. The plant is now becoming rare.

YELLOW LADY'S-SLIPPER (*Cypripèdium calcèolus*)
ORCHID FAMILY (Orchidàceae)   PLATE p. 122
Height: 1 to 2 feet.
Habit: An erect perennial with three to five large, bright green, elliptic to ovate basal leaves, 3 to 8 inches long, sheathing the stem, with blades conspicuously parallel-veined. The large, showy, faintly scented, terminal, nodding flower has an inflated saclike "slipper," 1 to 1½ inches long, golden yellow with delicate brown to purplish markings. The long, narrow lateral petals are spirally twisted and strongly marked with brownish purple.
Habitat: Low woods, bogs, swamps, rich woods. Maine to the mountains of Georgia, Louisiana; west to Tennessee and Missouri. Mid-April to mid-June.

SMALL YELLOW LADY'S-SLIPPER *(Cypripèdium calcèolus* var. *parviflórum)* PLATE p. 122
ORCHID FAMILY (Orchidàceae)

This plant is a variety of the preceding one, but with smaller leaves and flowers. The lateral petals are of a duller purplish brown. Flowers have a pungent fragrance.

Habitat: Swamplands (chiefly soil rich in lime). Newfoundland to Georgia (in mountains); west to Tennessee, Missouri, and Texas; but rare southward. April to mid-June.

PINK LADY'S-SLIPPER or MOCCASIN-FLOWER *(Cypripèdium acaùle)* PLATE p. 123
ORCHID FAMILY (Orchidàceae)

Height: 12 to 18 inches.

Habit: A low perennial with two nearly opposite, large, broad, bright green basal leaves, distinctly parallel-veined, sheathing the long, naked scape. The nodding flower rises well above the leaves. The large, deeply cleft pouch or "slipper," 1 to 1¼ inches long, is crimson to pink and veined with deeper rose. Lateral petals and sepals are yellowish brown.

Habitat: Wet woods, bogs, swamps. Quebec to North Carolina and Georgia; west to Missouri. June and July. One of the showiest of our wild orchids. The hairs on fresh plants can cause skin irritation, similar to poison ivy.

SHOWY LADY'S-SLIPPER *(Cypripèdium regìnae)*
ORCHID FAMILY (Orchidàceae) PLATE p. 123

Height: 12 to 30 inches.

Habit: A downy, erect perennial with three to seven large, ovate to elliptic leaves, 4 to 6 inches long and strongly ribbed. The leaves sheathe the stem, which bears one or two (rarely three) showy flowers. The "slipper" or lip, 1 to 1½ inches long, is rosy pink fading to white toward the base and underside. Both the lateral petals and broader sepals are white. The upper sepal arches over the lip.

Habitat: Wet woods, bogs, limy swamps. Quebec to mountains of North Carolina and Georgia; west to Tennessee, Missouri, and North Dakota. Mid-May to mid-August. One of our showiest wildflowers and in danger of extinction.

WATERARUM or WILD CALLA *(Cálla palùstris)*
ARUM FAMILY (Aràceae) PLATE p. 124

Height: 5 to 12 inches.

Habit: A water-loving perennial with thick, heart-shaped, deep green, long-stalked basal leaves. The white spathe partly clasps the golden spadix, on which the small flowers are clustered; the upper ones are male (staminate), the lower ones perfect (having both stamens and a pistil). Later, a cluster of red berries is produced.

Habitat: Cold bogs, sluggish streams. Newfoundland to New Jersey; west to Indiana, Wisconsin, and Minnesota. April to August. A naturalized plant.

DRAGON ARUM or DRAGON-ROOT (*Arisaèma dracóntium*)   PLATE p. 124
ARUM FAMILY (Aràceae)
Height: 1 to 3 feet.
Habit: An erect perennial with a solitary, long-stalked, compound leaf, palmately divided into seven to fifteen oblong, lance-shaped, pointed leaflets. At the base of the leaf is a short-stalked, greenish or purplish spathe, which partly sheathes the long tapering spadix, the "dragon's tongue," extending far above the spathe. Clustered at the base of the spadix are the tiny male (staminate) flowers; above are the female (pistillate) ones. Later, scarlet berries are produced.
Habitat: Rich bottoms, thickets, and woodlands. Quebec to Florida, locally in New Hampshire and Vermont; west to Minnesota and Texas. May and June.

BLUE FLAG or WILD IRIS (*Îris versícolor*)   PLATE p. 125
IRIS FAMILY (Iridàceae)
Height: 16 to 30 inches.
Habit: A stout perennial with erect or arching sword-shaped, parallel-veined leaves, 8 to 32 inches long, forming thick clumps from creeping rhizomes. The leafy stems are topped by one to several light blue flowers. The drooping blue to violet sepals, variegated with yellow and white (falls), are conspicuously veined; the small petals are erect.
Habitat: Wet meadows, swamps, edges of ponds. Northern part of our area, eastern Canada to Pennsylvania; west to Wisconsin and Minnesota. May to August. The common German iris of gardens is *I. germanica*.

VIPER'S BUGLOSS or BLUEWEED (*Échium vulgàre*)
BORAGE OR FORGET-ME-NOT FAMILY (Boraginàceae)
Height: 1 to 3 feet.   PLATE p. 125
Habit: A tall, erect, very rough-bristly, leafy plant, simple or branched. The lance-shaped, bristly, pointed leaves are up to 4½ inches long, progressively smaller and sessile upward. Strikingly showy, purplish blue, tubular flowers are bell-shaped, with five roundish lobes and projecting red stamens. The flowers are crowded on short, coiled stalks in upper leaf axils and bracts; later the stalks uncoil and straighten.
Habitat: Dry fields, waste places, roadsides. Throughout our range. June to September. A weed introduced from Europe, often in great abundance in open areas.

PASSIONFLOWER or MAYPOPS (*Passiflòra incarnàta*)
PASSIONFLOWER FAMILY (Passifloràceae)   PLATE p. 126
Height: Climbing or trailing up to 20 feet.
Habit: A rampant vine, climbing by tendrils, with lithe stems and alternate leaves, palmately divided into three to five lobes. The large, showy flowers, in the leaf axils, have five spreading, petallike sepals, 2 to 3 inches across, nearly white, with a three-rowed purple and flesh-colored crown. The parts of the flower are regarded as symbols of the crucifixion: the crown of thorns, in the fringes of the flower; nails, in the styles with their head-like stigmas; hammers to drive them, in the stamens; cords, in the tendrils. The edible fruit, as large as a hen's egg, is called maypop.
Habitat: Thickets and hedges or trailing on open ground. Maryland to Florida; west to Missouri and Oklahoma. June to September. The state flower of Tennessee.

MIAMI-MIST (*Phacèlia pùrshii*)   PLATE p. 127
WATERLEAF FAMILY (Hydrophyllàceae)
Height: 6 to 20 inches.
Habit: A small, erect or ascending to somewhat lax, slightly hairy annual, simple to bushy-branched. The leaves are deeply cleft into five to nine narrow lobes. The plant is topped by lavender blue (rarely white), tubular flowers with five equal, beautifully fringed lobes.
Habitat: Rich woods, clearings, and fields. Pennsylvania to Alabama; west to Ohio, Illinois, and Wisconsin. April to June.

SMALL-FLOWERED PHACELIA (*Phacèlia dùbia*)
WATERLEAF FAMILY (Hydrophyllàceae)   PLATE p. 127
Height: 4 to 16 inches.
Habit: A small annual, sparingly branched, with a rosette of simple to pinnately cleft basal leaves. The sessile stem leaves have seven to thirteen lobes. Pale bluish lavender flowers are widely bell-shaped, with five unfringed lobes.
Habitat: Rich woods, thickets, clearings. New York to Florida; west to Tennessee, Oklahoma, and Texas. April and May.

CYNTHIA (*Krìgia virgìnica*)   PLATE p. 127
COMPOSITE FAMILY (Compósitae)
Height: 8 to 12 inches.
Habit: This dwarf dandelion has a cluster of linear to oblanceolate leaves at the base, mostly pinnately lobed, up to 4½ inches long. The naked scape has a small yellow head of perfect ray flowers.
Habitat: Dry, poor soil; sandy fields. Maine to Florida; west to Michigan, Wisconsin, and Texas. April to August. Cynthia can

be distinguished from the common dandelion by its smaller head, bracts of equal length, and ring of scales surrounding the few long bristles.

CANCER-ROOT (*Orobánche uniflòra*)   PLATE p. 127
BROOM-RAPE FAMILY (Orobanchàceae)
Height: 6 to 10 inches.
Habit: A low, fleshy, leafless plant without green coloring. A single pale lavender to creamy white flower, with five equal wide-spreading lobes, is at the top of the naked stalk. Often there are several to many plants together. It is parasitic on the roots of other plants.
Habitat: Damp woods and thickets. Quebec to Florida; west to Mississippi and Texas. April to June.

SQUAWROOT (*Conópholis americàna*)   PLATE p. 127
BROOM-RAPE FAMILY (Orobanchàceae)
Height: 4 to 10 inches.
Habit: A plant with a thick, fleshy, conelike stalk covered with grayish, yellow, and brown soft, fleshy scales that later become hard and dry. From these scales emerge the grayish, tubular flowers, ½ inch long. The curved upper lip makes a narrow hood over the lower three-lobed lip.
Habitat: Rich woods. Nova Scotia to Florida; west to Louisiana and Wisconsin. April to July. Squawroot is parasitic on tree roots, especially beech and oaks.

PHILADELPHIA or DAISY FLEABANE (*Erigeron*
    philadélphicus)   PLATE p. 128
COMPOSITE FAMILY (Compósitae)
Height: 10 to 30 inches.
Habit: A tall, hairy-stemmed, short-lived, weedy perennial, much branched above. Its large basal leaves, up to 4½ inches long, are narrowly oblanceolate and coarsely toothed or lobed. The ovate stem leaves are clasping at the base, with pointed tips and wavy margins. Each of the numerous small, deep pink (to white) flowers has a yellow disk and 150 or more threadlike rays fading to white at the base.
Habitat: Fields, thickets, woodlands, shores, roadsides. Newfoundland to Florida; west to Louisiana and Texas. April to August. The fleabanes are distinguished from asters by blooming in spring and early summer and by possessing a single circle of same-length bracts instead of overlapping circles of varying-length bracts.

INDIAN PHYSIC or BOWMAN'S-ROOT (*Gillènia*
    trifoliàta)   PLATE p. 128
ROSE FAMILY (Rosàceae)
Height: 16 to 40 inches.

Habit: A simple to many-branched perennial of open habit, with leaves divided into three equal leaflets, each oblanceolate and tapering at both ends, finely toothed, and sessile. It is topped by a few white to pale pink flowers with twisted petals, ½ to 1 inch long.
Habitat: Rich upland woods or mountains. Ontario to Georgia; west to Alabama and Kentucky. May and June.

WILD GERANIUM (*Gerànium caroliniànum*) PLATE p. 128
  GERANIUM FAMILY (Geraniàceae)
Height: 18 to 24 inches.
Habit: A bushy annual with several stems from the base, freely branched and spreading; stalked leaves are palmately cleft into five to nine narrow lobes, each again three-lobed. The small, clustered flowers have five notched pink petals, each less than ½ inch long, and ten stamens. Later, beaked seedpods up to 1 inch long are produced.
Habitat: Poor or sandy soil, waste places. Maine to Florida; west to Texas and California. May to August.

YELLOW JESSAMINE (*Gelsèmium sempérvirens*)
  LOGANIA FAMILY (Loganiàceae) PLATE p. 129
Height: Up to 20 feet.
Habit: A climbing, twining, woody vine with many wiry, tangled branches and opposite, elliptic to ovate, evergreen leaves, 1½ to 3 inches long. The deliciously fragrant, bright yellow, tubular flowers, ½ to 1 inch long, have five equal lobes, widest at the tips and notched.
Habitat: Woods, thickets, sandy soil. A southern plant, southeastern Virginia to Florida; west to Arkansas and eastern Texas. Late March to early May.

FRINGED MILKWORT (*Polýgala paucifòlia*) PLATE p. 129
  MILKWORT FAMILY (Polygalàceae)
Height: 2 to 4 inches.
Habit: A dainty perennial with creeping stems up to 1 foot in length. The lower leaves are reduced to scales; the larger upper, elliptical to oval leaves, ¾ to 1½ inches long, may be crowded at the summit; they live through the winter. There are usually one to four flowers, each with two rose purple to magenta sepals, the "wings." The longer, white to pinkish petals are united in a tube, the lowest one fringe-tipped.
Habitat: Rich, moist woods; light soil. Quebec to the mountains of Georgia; west to Wisconsin, northern Illinois, and Minnesota. May to early June.

COMMON SUNDROPS (*Oenothèra fruticòsa*) PLATE p. 130
  EVENING-PRIMROSE FAMILY (Onagràceae)
Height: 1 to 2 feet.

Habit: An erect, downy, leafy perennial with few to many stems from the base, spreading by creeping rhizomes. Stem leaves are alternate, lance-shaped, up to 2½ inches long, short-stalked to sessile upward. The stem is topped by large bright yellow flowers, 1 to 2 inches across, with four petals, each ½ to 1 inch long, and orange stamens. The flowers close at night. Later, ribbed pods are produced.
Habitat: Marshes, fields, meadows. New England to Florida; west to Michigan and Missouri. May to August. Often cultivated in gardens for the showy flowers.

FRINGED LOOSESTRIFE *(Lysimáchia ciliàta)* PLATE p. 130
    PRIMROSE FAMILY (Primulàceae)
Height: 2 to 4 feet.
Habit: A much-branched, leafy perennial with smooth, opposite leaves, ovate to lance-shaped, 2½ to 3 inches long, broadly rounded at the base, with fringed stalks. The yellow, nodding flowers, on slender ascending stalks from the upper leaf axils, are wide open, ½ to 1 inch across, with five petals slightly toothed at the tip.
Habitat: Moist woods, damp meadows. Quebec to Florida; west to Texas and Arizona. May to August.

MONEYWORT *(Lysimáchia nummulària)*   PLATE p. 130
    PRIMROSE FAMILY (Primulàceae)
Height: 2 to 3 inches.
Habit: A perennial with long, creeping, leafy stems. The opposite leaves are roundish, ½ to 1 inch long, and almost as wide. The long-stalked, showy, yellow flowers, with five petals, are usually in pairs in the leaf axils.
Habitat: Damp ground. Newfoundland to Georgia; west to Kansas. July to September. A naturalized plant from Europe, sometimes grown in gardens as a ground cover.

WATER-WILLOW *(Justícia americàna)*   PLATE p. 130
    ACANTHUS FAMILY (Acanthàceae)
Height: 1 to 2 feet.
Habit: An erect, grasslike perennial with leafy stems and opposite narrow leaves, 3 to 6½ inches long. Small, dense heads of inconspicuous, purple and white, tubular flowers are borne on long stalks from the upper leaf axils. Often forms colonies.
Habitat: In water, edges of streams, shallow river beds. Quebec to Georgia; west to Wisconsin and Texas. June to October.

BLUE FALSE INDIGO *(Baptísia austràlis)*   PLATE p. 131
    PULSE OR BEAN FAMILY (Leguminòsae)
Height: 2 to 5 feet.
Habit: A robust, much-branched, smooth, bushy perennial with

alternate, compound leaves palmately divided into three obovate leaflets. The showy indigo blue, pealike flowers, $\frac{4}{5}$ to 1 inch long, are in dense, erect, terminal racemes.
Habitat: Rich, open woods; by streams. Pennsylvania to Georgia; west to Tennessee, Missouri, Nebraska, and Texas. May and June.

COMMON VETCH (*Vicia angustifòlia*)   **PLATE p. 131**
    PULSE OR BEAN FAMILY (Leguminòsae)
Height: Up to 40 inches.
Habit: A slender, straggling annual with alternate, compound leaves, each having two to five pairs of linear leaflets, $\frac{3}{5}$ to $1\frac{1}{4}$ inches long. The small, purple to white, pea-shaped flowers, $\frac{1}{4}$ to $\frac{1}{3}$ inch long, are usually paired in the upper leaf axils.
Habitat: Waste ground, roadsides. Throughout our area. March to October. A weedy plant introduced from Europe.

WOOD-VETCH (*Vicia caroliniàna*)   **PLATE p. 131**
    PULSE OR BEAN FAMILY (Leguminòsae)
Height: Up to 3 feet.
Habit: A slender, climbing or straggling perennial with alternate, compound leaves, having six to twelve pairs of narrow, pointed leaflets, each about $\frac{1}{2}$ inch long. The plant climbs by tendrils at the ends of the leaflets. Lavender to white, pea-shaped flowers, $\frac{1}{3}$ to $\frac{1}{2}$ inch long, are in seven to twenty flowered racemes.
Habitat: Woods and thickets. Southern Ontario, New York to Georgia and Florida; west to Wisconsin and Texas. April to June.

RED CLOVER (*Trifòlium praténse*)   **PLATE p. 132**
    PULSE OR BEAN FAMILY (Leguminòsae)
Height: 1 to 3 feet.
Habit: A tufted biennial or short-lived perennial with soft-hairy, ascending or erect stems and compound leaves, palmately divided into three oval to obovate, broadly triangular leaflets, $\frac{1}{4}$ to 1 inch long, each notched at the tip and marked with a paler green chevron. This is one of our most familiar clovers. Its dense, rounded heads of small crimson to pink, long-tubular, fragrant flowers, attract bumblebees.
Habitat: Roadsides, fields, clearings, waste ground. Throughout the United States. May to August. A naturalized plant from Europe, often used for hay.

WHITE CLOVER (*Trifòlium rèpens*)   **PLATE p. 132**
    PULSE OR BEAN FAMILY (Leguminòsae)
Height: 4 to 10 inches.
Habit: A low, creeping, smooth, leafy perennial with compound

leaves divided into three, sometimes four, elliptic to ovate leaflets, each faintly marked with a lighter green chevron. The
dense, rather flat, fragrant flower heads have numerous small,
pea-shaped, white to pinkish flowers, $1/4$ to $1/3$ inch long. The
outer flowers mature first, wither, and droop while the inner
ones are still blooming.
Habitat: Fields, lawns, roadsides, waste places. Throughout our
area. May to October. Introduced from Europe. Highly attractive to bees and a source of nectar for their honey.

YELLOW or HOP CLOVER (*Trifòlium agràrium*)

PULSE OR BEAN FAMILY (Leguminòsae)   **PLATE p. 132**
Height: 10 to 18 inches.
Habit: A light green, smooth-stemmed annual or biennial, with
ascending stems and compound leaves, palmately divided into
three narrow leaflets, $1/2$ to $3/4$ inch long. The dense, oval to
cylindrical heads of small, dull yellow flowers bloom from the
base of the head first, then dry and droop down, resembling
dried hops.
Habitat: Fields, roadsides. Common throughout our range.
June to September. Naturalized from Europe.

LOW HOP CLOVER (*Trifòlium procúmbens*) PLATE p. 132

PULSE OR BEAN FAMILY (Leguminòsae)
Height: 3 to 9 inches.
Habit: A low, wide-spreading, much-branched, downy annual
with compound leaves, palmately divided into three obovate
leaflets, notched at the tips; the middle leaflet is slightly stalked.
The short, compact flower heads have one to thirty tiny, yellow,
pea-shaped flowers, $1/10$ to $1/5$ inch long.
Habitat: Old fields and roadsides. Quebec to Georgia; west to
Arkansas, Mississippi, Kansas, and westward. May to September.
Naturalized from Europe. A plant similar to, but smaller than,
T. agrarium.

RABBIT'S-FOOT CLOVER (*Trifòlium arvénse*)

PULSE OR BEAN FAMILY (Leguminòsae)   **PLATE p. 132**
Height: 6 to 12 inches.
Habit: A soft-hairy, branched annual with few to several delicate stems and compound, short-stalked leaves, palmately divided into three linear-oblong leaflets, $1/4$ to $1/3$ inch long. The
oval to cylindrical, short-stalked, sweet-scented flower heads are
grayish pink and fuzzy. Long hairs of the sepals hide the small,
greenish white flowers.
Habitat: Poor soil, dry fields, waste ground, roadsides. Throughout our range. May to October. Naturalized from Europe.

BLACK-EYED SUSAN *(Rudbéckia hírta)*   **PLATE p. 133**
COMPOSITE FAMILY (Compósitae)
Height: 1 to 3 feet.
Habit: A tall, rough, hairy-stemmed perennial, simple or some-times branched. The basal leaves are ovate, spatulate, and coarsely toothed. The showy flower heads, borne singly on long stalks, have yellow notched and pointed rays and a raised, cone-shaped, purplish brown disk.
Habitat: Fields, meadows, roadsides. Massachusetts to Georgia and Alabama; west to Illinois. June to October. This is Mary-land's state flower.

TICKSEED *(Coreópsis verticillàta)*   **PLATE p. 133**
COMPOSITE FAMILY (Compósitae)
Height: 1 to 3 feet.
Habit: A tall, erect, smooth-stemmed, sparingly branched perennial, with opposite leaves divided into three segments, each again dissected into threadlike, slender divisions that seem to encircle the stem in whorls. One to several large flower heads have eight or more yellow rays, $\frac{1}{2}$ to 1 inch long, and tiny, yellow, tubular flowers.
Habitat: Dry woods, roadsides, clearings, waste ground. Mary-land to Florida and Alabama; west to Arkansas. June and July.

DAISY FLEABANE *(Erígeron ánnuus)*   **PLATE p. 134**
COMPOSITE FAMILY (Compósitae)
Height: 1 to 5 feet.
Habit: An erect, coarse, hairy annual or biennial, branched above and with large, ovate, coarsely notched or toothed leaves, up to 6 inches long, progressively smaller upward. The lower blades taper to a narrowly winged stalk; the upper ones are sessile. Branches at the summit have numerous small flower heads, $\frac{1}{2}$ to $\frac{3}{4}$ inch across, each with 80 to 125 tiny white rays (or tinted with pink or lavender) and a yellow disk. Outer greenish bracts are in one or two rows. In the closely related genus *Aster,* the outer greenish bracts are in many rows.
Habitat: Fields, waste places, and roadsides. Throughout our range. June to October.

CHICORY *(Cichòrium íntybus)*   **PLATE p. 134**
COMPOSITE FAMILY (Compósitae)
Height: 1 to 4 feet.
Habit: A tall, coarse, rigid perennial with a rosette of long-stalked leaves having deeply cut, backward-pointing segments. The smaller stem leaves, oblong or lance-shaped, are lobed or entire, and clasp the stem with earlike basal lobes. Numerous heads of showy, bright, lavender blue flowers, 1 to $1\frac{1}{2}$ inches

across, have twelve to twenty square-tipped and notched rays. The flower heads are sessile, occur singly or in twos and threes, and bloom only in the morning.
Habitat: Roadsides, waste ground, hayfields. Throughout our area and beyond. June to October. The ground-up taproot has been used as an adulterant for coffee. Naturalized from Europe.

YARROW or MILFOIL *(Achillèa millefòlium)* **PLATE p. 134**
  Composite Family (Compósitae)
Height: 1 to 3 feet.
Habit: A stiff, coarse, tough, erect, leafy, aromatic perennial with simple stems and alternate, finely divided, fernlike leaves, twice pinnately parted. The tiny grayish white heads of disk flowers, each with four to six rays, are tightly clustered in a flattish to rounded inflorescence. Flowers are occasionally rose-colored.
Habitat: Fields, roadsides, waste places. Commonly naturalized throughout our area. June to September. Introduced from Europe.

TALL BELLFLOWER *(Campánula americàna)* **PLATE p. 135**
  Bellflower Family (Campanulàceae)
Height: 2 to 5 feet.
Habit: A tall, erect annual or biennial with a simple, fine-hairy stem, usually unbranched. The thin leaves are narrowly ovate, toothed, and taper-pointed at both ends. A long, leafy spike bears light lavender blue tubular flowers, up to 1 inch across, that open quite flat and have five equal pointed lobes and a conspicuous long, curved style.
Habitat: Moist thickets, woods. Ontario to Florida and Alabama; west to Missouri and Minnesota. June to August.

VENUS'S LOOKING-GLASS *(Speculària perfoliàta)*
  Bellflower Family (Campanulàceae)   **PLATE p. 135**
Height: 6 to 24 inches.
Habit: A low, erect, weedy annual with a simple, rather weak ascending to reclining stem. The roundish, heart-shaped to ovate leaves, up to ¾ inch across, clasp the stem. Small blue to violet flowers, with five spreading pointed lobes, five stamens, and a three-lobed pistil, are borne singly in the upper leaf axils.
Habitat: Poor, dry hillsides; fields; open woods. Maine to Florida; west to Michigan, Wisconsin, and Minnesota. May to August. The common name refers to the shining mirrorlike seeds.

BLUE-EYED GRASS *(Sisyrínchium angustifòlium)*
  Iris Family (Iridàceae)   **PLATE p. 136**
Height: 6 to 24 inches.

Habit: A low, slender perennial with linear, folded, grasslike leaves in a loose tuft. The slightly twisted, flat scape bears one to a few deep blue flowers with six lobes, sepals and petals alike, each bristle-tipped, with a central golden yellow "eye," three stamens, and a prominent pistil. Flowers open only on sunny mornings and close by noon.
Habitat: Low, wet meadows; thickets. Newfoundland to Florida; west to Ohio, Indiana, Illinois, Missouri, and eastern Kansas. May to July.

GOLD-EYED GRASS or YELLOW STARGRASS
(*Hypóxis hirsùta*) PLATE p. 136
AMARYLLIS FAMILY (Amaryllidàceae)
Height: 5 to 10 inches.
Habit: A small, low perennial with hairy, pointed, grasslike, linear leaves in a tuft, 5 to 15 inches long and 1 to 1½ inches wide. One to seven flowers are borne on a naked scape shorter than the leaves; sepals and petals are alike, bright yellow within, greenish and hairy without, ½ to 1 inch across, with six stamens unequal in length.
Habitat: Open woods; meadows; dry, rocky ground. Maine to Florida; west to Ohio, Indiana, and Wisconsin. Late April to September.

WATERLEAF (*Hydrophýllum canadénse*) PLATE p. 136
WATERLEAF FAMILY (Hydrophyllàceae)
Height: 1 to 3 feet.
Habit: A nearly smooth perennial with large, broad, succulent, stalked leaves, palmately five-to-seven lobed, with a heart-shaped base, up to 3 inches long. White, bell-shaped, tubular flowers with five petals, five sepals, and five stamens projected beyond the petals are borne in clusters. The stalked inflorescence is shorter than the leaves.
Habitat: Damp, rich woods; along streams. Ontario to northern Alabama; west to Missouri and Michigan. June and July.

GOAT'S-BEARD (*Arúncus dioìcus*) PLATE p. 137
ROSE FAMILY (Rosàceae)
Height: 3 to 6 feet.
Habit: A tall, erect, unbranched perennial with a few large, mostly basal, compound leaves, having up to eleven small leaflets. The compound terminal panicle is formed of many tiny, narrow-petaled, yellowish white flowers crowded on slender spikes. Staminate (male) and pistillate (female) flowers are on separate plants.
Habitat: Rich woods, ravines. Pennsylvania to Georgia to Alabama; west to Kentucky, Oklahoma, and Idaho. Late May to July. This handsome plant is a good subject for a woodland garden.

PASTURE ROSE (*Ròsa carolìna*)   **PLATE p. 138**
  ROSE FAMILY (Rosàceae)
Height: 3 to 6 feet.
Habit: A low, slender shrub, spreading by underground runners, with scattered prickles and compound leaves with five to nine ovate, lance-shaped leaflets. The large, showy, pink, slightly fragrant flowers are 2½ to 3 inches across, with five petals, five sepals, and numerous stamens; they open flat and are mostly solitary on the branches. Later, they produce a red fruit, the hip, which is high in vitamin C.
Habitat: Open pastures; moist to dry, thin woods. Maine to Florida; west to Minnesota, Michigan, Wisconsin, Nebraska, and Texas. May to early July.

SWEETBRIAR ROSE (*Ròsa rubiginòsa*)   **PLATE p. 138**
  ROSE FAMILY (Rosàceae)
Height: 3 to 7 feet.
Habit: A many-stemmed shrub, disposed to climb and armed with strong, hooked prickles. The compound leaves have five to seven roundish to oval leaflets, downy and with russet glands beneath, giving a resinous aromatic fragrance. The lovely pink flowers, 1 to 2½ inches across, have five petals and numerous stamens. Later, pear-shaped hips are produced.
Habitat: Pastures, fence rows, waste ground. Throughout our range and west to Texas. June and July. Naturalized from Europe.

BLACK COHOSH or BLACK SNAKEROOT (*Cimicifuga racemòsa*)   **PLATE p. 139**
  CROWFOOT OR BUTTERCUP FAMILY (Ranunculàceae)
Height: 3 to 8 feet.
Habit: A tall, slender-stemmed, erect, stiff, smooth perennial growing from a knotted rhizome. It has large, alternate, compound leaves, divided and redivided into threes; the leaflets are irregularly incised and toothed, 1 to 3 inches long. A tall, naked stalk bears a terminal raceme, 6 inches to 2 feet in length, composed of small, delicate white flowers, with four to eight petals and numerous stamens. The plant has a fetid odor.
Habitat: Rich woods, woodland hillsides. Ontario to Georgia; west to Tennessee and Missouri. June to September.

TALL MEADOW-RUE (*Thalictrum polýgamum*)
  CROWFOOT OR BUTTERCUP FAMILY (Ranunculàceae)
Height: 2 to 10 feet.   **PLATE p. 139**
Habit: A tall, rather smooth-stemmed, graceful perennial with alternate, compound leaves divided into three roundish, thickish leaflets, each with three shallow lobes. The panicles, much-branched and rising above the leaves, with clusters of flowers

without petals, have a plumelike appearance. Some plants have complete flowers; others contain either pistils or stamens (polygamous).
Habitat: Sunny marshes, swamps, meadows, low thickets. Newfoundland to Georgia and Tennessee. June to August.

THIMBLEWEED *(Anemòne ripària)*   PLATE p. 140
  CROWFOOT OR BUTTERCUP FAMILY (Ranunculàceae)
Height: 1 to 4 feet.
Habit: A tall, erect perennial with fairly smooth stems and large, thin leaves with three to five oblanceolate to obovate lobed and cleft divisions. The single flower tops the long stalk with thin, white, petallike sepals (petals absent), broadly oblong to oval and rounded at the tip. The mounded, conelike center of the flower becomes the oval "thimble" containing numerous woolly seeds.
Habitat: Rocky ledges, banks of streams. New England to the mountainous part of Maryland; west to Illinois and Minnesota. May to July.

LEATHER-FLOWER *(Clématis viórna)*   PLATE p. 140
  CROWFOOT OR BUTTERCUP FAMILY (Ranunculàceae)
Height: 8 to 10 feet.
Habit: A rampant climber by means of coiling leafstalks, with opposite, compound leaves in three to seven ovate leaflets. Each long flower stalk bears a single, nodding, dull reddish, bell-shaped flower, ¾ to 1 inch long. The four thick sepals (no petals) are joined at the base, the narrow tips recurved showing the white inner surface. Later, seeds with very feathery tails develop.
Habitat: Rich woodlands, thickets. Pennsylvania to Georgia; west to Ohio, Indiana, Illinois, and Texas. May to August.

WHITE AVENS *(Gèum canadénse)*   PLATE p. 140
  ROSE FAMILY (Rosàceae)
Height: 1 to 4 feet.
Habit: A tall, straggling, branched perennial with slender, smooth or slightly hairy stems. The large, long-stalked basal leaves are simple or with three to five leaflets; upper stem leaves are three-cleft to simple and nearly sessile. The long-stalked, small, white flowers have five broadly ovate, inconspicuous petals, ⅕ to ⅓ inch long, and five sepals. Later, a bristly seed capsule is produced.
Habitat: Woods, thickets, along roadsides. Quebec to Georgia; west to Minnesota, South Dakota, and Texas. May and June.

BOUNCING BET or SOAPWORT *(Saponària officinàlis)*
  PINK FAMILY (Caryophyllàceae)   PLATE p. 141
Height: 1 to 3 feet.

Habit: A coarse, erect, smooth, many-stemmed, leafy perennial with opposite, oval to lance-shaped leaves. The pink to pale rose flowers are crowded in terminal clusters and in the upper leaf axils. The five petals, notched at the tip, are up to 1¼ inches long and reflexed. Plants with double flowers occur in the northern part of our range.
Habitat: Wastelands, roadsides. Throughout the United States. June to September. Naturalized from Europe. The leaves, crushed and mixed with water, can be used as soap.

DEPTFORD PINK (*Diánthus arméria*)   PLATE p. 141
   PINK FAMILY (Caryophyllàceae)
Height: 1 to 2 feet.
Habit: An erect, simple or slender-branched, weedy annual or biennial with narrow, pointed, hairy, erect leaves, 1½ inches long. The small rosy red flowers, about ¾ inch across, with whitish dots, are in clusters among the bracts at the tips of the branches. The petals are five-pointed and finely toothed.
Habitat: Waste places, dry fields. Quebec to Georgia; west to Kentucky, Missouri, and westward. May to July. Naturalized from Europe. The common name is from Deptford, England, where the plant grew abundantly.

STARRY CAMPION (*Silène stellàta*)   PLATE p. 141
   PINK FAMILY (Caryophyllàceae)
Height: 2 to 3 feet.
Habit: A perennial with stiff, ascending, leafy stems. The leaves are mostly in whorls of four, ovate to lance-shaped, 2 to 4 inches long. Flowers are in a long and loose panicle, forming a large, showy inflorescence; each flower has five white petals with deeply fringed margins and a bell-shaped, inflated calyx.
Habitat: Woods, thickets. Massachusetts to Georgia; west to Arkansas, Oklahoma, Texas, and Minnesota. July to September.

COMMON ST. JOHNSWORT (*Hypericum perforàtum*)
   ST. JOHNSWORT FAMILY (Hypericàceae)   PLATE p. 142
Height: 1 to 2 feet.
Habit: A leafy, much-branched, weedy perennial with opposite, sessile, elliptic leaves having scattered translucent dots. The golden yellow flowers, 1 to 1½ inches across, have a row of black dots on one side of the petal margins.
Habitat: Roadsides, waste places, fields. Throughout our area. A naturalized plant from Europe and Asia.

GOLDEN ST. JOHNSWORT (*Hypericum kalmiànum*)
   ST. JOHNSWORT FAMILY (Hypericàceae)   PLATE p. 142
Height: 1 to 3 feet.
Habit: A much-branched, shrubby perennial with papery,

whitish bark and opposite, sessile, whitish, linear to oblanceolate leaves. The flowers, $\frac{3}{4}$ to $1\frac{1}{4}$ inches across, have five
golden petals and many conspicuous stamens.
Habitat: Rocky, sandy soil. Near the Great Lakes, New York;
west to Ohio, Indiana, and Wisconsin. July and August. A plant
chiefly in the northern part of our area.

ST. ANDREW'S CROSS (*Áscyrum hypericoìdes*)

St. Johnswort Family (Hypericàceae)   PLATE p. 142
Height: 6 to 24 inches.
Habit: A low, leafy, much-branched, shrubby plant with opposite, narrow, oblong to linear leaves, $\frac{3}{4}$ to 1 inch long. The
bright yellow flowers are about $\frac{3}{4}$ inch across with two larger
and two smaller sepal lobes. They resemble the flowers of St.
Johnswort (*Hypericum*), but differ in having four petals and
four sepals.
Habitat: Sandy or rocky soil, thickets. Massachusetts to Florida;
west to Kansas and Texas. June to September.

SPOTTED ST. JOHNSWORT (*Hyperìcum punctàtum*)

St. Johnswort Family (Hypericàceae)   PLATE p. 142
Height: 1 to 3 feet.
Habit: An erect, little-branched, leafy perennial with small,
opposite, oblong-elliptic leaves, 1 to 2 inches long, sessile or
clasping the stem. The leaves have translucent dots. The small,
golden yellow flowers, $\frac{2}{5}$ inch long, are also marked with black
dots along the margins of their five petals, which are about twice
as long as the sepals.
Habitat: Moist or dry soil, fields, open woods. Quebec to Florida; west to Mississippi and Oklahoma. June to August.

JAPANESE HONEYSUCKLE (*Lonícera japónica*)

Honeysuckle Family (Caprifoliàceae)   PLATE p. 143
Height: Up to 20 feet.
Habit: A rapidly growing, rampant, very leafy, evergreen vine
with woody, hairy stems. It has opposite, ovate, glossy leaves,
1 to $1\frac{1}{2}$ inches long. The tubular flowers, 2 inches long, are
white or reddish, fading to yellow, with projecting stamens.
They later produce round, black fruits.
Habitat: Woods, fields, fence rows, road banks. Massachusetts to
Florida; west to Texas, Indiana, Missouri, Kansas, and Ohio,
but more common southward. A naturalized plant from Japan
and China. Densely tangled stems can smother and kill shrubs
and small trees.

TRUMPET-VINE (*Cámpsis radìcans*)   PLATE p. 143

Bignonia Family (Bignoniàceae)
Height: Up to 50 feet.

Habit: A vigorous, leafy, woody, high-climbing vine with hold-
fast rootlets that cling to the supporting plant. The opposite
leaves are pinnately divided, with five to thirteen ovate, sharp-
pointed and toothed leaflets. Large, showy, bright, leathery-
looking, orange red, tubular flowers, 2½ to 3 inches long, have
five equal rounded lobes. They later produce hanging, beanlike
pods, 4 to 6 inches long.
Habitat: Low woods, fence rows. Southern New Jersey to Florida; west to Missouri, Iowa, and Texas. July to September.

DAY-LILY (*Hemerocállis fúlva*)   PLATE p. 144
  LILY FAMILY (Liliàceae)
Height: 2 to 5 feet.
Habit: A tall perennial with numerous long-folded, keeled,
parallel-veined leaves in fans at the base of the scapes. Each
naked scape bears a cluster of large, showy, lilylike, funnel-
shaped, orange flowers, up to 5 inches across. Sepals and petals
are colored alike: the three inner ones are petals; the three
outer ones, sepals.
Habitat: Roadsides, borders of fields, along streams, thickets.
Throughout our area. June and July. Introduced from the Old
World. Does not produce seeds, but spreads rapidly by branching rhizomes and tuberous roots.

YELLOW MEADOW LILY (*Lilium canadénse*) PLATE p. 144
  LILY FAMILY (Liliàceae)
Height: 2 to 4 feet.
Habit: A tall perennial with an erect stem, having leaves in
scattered whorls of four to twelve. The narrow leaves are 3 to 6
inches long and lance-shaped. The stem is topped by one to
three showy yellow to orange, nodding flowers, with three sepals
and three petals alike, spotted and widely recurved.
Habitat: Moist meadows. Quebec to Maryland and upland Virginia; west to Kentucky and Ohio. June and July.

SPOTTED WINTERGREEN (*Chimáphila maculàta*)
  PYROLA FAMILY (Pyrolàceae)   PLATE p. 145
Height: 3 to 9 inches.
Habit: A low, stiffly erect perennial with a single whorl of thick,
glossy, evergreen leaves, ½ to 1½ inches long, the upper surface
dark green with light veinings. The long flower stalk may have
one to five white, waxy, nodding, very fragrant flowers, with
five wide-spreading petals and ten stamens.
Habitat: Dry woods, especially under pines; sandy soil. Massachusetts to Georgia and Alabama; west to Kentucky, northeast
Illinois, and Michigan. June to August.

PIPSISSEWA or PRINCE'S PINE (*Chimáphila umbellàta*)
PYROLA FAMILY (Pyrolàceae)   **PLATE p.** 145
Height: 3 to 10 inches.
Habit: A low, erect perennial with several whorls of evergreen, wedge-shaped leaves, 1 to 1¾ inches long, on the stem near the base. The long-stalked, nodding flowers rise from the leaf whorl with five wide-spreading white to pinkish petals and violet anthers. The two to eight flowers are in an open umbel.
Habitat: Sandy soil in dry woods. Quebec to Virginia; west to Indiana and Ohio. June to August.

INDIANPIPE (*Monótropa uniflòra*)   **PLATE p.** 145
PYROLA FAMILY (Pyrolàceae)
Height: 2 to 12 inches.
Habit: A smooth, waxy white plant without green coloring, the leaves reduced to scales. The stem is terminated by a single nodding, white (sometimes pink) flower with broadly oblong petals.
Habitat: Leaf mold in rich woods. Newfoundland to Florida and beyond our range. June to August. Plants are found singly or in extensive colonies. They are parasitic on roots or saprophytic on decomposing vegetable matter. The plant turns black later.

FALSE BEECHDROPS (*Monótropa hypópithys*) **PLATE p.** 145
PYROLA FAMILY (Pyrolàceae)
Height: 3 to 10 inches.
Habit: A small, erect, downy, tawny, fleshy-stemmed plant, without green coloring. It has small, scalelike leaves and a nodding flower of the same color, broadly tubular, saclike at the base, with scalelike petals and eight to ten stamens.
Habitat: Acid soil, woods. Newfoundland to Florida and beyond our range. June to September. It is parasitic on roots or saprophytic on decomposing vegetable matter. Turns black in drying.

GREAT MULLEIN (*Verbáscum thápsus*)   **PLATE p.** 146
FIGWORT OR SNAPDRAGON FAMILY (Scrophulariàceae)
Height: 3 to 6 feet.
Habit: A tall, stout, erect, woolly biennial producing a rosette of leaves in the autumn. The stem leaves, produced the following summer, are large, oblong, up to 10 inches long, decurrent on the stem, becoming winged. The stem is topped by a densely crowded spike, 6 to 30 inches long, of small yellow flowers.
Habitat: Fields, roadsides, gravel banks. Throughout our range and beyond. Late June to September. A naturalized weedy plant from Europe.

MOTH MULLEIN *(Verbáscum blattària)*   PLATE p. 146
FIGWORT OR SNAPDRAGON FAMILY (Scrophulariàceae)
Height: 3 to 5 feet.
Habit: A rather slender biennial with smooth green leaves; the
basal ones oblanceolate and stalked, the stem leaves narrow to
lance-shaped, sessile, and partly clasping. The stem is topped by
a raceme of yellow to white, open, five-lobed, tubular flowers,
the filaments bearded with violet wool.
Habitat: Roadsides, old fields, waste places. Throughout our
range and beyond. June to October. A naturalized plant from
Europe, established as a weed.

BUTTER-AND-EGGS *(Linària vulgàris)*   PLATE p. 146
FIGWORT OR SNAPDRAGON FAMILY (Scrophulariàceae)
Height: 1 to 2 feet.
Habit: An erect, smooth perennial with one to many stems and
numerous alternate, narrow, linear, pale green leaves, 1 to 2
inches long. The stems are topped by dense racemes of showy
spurred, tubular, yellow and orange flowers. Each flower has a
two-lobed upper lip, a three-lobed lower lip, and an orange
palate nearly closing the tubular throat.
Habitat: Roadsides and dry fields, waste ground. Throughout
our range and beyond. May to October. Naturalized from Europe. Spreads by underground runners.

SMOOTH FALSE FOXGLOVE *(Gerárdia laevigàta)*
FIGWORT OR SNAPDRAGON FAMILY (Scrophulariàceae)
Height: 2 to 4 feet.   PLATE p. 146
Habit: A tall, branched, stout perennial. Lower leaves may be
slightly lobed and ovate to lance-shaped; upper ones are uncut,
lance-shaped, and short-stalked. The large, yellow, tubular
flowers, 1¼ to 1½ inches long, have five equal rounded lobes.
Flowers are in the upper leaf axils.
Habitat: Chiefly in the mountains. Pennsylvania to Georgia;
west to Tennessee and Ohio. July to September.

HAIRY RUELLIA *(Ruéllia caroliniénsis)*   PLATE p. 147
ACANTHUS FAMILY (Acanthàceae)
Height: 1 to 3 feet.
Habit: A tall, simple or branched perennial, the stems covered
with fine, long hairs. The crowded leaves are opposite, lance-
shaped to ovate, 1 to 3½ inches long, and short-stalked. The
large, tubular, lavender blue flowers, 1 to 2 inches long, have
five spreading, equal lobes. Flowers are sessile in the leaf axils.
Habitat: Sandy woods, openings, clearings. New Jersey to Florida; west to Tennessee, Kentucky, Texas, Indiana, and Ohio.
June to September.

LIZARD'S-TAIL (*Saurùrus cérnuus*)　　　　**PLATE p. 147**
LIZARD'S-TAIL FAMILY (Saururàceae)
Height: 1 to 3 feet.
Habit: An erect perennial with jointed, leafy stems. Each leaf is heart-shaped and stalked. The flowers are in a dense, nodding terminal spike. The small, fragrant flowers have neither sepals nor petals, but appear white owing to the numerous white stamens.
Habitat: Swamps and marshes, shallow water. Quebec to Florida; west to Michigan, Minnesota, and Texas. June to September. A curious plant with only two species, one in North America and the other in eastern Asia.

PARTRIDGE-BERRY (*Mitchélla rèpens*)　　**PLATE p. 148**
MADDER FAMILY (Rubiàceae)
Height: 1 to 2 inches.
Habit: A creeping plant with opposite, smooth, glossy, round to ovate, evergreen leaves, $\frac{2}{5}$ to $\frac{4}{5}$ inch long. The white or very pale pink fragrant flowers are in leaf axils and at the ends of branches. The small tubular flowers are in pairs, each with four spreading lobes. Later, they produce scarlet, edible but insipid, berries that persist through the winter.
Habitat: Dry or moist woody slopes. Quebec to Florida; west to Minnesota and Texas. June and July. An excellent terrarium plant.

LARGE HOUSTONIA (*Houstònia purpùrea*)　　**PLATE p. 148**
MADDER FAMILY (Rubiàceae)
Height: 4 to 18 inches.
Habit: A tufted perennial with one to many stems from the base, bearing offsets. It has small, opposite, thin, sessile leaves, $\frac{2}{5}$ to 2 inches long. There are numerous short-stalked, pale purple to whitish, tubular flowers, each with four flat lobes.
Habitat: Dry woods, pine barrens. Pennsylvania to Georgia; west to Mississippi, Missouri, and Oklahoma. May to July.

ROUGH BEDSTRAW (*Gàlium aspréllum*)　　**PLATE p. 148**
MADDER FAMILY (Rubiàceae)
Height: 2 to 6 feet.
Habit: A weak, rough-stemmed perennial, ascending or lax with much-branched, square stems covered with hooked prickles. The leaves are in whorls of six, five, and four. The tiny white flowers are only $\frac{1}{10}$ to $\frac{1}{8}$ inch long and occur in branched clusters from the upper leaf axils.
Habitat: Damp soil, wet woods, along streams. Newfoundland to North Carolina; west to Minnesota and Missouri. May to August. The plant feels rough to the skin and catches freely on clothing.

WHITE WILD LICORICE (*Gàlium circaèzans*)
MADDER FAMILY (Rubiàceae)   PLATE p. 148
Height: 1 to 2 feet.
Habit: A slender, wiry-stemmed perennial, simple or branched
from the base, erect or ascending. It has oval to elliptic leaves,
⅘ to 2 inches long, in whorls of four. The tiny greenish white
flowers have four pointed lobes, their stalks usually once-forked.
Habitat: Dry woods and thickets. Maine to Florida; west to
Minnesota, Michigan, and Texas. June and July. Related to
Rough Bedstraw, but less rough and clinging.

NARROW-LEAVED VERVAIN (*Verbèna símplex*)
VERVAIN FAMILY (Verbenàceae)   PLATE p. 149
Height: 6 to 24 inches.
Habit: An unbranched or sparingly branched perennial with
rough-hairy stems and many opposite, linear to narrowly oblong,
roughish, sessile, ascending leaves, 1¼ to 4 inches long. The
stem is topped by tall spikes with small, crowded, lavender to
blue, tubular flowers, each solitary in the axil of a narrow bract.
Habitat: Dry woods, roadsides, rocky places, wasteland. Massachusetts to Florida; west to Mississippi, Louisiana, Oklahoma,
and Minnesota. June to August.

CURLY DOCK or YELLOW DOCK (*Rùmex crispus*)
BUCKWHEAT OR SMARTWEED FAMILY (Polygonàceae)
Height: 1 to 4 feet.   PLATE p. 149
Habit: A tall, smooth, erect, unbranched, weedy plant. The
lower leaves are blunt and rather heart-shaped at the base; the
upper ones, linear to lance-shaped; all are coarse and very wavy-
curled on the margins. Topping the stem are whorls of numerous small, inconspicuous flowers without petals, greenish
becoming brown. Later, they produce an abundance of three-
angled brownish seeds.
Habitat: Roadsides, fields, waste ground. Throughout the
United States. June to September. A common weed introduced
from Europe. Leaves are sometimes used for salad greens.

SHEEP SORREL (*Rùmex acetosélla*)   PLATE p. 149
BUCKWHEAT OR SMARTWEED FAMILY (Polygonàceae)
Height: 6 to 12 inches.
Habit: A low, slender, erect, simple or branched perennial with
a tuft of long-stalked, arrow-shaped leaves, each with two basal
spreading lobes. It is topped by racemes of tiny, inconspicuous,
reddish to yellowish, nodding flowers without petals.
Habitat: Lawns, worn-out fields, waste places, especially sour
soil. Throughout the United States. June to October. A pernicious weed, naturalized from the Old World. It is sour to the
taste; lower leaves can be used in salads.

QUEEN ANNE'S LACE *(Daùcus caròta)*   **PLATE p. 150**
PARSLEY FAMILY (Umbellíferae)
Height: 2 to 4 feet.
Habit: A tall, rough-hairy to bristly biennial, unbranched from
the base, with finely cut, palmately divided, fernlike leaves. The
beautiful flat-topped lacy umbels, 2 to 6 inches across, have
numerous tiny white flowers; the central flower is often purple.
Habitat: Dry fields, roadsides, waste places. Throughout the
United States. June to September. A naturalized weed from
Europe. The cultivated carrot is derived from this species.

HORSENETTLE *(Solànum carolinénse)*   **PLATE p. 150**
NIGHTSHADE FAMILY (Solanàceae)
Height: 1 to 3 feet.
Habit: An erect, leafy-branched, spiny-stemmed, simple or forking perennial. It has alternate, stalked, ovate, widely toothed
leaves, 2 to 4 inches long and ½ inch wide, with prickles beneath
along the midrib. It is topped by a cluster of white to pale
violet flowers with five pointed lobes, five stamens, and anthers
that form a cone around the style. Later, they produce yellow
berries.
Habitat: Fields, waste places, mostly sandy soil. Ontario to
Florida; west to Illinois, Nebraska, and Texas. May to October.
A weed difficult to eradicate. Native to the southern states; introduced elsewhere. Both potatoes and tomatoes are in the
family.

GRASS-OF-PARNASSUS *(Parnássia glaùca)*   **PLATE p. 151**
SAXIFRAGE FAMILY (Saxifragàceae)
Height: 9 to 20 inches.
Habit: A smooth perennial with a rosette of large, leathery,
blue green leaves, 1 to 2 inches long, and a long scapelike stem
with a single, small, sessile leaf near the base. Each stem is
topped by a single large flower up to 1½ inches across. The five
white petals have greenish veining; five fertile stamens are between the petals, and a number of barren stamens surround the
pistil.
Habitat: Wet fields and meadows. Quebec to Pennsylvania; west
to Ohio, Indiana, and South Dakota. Late July to October.
Found only in the northern part of our range.

WOOD-BETONY or COMMON LOUSEWORT
    (Pediculàris canadénsis)   **PLATE p. 151**
FIGWORT OR SNAPDRAGON FAMILY (Scrophulariàceae)
Height: 6 to 12 inches.
Habit: A low, hairy-stemmed perennial with mostly basal alter-
nate, long-stalked, segmented leaves. The stem leaves are red-
dish, pinnatifid, reduced in size upward, and becoming sessile.

The plant has a dense, oval head with many small bracts, among which are the yellowish or greenish to purplish tubular flowers, each with a hooded upper lip and a three-lobed lower lip.
Habitat: Upland woods, clearings. Maine to Florida; west to Mississippi, Louisiana, and Texas. April to June. The species name comes from the Latin *pediculus,* meaning "louse."

ROSE POGONIA (*Pogònia ophioglossoìdes*)   PLATE p. 152
  ORCHID FAMILY (Orchidàceae)
Height: 2 to 6 inches.
Habit: A small perennial with a slender, erect stem, having a single sessile leaf, 1 to 3 inches long, about midstem and a small bracteal leaf under the nodding, fragrant, rose pink flower. Sepals and petals are alike except for a distinctive lower, drooping lip, bearded and fringed with three rows of hairs.
Habitat: Bogs, swamps, wet meadows. Newfoundland to Florida; west to Minnesota and Texas. May to July.

YELLOW MILKWORT (*Polýgala lùtea*)   PLATE p. 152
  MILKWORT FAMILY (Polygalàceae)
Height: 6 to 12 inches.
Habit: A small biennial with one to several stems, branched or unbranched, and a rosette of obovate to spatulate leaves, ¾ to 1½ inches long, almost stalkless. The stems have lance-shaped, sessile leaves. The plant is topped by a headlike raceme of very small orange yellow flowers, with two similar upper petals and a keel-shaped and crested lower one.
Habitat: Wet, acid soil; sandy swamps and bogs. New York (Long Island) to Florida and Louisiana. June to August.

SENECA SNAKEROOT (*Polýgala sénega*)   PLATE p. 152
  MILKWORT FAMILY (Polygalàceae)
Height: 6 to 18 inches.
Habit: A perennial, usually unbranched, with one to several slightly hairy, leafy stems from a thick crown. The lowest leaves are bracteal; stem leaves are linear to lance-shaped, 1½ to 2¾ inches long, and short-stalked. The stem is topped by a raceme of small, rounded, white flowers with nearly round wings (two inner sepals) .
Habitat: Dry soil, rocky land. New Brunswick to Georgia; west to Arkansas, Tennessee, and South Dakota. May and June.

GRASS-PINK (*Calopògon pulchéllus*)   PLATE p. 153
  ORCHID FAMILY (Orchidàceae)
Height: 8 to 15 inches.
Habit: A slender-stemmed perennial with one, rarely two, linear, grasslike. nearly basal leaves, up to 14 inches long. It has four to ten large, rose purple, sweet-scented, showy flowers;

petals and sepals are colored alike. The fan-shaped, yellow-bearded lip is erect.

Habitat: Acid bogs and swamps, peaty meadows. Ontario to Florida; west to Minnesota and Texas. May to August.

LARGE PURPLE-FRINGED ORCHIS (*Habenària fimbriàta*)　　　　　　　　　　　　　　**PLATE p. 153**
ORCHID FAMILY (Orchidàceae)
Height: Up to 45 inches.
Habit: A perennial with a simple stem and alternate leaves. Lower leaves are lance-shaped to oval, up to 12 inches long and 3½ inches wide; upper leaves, linear to lance-shaped and much smaller. A densely flowered raceme bears handsome lavender to purple, fragrant flowers. Sepals and petals are colored alike; sepals erect and oval, petals with a drooping, three-parted lip almost 1 inch wide and fringed. There is a curved green spur.
Habitat: Borders of wet woods, moist meadows, and thickets. Quebec to North Carolina (usually in the mountains). June to August.

NARROWLEAF PLANTAIN (*Plantàgo lanceolàta*)
PLANTAIN FAMILY (Plantaginàceae)　　　　　　**PLATE p. 154**
Height: 8 to 12 inches.
Habit: A weedy plant with a basal tuft of narrow, ribbed, lance-shaped leaves, tapering at both ends. The tiny, whitish to purplish, dry, papery corollas, with the anthers extending beyond the flower, are in very dense spikes on long scapes.
Habitat: A common and troublesome weed of open sunny areas, lawns, waste places. Throughout the United States. May to October.

COMMON MALLOW (*Málva neglécta*)　　　　**PLATE p. 154**
MALLOW FAMILY (Malvàceae)
Height: Up to 40 inches long.
Habit: A prostrate, spreading, or ascending biennial. The long-stalked leaves have five to nine shallow lobes and are rather rounded and indented at the base. Small, stalked, axillary flowers, white or tinged with pink or lavender, have five notched petals, each lined with darker purple. The seed case is round and flat in the shape of a tiny cheese.
Habitat: A common weedy plant of waste places and roadsides. Widely established throughout temperate North America. May to October. Naturalized from Europe.

BLUE LUPINE (*Lupìnus perénnis*)　　　　　　**PLATE p. 154**
PULSE OR BEAN FAMILY (Leguminòsae)
Height: 8 to 24 inches.
Habit: An erect perennial with few to many stems from the

base. The leaves are round in general outline, palmately divided, with seven to eleven leaflets, each widest near the rather blunt tip. Showy, erect racemes of pea-shaped flowers are blue purple.
Habitat: Sandy soil, fields, open woods. Maine to Florida and Louisiana. May and June. Many species are found in the western states but only one species in the East.

FOUR-LEAVED LOOSESTRIFE (*Lysimáchia quadrifòlia*)
PRIMROSE FAMILY (Primulàceae)   PLATE p. 155
Height: 1 to 3 feet.
Habit: A tall, erect, rarely branched perennial. The leaves are in whorls of four at intervals on the stem decreasing in size upward, narrowly or broadly lance-shaped, and wide-spreading. Four long-stalked yellow flowers are in the axils of the leaf whorls. The five spreading corolla lobes are pointed and dotted with a deeper orange color. The stamens and pistil are in a cone-shaped projecting cluster.
Habitat: Sandy or lime soil, bogs, shores. Maine to Georgia and Alabama; west to Tennessee and Illinois. May to August.

SWAMP CANDLE (*Lysimáchia terréstris*)   PLATE p. 155
PRIMROSE FAMILY (Primulàceae)
Height: 1 to 3 feet.
Habit: A tall, erect, smooth-stemmed perennial, usually unbranched, with opposite, narrowly lance-shaped leaves, $1\frac{1}{2}$ to 4 inches long, becoming smaller upward. All have pointed tips and smooth margins. The stem is topped by a tall raceme of small, long-stalked, yellow flowers with five pointed petals, dotted or streaked with darker yellow or orange.
Habitat: Open swamps, wet soil, shores. Newfoundland to Georgia; west to Kentucky and Iowa. June to August.

SWAMP MILKWEED (*Asclèpias incarnàta*)   PLATE p. 156
MILKWEED FAMILY (Asclepiadàceae)
Height: 2 to 4 feet.
Habit: A tall, smooth, erect perennial with branching stems and milky juice. It has numerous opposite, lance-shaped to linear-oblong, short-stalked, smooth leaves. The numerous umbels of deep pink to rose purple flowers, $1\frac{1}{2}$ to 2 inches across, have the corolla lobes strongly reflexed. The stamens are in a ring with an erect or earlike appendage (hood) behind each anther. The anthers surround and partly adhere to the stigma.
Habitat: Swamps, wet meadows. Quebec to Florida; west to Louisiana and New Mexico. June to August.

BUTTERFLY-WEED (*Asclèpias tuberòsa*)   PLATE p. 156
MILKWEED FAMILY (Asclepiadàceae)
Height: 1 to 3 feet.

Habit: A perennial with few to many erect or ascending hairy stems, simple below and branched above. It has numerous slightly hairy, alternate, opposite, or even whorled leaves, linear to oblong, 2 to 4 inches long, with milky juice. Each stem is topped by a spreading umbel, 1½ to 2 inches across, of flowers that are bright orange red, yellow with orange hoods, or occasionally yellow throughout. For details see Swamp Milkweed.

Habitat: Dry fields, roadsides, open ground, especially sandy soil. Ontario to Florida; west to Kentucky, Mississippi, Texas, Arizona, Colorado, Michigan, and Minnesota. June to August. One of our showiest wildflowers and frequently cultivated; attractive to butterflies.

COMMON MILKWEED (*Asclèpias syrìaca*) PLATE p. 156
Milkweed Family (Asclepiadàceae)

Height: 2 to 6 feet.

Habit: A tall, stout, hairy perennial, usually unbranched, with numerous opposite, broadly elliptic to ovate leaves, 4 to 6 inches long, soft-hairy beneath and distinctly stalked. The rounded, many-flowered umbels are at the top and in upper leaf axils. The purplish reflexed corollas have paler dusty rose hoods, not so erect and spreading, each long-stalked, lax, and heavily fragrant.

Habitat: Roadsides, meadows, thickets, edges of woods. Canada to Georgia; west to Tennessee and Kansas. Can become a troublesome weed.

HEDGE BINDWEED or WILD MORNING-GLORY
(*Convólvulus sèpium*) PLATE p. 157
Convolvulus or Morning-Glory Family (Convolvulàceae)

Height: Up to 10 feet.

Habit: An extensively branched, twining or trailing perennial with alternate, stalked, triangular to arrow-shaped leaves. Each large, trumpet-shaped flower has a pink tube and a spreading white limb, 1½ to 2⅘ inches across. Flowers are borne in the leafy axils.

Habitat: Roadsides, fence rows, shores. Newfoundland to Florida; west to Texas and Oregon. July to September. Often a noxious weed difficult to eradicate.

MORNING-GLORY (*Ipomoèa hederàcea*) PLATE p. 157
Convolvulus or Morning-Glory Family (Convolvulàceae)

Height: Up to 7 feet.

Habit: A twining annual with fine-hairy stems and alternate three-lobed leaves, the central lobe largest. The leaves are stalked and hairy, 2 to 4 inches wide. The flower has a funnel-shaped corolla, the tube white and nearly 2 inches long, the spreading limb first blue, soon becoming rose purple.

Habitat: A weed in waste places, along roads, in cornfields. New York to Florida; west to Ohio, Indiana, Illinois, Minnesota, and North Dakota. Naturalized from tropical America.

COMMON DODDER (*Cuscùta gronòvii*)   **PLATE p.** 157
  CONVOLVULUS OR MORNING-GLORY FAMILY (Convolvulàceae)
Height: 4 to 5 feet.
Habit: A parasitic plant, lacking green color, resembling threads of yellowish to reddish yarn, intertwining over herbs and bushes, robbing them of their juices. The leaves are reduced to tiny scales. The plant has many dense clusters of small, waxy, five-lobed flowers, at first spreading, but becoming reflexed with age.
Habitat: Parasitic on many different hosts, mainly herbaceous plants. Canada to Florida, Texas, and westward. This is our commonest species. July to October. Often a bad weed in crops.

MOUNTAIN PHLOX (*Phlóx ovàta*)   **PLATE p.** 158
  PHLOX FAMILY (Polemoniàceae)
Height: 2 to 4 feet.
Habit: A tall, erect, smooth perennial with tufted, elliptic to ovate basal stem leaves and chiefly opposite, oblanceolate to elliptic upper stem leaves, 1½ to 4 inches long, smaller and sessile upward. The deep pink to reddish purple tubular flowers, ½ to ¾ inch long, have flat, open, rounded lobes. Flowers are in a crowded corymb at the top of the stem and upper leaf axils.
Habitat: Open woods, thickets, meadows. Southeastern Pennsylvania to upland North Carolina, Alabama, and Indiana. Mid-May to early July.

COMMON or SCARLET PIMPERNEL (*Anagállis
    arvénsis*)   **PLATE p.** 158
  PRIMROSE FAMILY (Primulàceae)
Height: 6 to 12 inches.
Habit: A low, diffusely branched annual, with slender, leafy stems and opposite, sessile, elliptic to ovate leaves, ⅜ to ⅝ inch long. The small, stalked, orange red flowers, ⅓ inch across, in the leaf axils, have five broad petals fringed with minute glandular teeth, and a very short corolla tube.
Habitat: A weed in gardens, lawns, roadsides, waste places. Throughout most of the United States. May to August. A naturalized plant from Europe. The flowers open only in fair weather and close on the approach of bad weather, hence the name Poor Man's Weatherglass.

LOPSEED (*Phrýma leptostáchya*)   **PLATE p.** 158
  LOPSEED FAMILY (Phrymàceae)
Height: 12 to 30 inches.
Habit: A low, erect, slender perennial with simple to few-

branching, leafy stems and opposite, bright green, ovate leaves, 2 to 4 inches long, with pointed tips. The lower leaves are long-stalked, progressively shorter-stalked upward. The opposite, tiny, lavender and white, tubular flowers are in a slender, elongated terminal spike and droop or lop down after blooming.
Habitat: Moist woods. Quebec to Florida; west to Tennessee, Oklahoma, and Texas. A unique plant, the only member of the family.

WHORLED ROSINWEED (*Silphium trifoliàtum*)
COMPOSITE FAMILY (Compósitae)   PLATE p. 159
Height: 3 to 5 feet.
Habit: A tall, coarse, smooth-stemmed, leafy perennial. Leaves, 2 to 6 inches long, are usually arranged in whorls of three or four, but may be opposite or alternate. They are rough and often slightly hairy on the midrib beneath. Each of the several to numerous large, golden yellow flower heads has eight to fifteen spreading, overlapping rays, ½ to 1½ inches long, and a yellow disk, up to ½ inch across.
Habitat: Woodlands, thickets, waste ground. Pennsylvania to Georgia; west to Alabama and Indiana. July to September.

SHARP-LEAVED GOLDENROD (*Solidàgo argùta*)
COMPOSITE FAMILY (Compósitae)   PLATE p. 159
Height: 2 to 4 feet.
Habit: A perennial with a solitary, erect, leafy stem and tufted, persistent basal leaves, 4 to 12 inches long, narrowly to broadly elliptic, and long-stalked. The stem leaves are sharp-pointed and finely toothed, somewhat rough and becoming sessile toward the top. The spreading, branched, wandlike, golden yellow panicle has numerous small heads of both tubular and ray flowers.
Habitat: Open woods, dry meadows. Maine to North Carolina. July to October. Almost a hundred species of goldenrod are native to North America. They are difficult to differentiate.

DROPSEED (*Galinsòga parviflòra*)   PLATE p. 159
COMPOSITE FAMILY (Compósitae)
Height: 1 to 2 feet.
Habit: A freely branched, erect, smooth-stemmed annual with opposite, oval to lance-ovate, coarsely toothed leaves. The small, inconspicuous flower heads, with five white, three-lobed rays, are in the axils of the upper leafy bracts.
Habitat: Waste places, cultivated ground, moist banks. A weed throughout our area. June to November. Naturalized from tropical America.

IRONWEED (*Vernònia altíssima*)   PLATE p. 160
COMPOSITE FAMILY (Compósitae)
Height: 3 to 10 feet.

Habit: A tall, coarse, leafy perennial, usually unbranched and with numerous veiny, spreading, narrowly ovate leaves, 6 to 10 inches long, pointed and sharply toothed, smooth above and minutely hairy beneath. The large, flat, showy, purplish red terminal flower clusters may be up to 20 inches across; each head contains thirteen to thirty rayless flowers.

Habitat: Moist woodlands, meadows, fence rows. Western New York to Georgia and Louisiana; west to Michigan and Nebraska. August to October.

PEARLY EVERLASTING (*Anáphalis margaritàcea*)
COMPOSITE FAMILY (Compósitae)   PLATE p. 160
Height: 1 to 3 feet.
Habit: An erect, usually unbranched, leafy, white-woolly perennial with narrow, linear, uncut, sessile, spreading, alternate leaves, 1 to 1½ inches long, only slightly reduced in size upward; the basal leaves soon wither and become brownish. The upper leaf surface is much less woolly than beneath. The stems are corymbose at the top, with clusters of short-stalked, more or less flat-topped to rounded flower heads, each ¼ to ½ inch across. The flower heads are numerous (the pistillate and staminate on separate plants), each with many dry, papery, pearly white involucral bracts; corollas are yellow.

Habitat: Usually dry, open ground; often in sand or gravel. Newfoundland to North Carolina; west to Kansas. July to September. This is a small genus of North America and northeastern Asia. Sometimes cultivated in gardens.

WHITE-TOPPED ASTER (*Seriocárpus asteròides*)
COMPOSITE FAMILY (Compósitae)   PLATE p. 160
Height: 6 to 24 inches.
Habit: A tufted, somewhat hairy perennial with few to many stems from the base and broadly oblanceolate, stalked leaves, up to 3 inches long. The upper leaves are more or less toothed and become smaller and sessile. There is a rather flat-topped cluster of twelve to twenty tiny flower heads, each with four to eight white rays.

Habitat: Dry woods, clearings. Southern Maine to Florida, Alabama, and Mississippi; west to Michigan. June to August.

JOE-PYE-WEED (*Eupatòrium purpùreum*)   PLATE p. 160
COMPOSITE FAMILY (Compósitae)
Height: 2 to 7 feet.
Habit: A tall, erect, coarse perennial with large, lance-shaped to elliptic leaves, 2½ to 9 inches long, in whorls of five and six. Each leaf is smooth above, soft-hairy beneath, and very veiny. The pale, pinkish lavender flower heads are in large, compound,

domed clusters. Each head contains three to seven rayless flowers. The plant is sweetly vanilla-scented when bruised.
Habitat: Thickets, open woods. New Hampshire to northern Florida; west to Tennessee, Arkansas, Oklahoma, Nebraska, and Minnesota. Mid-July to mid-September.

MISTFLOWER *(Eupatòrium coelestìnum)*   **PLATE p. 161**
   COMPOSITE FAMILY (Compósitae)
Height: 1 to 3 feet.
Habit: A fine-hairy, leafy, branched perennial with opposite, broadly to narrowly triangular, somewhat heart-shaped leaves, 1 to 3 inches long, and coarsely toothed. Flat-headed flower clusters terminate the upper branches; each head contains thirty-five to seventy light blue to violet disk flowers without rays.
Habitat: Moist meadows, stream banks, fields. New Jersey to Florida; west to Kansas and Texas. June to October. This plant often makes a carpet of blue. It resembles the garden *Ageratum.*

PURPLE CONEFLOWER *(Echinàcea pállida)*   **PLATE p. 161**
   COMPOSITE FAMILY (Compósitae)
Height: 2 to 3 feet.
Habit: A coarse, hairy, unbranched perennial with a few, mostly alternate, parallel-veined, narrow leaves, up to 8 inches long, gradually tapering to a long, narrow base. The stem is topped by a large, purple, conelike flower head having many crowded tiny flowers and drooping purple rays, toothed at the tips, 1 to 2½ inches long.
Habitat: Fields, fence rows, rich soil, dry woods. Casual as an immigrant in the Atlantic states; native to Alabama and Louisiana; west to Texas; north to Nebraska and Michigan. June and July.

TANSY *(Tanacètum vulgàre)*   **PLATE p. 161**
   COMPOSITE FAMILY (Compósitae)
Height: 2 to 5 feet.
Habit: A strongly aromatic, coarse, densely tufted perennial with alternate, deep green, finely divided, fernlike leaves, one to three pinnately dissected, 3 to 9 inches long. The stem is terminated by flat-topped clusters of numerous yellow, buttonlike flower heads composed of disk flowers only, ¼ to ⅓ inch across.
Habitat: Fields, fence rows, roadsides. Newfoundland and northern parts of our area and beyond. July to September. A naturalized plant from Europe.

DOG-FENNEL or STINKING CHAMOMILE *(Anthemis còtula)*   **PLATE p. 161**
   COMPOSITE FAMILY (Compósitae)
Height: 8 to 20 inches.

Habit: A strongly aromatic, ill-scented annual, unbranched to bushy-branched with many alternate, finely cut leaves, two to three times pinnately divided into very narrow leaflets or segments. The plant is terminated by long-stalked flower heads composed of mounded or cone-shaped golden disks and ten to twenty white rays.

Habitat: A common weed in fields, waste places, fence rows, along roadsides. Throughout our range and beyond. A plant naturalized from Europe.

BLACK MUSTARD (*Brássica nìgra*) PLATE p. 162
MUSTARD FAMILY (Crucíferae)

Height: 2 to 5 feet.

Habit: A tall, coarse annual with a simple or branched, short-hairy or nearly smooth leafy stem. The lower leaves are deeply lobed, with one terminal large lobe and two to four smaller lateral lobes; the upper ones smaller and sometimes only toothed; all with short stalks. Clusters of small, bright yellow flowers with four petals wider and indented at the tip, 1/3 to 1/2 inch across, are borne on terminal racemes that elongate with age. Flowers produce short, erect, four-angled pods.

Habitat: Fields, roadsides, waste places. Throughout the United States. June to October. Naturalized plant from Europe. The mustard family gives us cabbage, Brussels sprouts, cauliflower, turnips, and mustard.

ENCHANTER'S NIGHTSHADE (*Circaèa quadrisulcàta* var. *canadénsis*) PLATE p. 162
EVENING-PRIMROSE FAMILY (Onagràceae)

Height: 2 to 4 feet.

Habit: A tall, slender, erect, branching perennial with opposite, thin, oblong-ovate leaves, widest at the base, 1 3/4 to 3 1/2 inches long. Tiny, stalked, white flowers, 1/4 inch across, are in terminal and lateral racemes, up to 6 inches long. A pod is later produced, reflexed downward and covered with stiff, hooked hairs.

Habitat: Moist woods, thickets, ravines. Quebec to North Carolina and Georgia; west to Tennessee, Missouri, and Oklahoma. June to August.

WINTERGREEN or CHECKERBERRY (*Gaulthèria procúmbens*) PLATE p. 162
HEATH FAMILY (Ericàceae)

Height: 2 to 5 inches.

Habit: A low, subshrub with short, erect, stiff, brownish stems and smooth, leathery, glossy, elliptic to ovate, evergreen leaves, often crowded at the top of the plant. The small, drooping, white, bell-like, waxy, tubular flowers have five shallow lobes, 1/4 to 1/3 inch long, and grow from the leaf axils. Later, they produce a round, red, edible, aromatic berry.

Habitat: Acid soil, woods, hillsides. Newfoundland to Virginia
and mountains of Georgia; west to Kentucky and Minnesota.
July and August. The bruised leaves have the flavor of wintergreen.

POKEBERRY (*Phytolácca americàna*) **PLATE p. 162**
POKEWEED FAMILY (Phytolaccàceae)
Height: 4 to 12 feet.
Habit: A large, coarse, stout, smooth, leafy perennial with thick,
fleshy reddish stems and alternate, large, uncut, ovate leaves, up
to 10 inches long. Long racemes of tiny, inconspicuous flowers
are opposite the upper leaf axils. Each flower has five greenish
white sepals (petals absent) and ten stamens; later, reddish
purple, juicy berries are produced on drooping stalks.
Habitat: Fence rows, clearings, low fields, waste places. Maine
to Florida; west to Minnesota and Texas. July to September.
The young shoots can be cooked for greens, but the roots and
mature leaves are poisonous.

BUTTERFLY PEA (*Clitòria mariàna*) **PLATE p. 163**
PULSE OR BEAN FAMILY (Leguminòsae)
Height: 3 feet or more.
Habit: A smooth, slender perennial vine, twining by tendrils,
with alternate, compound leaves, the three leaflets ovate to
ovate-oblong, each 1 to 1¾ inches long. The large, solitary, pea-
shaped flower, in the leaf axil, is pale lavender, 1½ to 2 inches
long, with an inflated standard, notched at the top, and much
smaller, incurved, keel-shaped petals.
Habitat: Dry upland woods, on bushes and rocks. New York to
Florida; west to southern Indiana and southern Illinois. June
to August.

WILD INDIGO or RATTLEWEED (*Baptisia tinctòria*)
PULSE OR BEAN FAMILY (Leguminòsae) **PLATE p. 163**
Height: 1 to 3 feet.
Habit: A tall, widely spreading, bushy-branched perennial with
small, compound leaves, palmately divided into three wedge-
shaped, nearly sessile leaflets, each ¼ to ⅓ inch long. It has
many small racemes, each with a few yellow, pea-shaped flowers,
¼ to ½ inch long, that later produce thick, somewhat inflated
pods.
Habitat: Dry, open woods; sandy soil; clearings. Maine to Florida; west to Tennessee, Indiana, Michigan, and Minnesota. Late
May to September.

WHITE SWEET CLOVER or MELILOT (*Melilòtus
álba*) **PLATE p. 163**
PULSE OR BEAN FAMILY (Leguminòsae)
Height: Up to 6 feet.

Habit: A coarse, erect, open-branched perennial with small, stalked, compound leaves with three narrow leaflets, ¼ to ¾ inch long. The numerous small, white, pea-shaped flowers, ⅛ to ⅙ inch long, are in terminal racemes.

Habitat: Waste places, roadsides, fields. Widely distributed throughout the United States. May to October. Introduced from Europe. Plants are fragrant on a bright sunny day, also when cut and dried.

YELLOW MELILOT or YELLOW SWEET CLOVER
(Melilòtus officinàlis)   PLATE p. 163
PULSE OR BEAN FAMILY (Leguminòsae)

Height: Up to 5 feet.

Habit: Another species similar to *M. alba* but usually not so tall, with the same habit and similar leaves, but with small, bright yellow flowers, ¼ to ⅜ inch long, borne in spikelike racemes, 2 to 6 inches long.

Habitat: Waste ground, fence rows, roadsides. Throughout our range, but less common in the southern region. Late May to October. Naturalized from Europe. Often *M. alba* and *M. officinalis* are found growing together.

PINK WILD BEAN *(Strophostỳles umbellàta)*   PLATE p. 163
PULSE OR BEAN FAMILY (Leguminòsae)

Height: Up to 6 feet long.

Habit: A trailing perennial with three-divided leaves, each leaflet narrowly oblong to lance-shaped, ½ to 2 inches long. The small, pink to purple, pealike flowers, ½ to ¾ inch long, are on a headlike, stalked raceme extending above the leaves. Later, the flowers form a long beanlike pod that twists after opening.

Habitat: Dry, sandy, upland woods; sandy fields; clearings. New York to Florida; west to Indiana, Oklahoma, and Texas. July to October.

RATTLEBOX *(Crotalària sagittàlis)*   PLATE p. 164
PULSE OR BEAN FAMILY (Leguminòsae)

Height: 6 to 24 inches.

Habit: A low, hairy annual, simple or branched above, with small, uncut, blunt, lance-shaped to linear, sessile leaves, 1 to 2½ inches long. The stalked, yellow, pea-shaped flowers, ¼ to ½ inch long, are in few-flowered racemes from the leaf axils and ends of branches. The flowers later produce inflated pods, ½ to 1 inch long, in which the seeds rattle after drying; hence, the name Rattlebox.

Habitat: Dry, sandy soil; wasteland. Massachusetts to Florida; west to Minnesota, South Dakota, and Texas. June to September.

PARTRIDGE-PEA or GOLDEN CASSIA (*Cássia fasciculàta*)   **PLATE p. 164**
PULSE OR BEAN FAMILY (Leguminòsae)
Height: 1 to 3 feet.
Habit: A tall, erect annual with ascending, rather spreading, fine-hairy branches and many fernlike, pinnately divided leaves with six to eighteen pairs of leaflets, each ⅓ to ¾ inch long, and tipped with a tiny bristle. The one to six large, bright yellow, showy, axillary flowers have five petals, each ½ to ¾ inch long, usually spotted with a darker color at the base. Later, a narrow, straight pod is produced.
Habitat: Moist or dry sandy fields, upland woods, roadsides, old fields. Massachusetts to Florida; west to Minnesota, South Dakota, and Texas. July to September.

TICK-TREFOIL (*Desmòdium nudiflòrum*)   **PLATE p. 164**
PULSE OR BEAN FAMILY (Leguminòsae)
Height: 1 to 2 feet.
Habit: A tall, slender, lax perennial with several stems from the base and upper clusters of compound, three-divided leaves; leaflets are rounded at the base and the middle segment is much the largest. The lavender to pink, inconspicuous, pea-shaped flowers, about ¼ inch long, are widely spaced along the terminal raceme.
Habitat: Rich woods, wasteland. Maine to Florida; west to Wisconsin and Texas. July to September. Tick-trefoils produce stickers—triangular pods joined only at the upper corners and covered with tiny hooked hairs, which cling to clothing.

PENCIL FLOWER (*Stylosánthes biflòra*)   **PLATE p. 164**
PULSE OR BEAN FAMILY (Leguminòsae)
Height: 4 to 16 inches.
Habit: An erect, ascending, or spreading, wiry-stemmed perennial, branched from the base, with small, three-divided leaves, each leaflet narrowly oblong, ¾ to 1¼ inches long. The inconspicuous, orange yellow, pea-shaped flowers, ¼ to ⅓ inch long. are usually in pairs in the upper leaf axils.
Habitat: Dry or rock woods. New York to Florida; west to Illinois, Kansas, and Texas. June to August.

FALSE DRAGONHEAD (*Physostégia virginiàna*)
MINT FAMILY (Labiàtae)   **PLATE p. 165**
Height: 1 to 4 feet.
Habit: A tall, stiffly erect, smooth, square-stemmed perennial with opposite, narrow, rigid, grayish green leaves, 2 to 5 inches long, widely separated on the stem. There is a spike of large, showy, pink to purple, tubular flowers, 1 to 1¼ inches long, each with a straight upper lip and a three-lobed lower lip.

Habitat: Waste places along stream banks, swampy thickets. Quebec to North Carolina; west to Tennessee, Missouri, and Minnesota. June to September. Often cultivated in gardens. Mostly in the western part of our range.

AMERICAN GERMANDER or WOOD-SAGE (*Teùcrium canadénse*)   PLATE p. 165
MINT FAMILY (Labiàtae)
Height: 1 to 2 feet.
Habit: A stiff, erect, downy, square-stemmed, leafy perennial, branched or unbranched, with ovate to lance-shaped leaves, ½ to 1 inch, broad and rounded at the base, usually not whorled. The stem is topped by a tall raceme of crowded, purplish pink or creamy, tubular flowers, each ¾ inch long, with stamens that project through an opening in the upper lip.
Habitat: Thickets, woods, shores. Maine to Florida and in the Mississippi valley to Oklahoma. July to September.

BASIL (*Saturèja vulgàris*)   PLATE p. 165
MINT FAMILY (Labiàtae)
Height: 8 to 24 inches.
Habit: An erect, simple, perennial with a fine-hairy, square stem, occasionally branched above. The opposite leaves are ovate-oblong to lance-shaped, entire or with a few fine teeth on the leaf margins, and short-stalked. Numerous flowers are in dense clusters (verticils) at the top of the plant and in the upper leaf axils, the upper and terminal verticils usually largest. The small tubular flowers are lavender, rose purple, or pink (rarely white) ; the tube gradually passes into the throat, with an upper lip and a wider lower lip.
Habitat: Woods, thickets, alluvial shores, roadsides, pastures. Quebec to North Carolina; west to Tennessee, Kansas, Arizona, and New Mexico. June to September. This is both a native and an introduced plant from Europe.

WILD BERGAMOT (*Monárda fistulòsa*)   PLATE p. 166
MINT FAMILY (Labiàtae)
Height: 2 to 4 feet.
Habit: A tall, erect perennial with thin, opposite leaves, broad at the base and pointed at the tip, 2 to 6 inches long. The pale pink or deeper magenta purple tubular flowers are clustered in a leafy head; each flower is distinctly two-lipped, the upper one straight, the broader lower lip curving downward.
Habitat: Dry ground, open woods, roadsides. Quebec to Georgia; west to Louisiana, Arizona, and Texas. June to September. It has an aromatic odor.

SELFHEAL *(Prunélla vulgàris)* PLATE p. 166
MINT FAMILY (Labiàtae)
Height: 8 to 24 inches.
Habit: A low, simple or branched perennial with stout, slightly hairy, four-angled stems and opposite, lance-shaped to ovate leaves, 1 to 4 inches long and half as wide. The sessile, bluish violet or lavender, hooded, tubular flowers are in the axils of bractlike leaves, forming a dense oblong head. Only a few flowers bloom at a time.
Habitat: Roadsides, waste ground, borders of fields. Throughout the United States. May to October. Naturalized from Europe.

ROUGH HEDGE-NETTLE *(Stáchys nuttállii)*
MINT FAMILY (Labiàtae) PLATE p. 166
Height: 2 to 4 feet.
Habit: A tall, erect perennial with sticky-hairy square stems and opposite, narrowly ovate to oblong leaves, hairy above and on the veins beneath, 1 to 4 inches long. In the axils of the upper bracts are whorls of small, pink or lavender, tubular flowers, spotted with a deeper shade of the same color. The upper lip is hooded; the wider, three-lobed lower lip droops.
Habitat: Mountain forests. Virginia and North Carolina; west to Kentucky, Arkansas, and Oklahoma. June and July.

HEMP-NETTLE *(Galeópsis tetràhit)* PLATE p. 166
MINT FAMILY (Labiàtae)
Height: 1 to 2 feet.
Habit: A simple or branching annual with four-angled, rough, hairy stems and opposite, ovate leaves, rounded near the base. The small, pale purple to pink and white, tubular flowers are in dense whorls at the top of the stem, usually in the axils of floral leaves, but these are sometimes absent, as in the illustration in this book. There are white bristles on the outer surface of the upper lip.
Habitat: Roadsides, gardens, waste fields. Quebec to North Carolina; west to Ohio, Michigan, and Wisconsin. July to September. Naturalized from Europe.

TALL BUTTERCUP *(Ranùnculus ácris)* PLATE p. 167
CROWFOOT OR BUTTERCUP FAMILY (Ranunculàceae)
This is another form of *R. acris,* which is a variable plant. The leaf segments are wider and variable. The flower is a lighter soft yellow. See p. 25 for full description of *R. acris.*

THIMBLEWEED *(Anemòne virginiàna)* PLATE p. 167
CROWFOOT OR BUTTERCUP FAMILY (Ranunculàceae)
Height: 2 to 3 feet.

Habit: A tall perennial with a few long-stalked basal leaves, deeply divided into three or five segments. The stem leaves are in whorls of three, the uppermost in pairs, on the erect stem. A single flower, up to 1 inch across, with five petallike sepals, white within and green without, tops the stem. Later, a thimble-shaped head covered with densely woolly seeds is produced. *Habitat:* Dry or open woods, thickets, rocky banks. Quebec to Georgia and Alabama; west to Arkansas, Kansas, and Minnesota. June to August.

VIRGIN'S-BOWER *(Clématis virginiàna)*   PLATE p. 167
  CROWFOOT OR BUTTERCUP FAMILY (Ranunculàceae)
Height: 8 to 12 feet.
Habit: A climbing, woody vine with leaves divided into three distinct leaflets and clusters, in the leaf axils, of small fragrant flowers with creamy white petallike sepals. Feathery-tailed seeds are produced in late summer.
Habitat: Draped over bushes, along roadsides, moist places. Quebec to Georgia, Alabama, Mississippi, and Louisiana; west to Kansas. July to September.

MONKEY-FLOWER *(Mímulus alàtus)*   PLATE p. 168
  FIGWORT OR SNAPDRAGON FAMILY (Scrophulariàceae)
Height: 1 to 3 feet.
Habit: A tall, erect, smooth perennial with four-angled stems, narrowly winged along the angles, and opposite, large, stalked leaves, lance-shaped to ovate, 2 to 4 inches long. The axillary, large, violet, pink, or white, tubular flowers, 1 inch long, have the lobes of the upper lip recurved and a wider spreading lower lip. The tubular calyx, with pointed lobes, is conspicuous.
Habitat: Wet woods, swamps, along streams. Ontario to Florida; west to Texas, Iowa, and Michigan. July and August. *M. ringens* is closely related and similar, but has sessile leaves.

CULVER'S-ROOT *(Veronicástrum virgínicum)* PLATE p. 168
  FIGWORT OR SNAPDRAGON FAMILY (Scrophulariàceae)
Height: 2 to 6 feet.
Habit: A tall, erect perennial with narrow, pointed leaves in whorls of three to six around the stem. The spikes of crowded, tiny, white, tubular flowers, each with two projecting stamens, give the inflorescence a lacy, fuzzy appearance.
Habitat: Meadows, rich woods, thickets, roadsides. Manitoba to western Florida; west to Texas. June to September.

FALSE PIMPERNEL *(Lindérnia dùbia)*   PLATE p. 168
  FIGWORT OR SNAPDRAGON FAMILY (Scrophulariàceae)
Height: 4 to 8 inches.
Habit: A small annual, usually branched or spreading, with

opposite, oblong or obovate leaves, about 1 inch long. Small, pale lavender to violet, tubular flowers, ⅓ to ½ inch long, are in the upper leaf axils. They may fertilize themselves without opening.
Habitat: Damp soil, sandy or muddy shores. Quebec to Florida; west to North Dakota and Texas. June to October.

JEWELWEED or TOUCH-ME-NOT (*Impàtiens capénsis*)
JEWELWEED OR TOUCH-ME-NOT FAMILY (Balsaminàceae)
Height: 2 to 5 feet.   PLATE p. 169
Habit: A tall, smooth annual with succulent stems, much-branched above, and alternate, soft, pale green, ovate leaves, 1½ to 3½ inches long. Each drooping, spotted, orange yellow, tubular flower has a saclike sepal with a recurved basal spur. Later, a capsule, up to 1 inch long, is produced, which when mature, springs open at the slightest touch, scattering the seeds.
Habitat: Moist woods, stream banks, ravines. Quebec to South Carolina and Alabama; west to Arkansas and Oklahoma. June to September.

PALE JEWELWEED (*Impàtiens pállida*)   PLATE p. 169
JEWELWEED OR TOUCH-ME-NOT FAMILY (Balsaminàceae)
Height: 2 to 6 feet.
Habit: Similar to *I. capensis* in having tubular and spurred flowers, but a taller plant with slightly larger leaves and pale yellow flowers, with or without spots. The capsule is also a bit longer.
Habitat: Wet woods, meadows, wet shady ground. Quebec to North Carolina; west to Tennessee and Missouri. June to September. It is usually less abundant than *I. capensis.*

FLOWERING SPURGE (*Euphórbia corollàta*)   PLATE p. 169
SPURGE FAMILY (Euphorbiàceae)
Height: 2 to 5 feet.
Habit: A tall, smooth perennial with milky juice, much-branched above, with small, alternate, linear to elliptic stem leaves, ¾ to 1 inch long, and a whorl of leaves just under the rather flat inflorescence, which is loosely branched and can be up to 12 inches across. Many tiny flowers, each with five petal-like appendages, surround a greenish ovary (young seedpod).
Habitat: Dry woods, old fields, roadsides. Massachusetts to Florida; west to Texas, Nebraska, and Minnesota. June to October.

WATER-PARSNIP (*Sìum suàve*)   PLATE p. 170
PARSLEY FAMILY (Umbellíferae)
Height: 2 to 6 feet.
Habit: A tall, branched perennial, usually growing in marshes,

with stout strongly angled stems. The leaves are variable: underwater leaves, if present, may be finely divided and long-stalked; stem leaves are divided into seven to seventeen pinnately compound, narrow leaflets; uppermost leaves may be undivided. The small, white, fragrant flowers are crowded in umbels, 1 to 4 inches across.

Habitat: Swamps, marshes, wet meadows, streams. Newfoundland to Florida and Louisiana; west to Ohio, Indiana, Illinois, Missouri, and eastern Kansas. June to September.

NEW JERSEY TEA (*Ceanòthus americànus*)   PLATE p. 171
    BUCKTHORN FAMILY (Rhamnàceae)
Height: 2 to 4 feet.
Habit: A much-branched shrub with coarse, woody stems and alternate, undivided, narrowly to broadly ovate leaves, 1 to 3 inches long, with three prominent veins. The small, white, clustered flowers, each with five slender petals, are in cone-shaped, fluffy, headlike inflorescences and have a slight odor.
Habitat: Upland woods; dry, open fields; gravel banks. Quebec to Florida; west to Minnesota and Missouri. June and July. Revolutionary War soldiers made an indifferent tea from the dried leaves.

FOG-FRUIT (*Lìppia lanceolàta*)   PLATE p. 171
    VERVAIN FAMILY (Verbenàceae)
Height: 6 to 9 inches.
Habit: A weak, open-branched perennial with prostrate, sprawling, or ascending stems often rooting at the nodes. The leaves are opposite, lance-shaped to ovate, and short-stalked to sessile. Long-stalked, many-flowered heads, 1/2 inch across, have tiny pink, bluish, or white flowers surrounded by pointed bracts. The heads later elongate and become conelike.
Habitat: Moist river bottoms, coastal marshes, meadows. Ontario to Florida; west to Kansas and Minnesota. May to October.

EVENING LYCHNIS or WHITE CAMPION (*Lýchnis
    álba*)   PLATE p. 171
    PINK FAMILY (Caryophyllàceae)
Height: 1 to 2 feet.
Habit: A tall, fine-hairy, sticky-stemmed, open-branched perennial with up to ten pairs of opposite, broadly elliptic leaves, 1 to 3¼ inches long. The lower leaves are stalked; the upper ones, sessile. Single, fragrant, white to pink flowers, with five deeply notched petals, are borne at the tips of the branches.
Habitat: Roadsides, borders of fields, waste places. Quebec to Georgia; west to Indiana, Illinois, Missouri, and Kansas. Late May to September. Naturalized from Europe. Flowers open only in the evening.

CORN-COCKLE (*Agrostémma githàgo*)   PLATE p. 171
PINK FAMILY (Caryophyllàceae)
Height: 1 to 3 feet.
Habit: A tall, erect, downy annual with opposite, linear, pointed leaves. The large, bright, rose to purplish flowers have five petals and may be spotted with black at the outer, wider margins. The ribbed calyx is prominent, and the five narrow teeth extend beyond the petals.
Habitat: A weed of grainfields, waste places, roadsides. More abundant in the northern part of our range. July to September. Naturalized from Europe and widely established in this country.

WILD GARLIC (*Allium canadénse*)   PLATE p. 172
LILY FAMILY (Liliàceae)
Height: 6 to 24 inches.
Habit: From a bulb, with narrowly linear, keeled, thick basal leaves. The long, naked scape has an umbel of whitish to purplish bulblets, mixed occasionally with a few flowers.
Habitat: Moist or dry woods, fields. Maine to Florida; west to Texas, Wisconsin, and Minnesota. May to July. Plant has a strong odor of garlic when bruised.

NODDING WILD ONION (*Allium cérnuum*)   PLATE p. 172
LILY FAMILY (Liliàceae)
Height: 6 to 24 inches.
Habit: A perennial from a bulb. Narrow, flat, fleshy, basal leaves are shorter than the tall, naked, flowering scape that arches at the top, with a loose head of small, pink or white, nodding flowers.
Habitat: Dry woods, ledges, gravel. New York to Georgia; west to Tennessee, Missouri, and Texas. July and August. Bulbs and leaves have a strong odor of onion when bruised.

WOOD LILY (*Lilium philadélphicum*)   PLATE p. 172
LILY FAMILY (Liliàceae)
Height: 1 to 3 feet.
Habit: A perennial from a bulb, with narrow, lance-shaped or linear leaves in two to six whorls of four to seven leaves each. The stem is topped by one to three orange red flowers, with petals and sepals colored alike, narrowed at the base to a "claw" and widening out to form a rather spreading cup with pointed tips and lined inside with purple dots.
Habitat: Damp, sandy soil; thickets; open woods; clearings. Maine to North Carolina and Kentucky. Mid-June to mid-August.

WATER-PLANTAIN (*Alísma plantágo-aquática*)
WATER-PLANTAIN FAMILY (Alismatàceae)   PLATE p. 173
Height: 4 to 40 inches.

Habit: A perennial of marshes, ponds, and streams, with long-stalked, elliptic to broadly ovate basal leaves, 1 to 6 inches long. The tall, naked scape is topped by whorls of tiny, white to pinkish, three-petaled, stalked flowers.
Habitat: Marshes, ponds, sluggish streams, shallow water, swamps. Quebec to southern New York; west to Michigan, Wisconsin, and westward. June to October.

ARROWHEAD *(Sagittària austràlis)*   PLATE p. 173
    WATER-PLANTAIN FAMILY (Alismatàceae)
Height: 2 to 4 feet.
Habit: A stout, aquatic perennial with long-stalked, arrow-shaped leaves and a thick scape projecting above the leaves with stalked whorls of three to ten showy white flowers; each has three petals, $\frac{3}{16}$ to $\frac{1}{4}$ inch long. The upper flowers are male (staminate) ; the lower ones female (pistillate) .
Habitat: Shallow water, swamps, ponds, springs. New Jersey to Florida and Alabama; west to Indiana and Missouri. July to October. More robust, with broader-lobed leaves, in the southern part of its range.

ARROWHEAD *(Sagittària rígida)*   PLATE p. 174
    WATER-PLANTAIN FAMILY (Alismatàceae)
Height: 1 to 2 feet.
Habit: An erect or lax, emersed or submersed perennial with variable leaves, mostly lance-shaped and uncut (a few arrow-shaped) , with poorly developed small basal lobes, all long-stalked. The erect scape has two to eight whorls of white flowers, with three petals, $\frac{1}{2}$ to 1 inch long. The upper flowers are male (staminate) ; the lower ones female (pistillate) .
Habitat: Swamps, ponds, shallow water. Quebec to Delaware; west to Tennessee, Kentucky, Ohio, and Nebraska. July to October. Plants are extremely variable, according to habitat.

ARROWHEAD *(Sagittària latifòlia)*   PLATE p. 174
    WATER-PLANTAIN FAMILY (Alismatàceae)
Height: 2 to 3 feet.
Habit: A large, coarse, erect, aquatic perennial with variable leaves, all basal and large, up to 16 inches long and 10 inches wide, with lobes varying from broadly ovate to linear. The naked scapes, up to 4 feet high, are simple or branched, with two to fifteen whorls of pure white, three-petaled, showy flowers, up to 1 inch across.
Habitat: Swamps, ponds, streams. Nova Scotia to Florida and Louisiana; west to Kansas. July to October.

PICKERELWEED (*Pontedèria cordàta*)   PLATE p. 175
PICKERELWEED FAMILY (Pontederiàceae)
Height: 1 to 4 feet.
Habit: A stout perennial water plant, often forming large colonies, with variable, large, thick, glossy leaves, more than 7 inches long, and heart-shaped, arrow-shaped, or narrowed at the base. The long flower stalk is sheathed by a single leaf and topped by a spikelike panicle of crowded, violet blue, tubular flowers.
Habitat: Sluggish streams, ponds, shallow margins of lakes. Nova Scotia to South Carolina; west to Texas and Minnesota. June to September.

WATER-STARGRASS (*Heteranthèra dùbia*)   PLATE p. 175
PICKERELWEED FAMILY (Pontederiàceae)
Height: 2 to 3 feet.
Habit: An aquatic plant with submerged branching, grasslike, long, translucent sessile leaves. The naked scape usually has a single small, pale yellow flower at or above the surface of the water, with a threadlike tube and six pointed, starlike lobes. It is often fertilized in the bud.
Habitat: Sluggish streams, quiet waters, shallow lake margins. Quebec to North Carolina; west to Minnesota, Arkansas, New Mexico, and Texas. June to September.

WATER-LILY (*Nymphaèa odoràta*)   PLATE p. 176
WATER-LILY FAMILY (Nymphaeàceae)
Height: Leaves and flowers float on the water surface.
Habit: An aquatic perennial with long-stalked, leathery, roundish leaves, 4 to 8 inches wide, green above and purplish beneath. The solitary, fragrant flower is large and showy, 1½ to 9 inches across, with numerous narrow, pointed, white petals and conspicuous yellow stamens. Both flowers and leaf blades float on the water surface. Each blossom opens in the morning only for three or four days.
Habitat: Ponds, still water, bogs. Throughout most of our range. June to September.

YELLOW POND-LILY (*Nùphar ádvena*)   PLATE p. 176
WATER-LILY FAMILY (Nymphaeàceae)
Habit: An aquatic plant with large, erect, oval, heart-shaped leaves, 6 to 12 inches long, green above and purplish red beneath. The flower, with green, curving outer sepals and inner yellow-tipped sepals, forms a cup, 1½ to 2 inches across. Numerous small scalelike petals are shorter than the stamens.
Habitat: Ponds, still water, swamps. Maine to North Carolina;

west to Arkansas, Kentucky, Texas, Wisconsin, and Nebraska.
June to October.

RATTLESNAKE-PLANTAIN (*Goodyèra pubéscens*)
  ORCHID FAMILY (Orchidàceae)   PLATE p. 177
Height: 6 to 18 inches.
Habit: A low perennial with a flat rosette of ovate leaves, 1 to
2½ inches long, conspicuously marked with light-colored, netted
veinlets. The flowering stem is erect and downy, with a few
scalelike bracts and a spikelike raceme, 1½ to 4 inches long, of
small, densely crowded, white flowers, each having a straight,
blunt lower lip.
Habitat: Dry or moist, rich woodlands. Quebec to Florida and
Alabama; west to Tennessee and southeastern Missouri. July to
early September. The plants may be in colonies; leaf rosettes
persist and are attractive throughout the winter.

NODDING LADIES'-TRESSES (*Spiránthes cérnua*)
  ORCHID FAMILY (Orchidàceae)   PLATE p. 177
Height: 4 to 24 inches.
Habit: A slender perennial with mostly narrow basal leaves, up
to 10 inches long, and an erect flowering stem with several scale-
like leaves. The small, white, nodding, vanilla-scented, tubular
flowers, ⅓ to ½ inch long, are in a more or less spirally twisted
raceme, up to 6 inches long.
Habitat: Damp, acid soil; open woods, fields, and meadows.
Quebec to Florida; west to Texas, South Dakota, and Minnesota.
Mid-August to early November.

SPRING LADIES'-TRESSES (*Spiránthes vernàlis*)
  ORCHID FAMILY (Orchidàceae)   PLATE p. 177
Height: 6 to 28 inches.
Habit: A slender, erect perennial with narrow basal leaves, 2 to
6 inches long, firm and ascending. The tall, flowering stem has
scalelike leaves. Small, downy, white, fragrant flowers, ¼ to ½
inch long, are in a spirally twisted terminal raceme.
Habitat: Dry or moist soil, in grassy clearings, on or near the
coastal plain. Massachusetts to Florida; west to Texas and Missouri. May to August.

TEASEL (*Dipsacus sylvéstris*)   PLATE p. 178
  TEASEL FAMILY (Dipsàcaceae)
Height: 2 to 6 feet.
Habit: A tall, stout, erect, coarse, prickly biennial, little-
branched, with opposite, sessile leaves, up to 4 inches long,
prickly on the midvein beneath. The stem is terminated by a
stout, dense, prickly, cylindrical head, 3 to 5 inches long. The
purple to lavender flowers, with four petals and four stamens,

are in the axils of spiny bracts projecting beyond the flower. Blooming flowers encircle the head in one or more bands.

Habitat: Roadsides and waste ground. Quebec to North Carolina; west to Tennessee, Missouri, and Michigan. A naturalized European weed. The mature flower head was used in early times for carding wool.

DEVIL'S-BIT or FAIRY WAND (*Chamaelirium luteum*)
LILY FAMILY (Liliàceae)   PLATE p. 178
Height: 2 to 4 feet.

Habit: A tall, delicate perennial with numerous spatulate to obovate basal leaves, 3 to 6 inches long. The erect stem has a few smaller alternate leaves that become narrowed upward, the uppermost linear. Plants are male and female, with racemes of small, frothy, white flowers having very narrow sepals and petals. Male flowers are in spreading racemes, 1 to 4 inches long; the female racemes are slender, up to 9 inches long, and erect or ascending.

Habitat: Moist woods, bogs, meadows, thickets. Ontario to Florida; west to Mississippi and Arkansas. May to July.

ROUND-LEAVED SUNDEW (*Drósera rotundifòlia*)
SUNDEW FAMILY (Droseràceae)   PLATE p. 179
Height: 8 to 12 inches.

Habit: A low perennial having a basal rosette of roundish, long-stalked, spreading leaves, 1/4 to 3/4 inch across, with gland-tipped hairs that exude a sticky secretion. A tall, naked, slender scape, branched or unbranched, has small, inconspicuous, white flowers at the top, each up to 1/2 inch across. They open only in sunshine.

Habitat: Peaty or moist acid soil, bogs, swamps. Throughout the United States. June to September. Belongs to a family of insectivorous plants. Insects are trapped by the sticky glands on the leaves, and the hairs bend around them. A digestive juice is exuded that enables the plant to feed on its victim.

VENUS'S-FLYTRAP (*Dionaèa muscìpula*)   PLATE p. 179
SUNDEW FAMILY (Droseràceae)
Height: 6 to 8 inches.

Habit: A remarkable predatory plant with rosettes of leaves on flat stalks of varying lengths. The double-sided blade, 2 to 3 inches long, is fringed with prominent, eyelash-like teeth and hinged at the midrib. An insect touching the inner hairs causes the double leaf to close and the teeth to interlace. The plant then secretes a digestive juice and opens to release indigestible insect parts. Small white flowers, 3/4 to 1 inch across, are at the top of a tall, naked scape.

Habitat: Found only on the coast of North and South Carolina, especially in the vicinity of Wilmington, N.C. May and June.

MEADOW-BEAUTIES (*Rhéxia* spp.)   **PLATE p. 180**
 MELASTOMA FAMILY (Melastomatàceae)
The illustrations represent three different species of the genus, but their exact identification is difficult. The following is a composite description of the group in our area.
Height: 8 to 24 inches.
Habit: Erect, simple or branched perennials with four-angled stems and sessile or short-stalked, ovate leaves, smooth to hairy, ½ to 1¼ inches long, spreading to ascending. The handsome rose pink flowers have four petals and eight stamens. The unusual anthers, ⅕ to ¼ inch long, are curved and attached at the middle with a minute spur.
Habitat: Pine woods, moist meadows, acid bogs. There are about half a dozen species throughout our range. July to September. These plants, with their showy flowers, are often abundant in late summer.

BLACKBERRY-LILY (*Belamcánda chinénsis*)   **PLATE p. 181**
 IRIS FAMILY (Iridàceae)
Height: 2 to 3 feet.
Habit: A perennial with swordlike, narrow, flat leaves, 2 to 3 feet long, and pointed. The stem rises well above the leaves, up to 40 inches tall, and bears several large, bright orange yellow flowers, three petals and three sepals alike, spotted with brownish crimson, 1½ to 2¼ inches across, and three conspicuous stamens.
Habitat: Escaped from cultivation and thoroughly established along roadsides, pastures, thickets. Connecticut to Georgia; west to Kansas. July to September. Introduced from Asia.

EVENING-PRIMROSE (*Oenothèra biénnis*)   **PLATE p. 182**
 EVENING-PRIMROSE FAMILY (Onagràceae)
Height: 3 to 5 feet.
Habit: A stout, erect biennial with a rosette of long leaves, the second year producing a soft-hairy, leafy stem with lance-shaped pointed leaves. The large, showy, lemon-scented, pure yellow flowers have four large, broad, notched petals, ¾ to 1 inch long. The flowers open only in the evening and are ephemeral.
Habitat: Waste places; fields; roadsides; open, dry ground. Quebec to northern Florida; west to Tennessee, Arkansas, and North Dakota. June to September. Early introduced from Europe and now widely naturalized.

BIENNIAL GAURA (*Gaùra biénnis*)   **PLATE p. 182**
 EVENING-PRIMROSE FAMILY (Onagràceae)
Height: 3 to 5 feet.

Habit: A downy, open-branched, slender biennial with a rosette of spatulate leaves and alternate stem leaves, tapering at each end, 1 to 3 inches long. The long, tubular, white flowers (pink when fading) are in clusters blooming a few at a time. The four petals are reflexed and narrowed at the base. There are eight stamens and a long stigma in the shape of a cross.
Habitat: Damp shores, meadows, open woods. Massachusetts to North Carolina; west to Louisiana, Tennessee, Illinois, and Nebraska. August and September.

SEEDBOX *(Ludwígia alternifòlia)*   PLATE p. 182
   EVENING-PRIMROSE FAMILY (Onagràceae)
Height: 1 to 3 feet.
Habit: A smooth, erect, branched perennial with alternate, narrow leaves, tapering at each end, 2 to 4 inches long. The light yellow flowers, in the upper leaf axils, are about $3/4$ inch across, with four petals and four green sepals of equal length showing between the petals. A four-sided seed capsule is later produced, in which the seeds rattle when dried.
Habitat: Swamps, wet soil. Ontario to Florida; west to Texas, Kansas, Michigan, and Illinois. June to August.

MARSH MALLOW *(Hibíscus militàris)*   PLATE p. 183
   MALLOW FAMILY (Malvàceae)
Height: 2 to 6 feet.
Habit: A large, coarse perennial with few to many stems and triangular leaves, the small lower lobes widely divergent, the terminal lobe much the largest, all pointed. The large, showy flowers, 4 to 5 inches across, are soft pink with a darker purplish base; the stamens are arranged in a cylinder around the style.
Habitat: Marshes, shallow water, wooded swamps, wet river banks. Pennsylvania to Florida; west to Ohio, Minnesota, Nebraska, Illinois, and Texas. August and September.

MUSK MALLOW *(Málva moschàta)*   PLATE p. 184
   MALLOW FAMILY (Malvàceae)
Height: 1 to 2 feet.
Habit: A tall, erect, rough-hairy perennial with firm stems. The basal leaves are rounded, unlobed or shallowly cleft; the lower stem leaves are similar; the upper ones have five to seven lobes and the segments are pinnatifid. The white to rose pink flowers are terminal and in the upper leaf axils. Notched triangular petals are $4/5$ to $1\frac{1}{4}$ inches long and veined; the stamens are in a column around the style.
Habitat: Along roadsides, waste places, escaped from cultivation. Quebec to Virginia; west to Missouri. June to September. A native of Europe, now thoroughly naturalized.

CRIMSON-EYE ROSE-MALLOW   (*Hibíscus moscheùtos*)
   MALLOW FAMILY (Malvàceae)   PLATE p. 184
Height: 2 to 6 feet.
Habit: A many-stemmed, erect to ascending perennial growing in marshes and shallow water. The stalked leaves are broadly rounded at the base, irregularly toothed and pointed at the tip. Beautiful showy flowers, 3 to 6 inches across, are white, rarely pale pink, usually with a red or purple center; they have the characteristic stamen column and a musky odor.
Habitat: Marshes and shallow water, inland and along the coast. Maryland to Florida and Alabama; west to Ohio and Indiana. July to September. Showy hybrids of this plant are cultivated in gardens.

JERUSALEM ARTICHOKE   (*Heliánthus tuberòsus*)
   COMPOSITE FAMILY (Compósitae)   PLATE p. 185
Height: 3 to 10 feet.
Habit: A tall, stout-stemmed, rather hairy perennial. The lower leaves, sometimes opposite, becoming alternate upward, are rough, broadly lance-shaped to ovate, 4 to 10 inches long, often with winged stalks. Several to numerous large, showy flower heads have yellow disks, $\frac{1}{2}$ to 1 inch across, and ten to twenty yellow rays, 1 inch or more long.
Habitat: Waste places, moist soil. Throughout our range and west to the Rocky Mountains. August to October. The plant was cultivated by the Indians for the edible tubers.

SNEEZEWEED   (*Helénium autumnàle*)   PLATE p. 185
   COMPOSITE FAMILY (Compósitae)
Height: 2 to 5 feet.
Habit: A tall, smooth to fine-hairy, bushy perennial with numerous elliptic to narrowly ovate leaves, narrowed to a sessile base, and continuing along the stalk as "wings." The lower leaves have withered at blooming time. Several to numerous showy flower heads have hemispheric disks, greenish in color, $\frac{1}{3}$ to $\frac{3}{4}$ inch across, and ten to twenty yellow, wedge-shaped rays, narrower at the base and notched at the wide tip.
Habitat: Low, moist ground; rich thickets; meadows; shores. New England to North Carolina; west to Kentucky, Missouri, and Minnesota. August to November.

TALL CONEFLOWER (*Rudbéckia laciniàta*)   PLATE p. 186
   COMPOSITE FAMILY (Compósitae)
Height: 2 to 10 feet.
Habit: A tall, coarse, smooth-stemmed perennial from a woody base, with large stalked leaves, variously toothed and divided into three to seven leaflets. The lower leaves are long-stalked, up to 5 inches long; the upper ones are sessile and reduced in

size. The large, golden yellow flower heads have dull, greenish yellow disks, which elongate in maturity, and six to sixteen rays, up to 2 inches long, which droop as the plant matures.
Habitat: Moist places; rich, low grounds. Quebec to northern Florida; west to Montana, Idaho, and Arizona. July to September. A form with double petals, grown in gardens, is Golden Glow.

TALL TICKSEED (*Coreópsis trípteris*)   PLATE p. 186
COMPOSITE FAMILY (Compósitae)
Height: 2 to 3 feet.
Habit: A tall, smooth-stemmed perennial with the lower leaves divided into three narrowly elliptic leaflets, 1½ to 3 inches long; the lowest leaves may have the terminal leaflet again divided. Several to numerous light yellow flower heads have brownish or purplish disks surrounded by rays, ¾ to 1 inch long. Flowers have the odor of anise.
Habitat: Thickets, borders of woods. Massachusetts to Florida; west to Wisconsin, Kansas, and Texas. July to September.

TALL SUNFLOWER (*Heliánthus gigantèus*)   PLATE p. 187
COMPOSITE FAMILY (Compósitae)
Height: 4 to 10 feet.
Habit: A tall, coarse, rough perennial, much-branched near the top and with large, uncut, lance-shaped, rough leaves, 2¼ to 4½ inches long, narrowed to a short-stalked or sessile base. The lowest leaves may be opposite; all others are alternate. The stem is topped by several to many heads of flowers, each with ten to twenty lemon yellow rays, 2 to 2½ inches long, and a yellow disk, ⅘ to 1 inch across. Under the rays are thin, narrow, green bracts, half as long as the rays. The flower heads tend to face the sun.
Habitat: Swamps and moist places. Maine to Florida and beyond our limits. July to October.

ROSINWEED (*Sílphium integrifòlium*)   PLATE p. 187
COMPOSITE FAMILY (Compósitae)
Height: 2 to 6 feet.
Habit: A tall, coarse, rough, resinous perennial with opposite, lance-shaped to elliptic leaves, 2½ to 4½ inches long. The large flower heads have narrow, pale yellow rays, ¾ to 1½ inches long. The ray flowers are fertile; the disk flowers, sterile.
Habitat: Dry woodlands, prairies, roadsides. Ohio to Minnesota and Nebraska; south to Mississippi and Alabama. July to September.

LEAFCUP (*Polýmnia uvedàlia*)   PLATE p. 188
COMPOSITE FAMILY (Compósitae)
Height: 10 to 15 feet.

Habit: A tall, coarse, sticky-hairy, branching perennial with large, opposite, palmately lobed lower leaves, abruptly narrowed to winged stalks. The uppermost leaves are alternate, broadly ovate, and nearly sessile. All leaves are rough-hairy above and fine-hairy beneath. Several to numerous heads of yellow flowers have ten to fifteen light yellow rays, ¾ inch long, and rather rounded disks.

Habitat: Woodlands and meadows. New York to Florida; west to Illinois, Missouri, and Texas. July to September.

TICKSEED-SUNFLOWER (*Bìdens aristòsa*)   PLATE p. 188
    COMPOSITE FAMILY (Compósitae)
Height: 1 to 4 feet.

Habit: A tall, erect, smooth, slender, freely branching annual or biennial with opposite pinnate leaves, 2 to 6 inches long, divided into three to seven leaflets, coarsely and variously toothed and incised, the terminal segment largest. Numerous heads of spreading, showy flowers with yellow rays, ½ to 1 inch long, and yellow disks up to ½ inch across, later produce black seeds with two barbed awns.

Habitat: Low fields, wet places. Maine to Virginia and Alabama; west to Minnesota and Texas. August to November.

THIN-LEAVED CONEFLOWER (*Rudbéckia tríloba*)
    COMPOSITE FAMILY (Compósitae)   PLATE p. 189
Height: 2 to 5 feet.

Habit: A moderately spreading and branching, short-lived perennial, with hairy to rather smooth stems, more leafy at the base. Basal leaves are broad, ovate, deeply three-lobed; stem leaves are narrower with shallow lobes. Numerous flower heads have dark brownish purple, cone-shaped disks, ¼ to ¾ inch across, and deep yellow rays, orange yellow to brown at the base.

Habitat: Open woods, thickets, fields. New York to Georgia; west to Tennessee, Arkansas, Kansas, and Michigan. July to October.

YELLOW IRONWEED or WINGSTEM (*Actinómeris*
    alternifòlia)   PLATE p. 189
    COMPOSITE FAMILY (Compósitae)
Height: 5 to 10 feet.

Habit: A tall, branching perennial with long, elliptic, sometimes ovate leaves, tapering to the base and decurrent on the hairy stem. The leaves may be alternate, opposite, or in threes, rough-hairy and up to 10 inches long. The flower heads have only two to eight narrow yellow rays, unequal in length, spreading outward and downward; the yellow disk flowers also are loosely spreading.

Habitat: Roadsides, woodlands, waste places. New York to

Florida and Louisiana; west to Illinois, Iowa, and Oklahoma. August and September. The plant is easily identified by the winged stems.

CROWN-BEARD (*Verbesìna occidentàlis*)   PLATE p. 189
COMPOSITE FAMILY (Compósitae)
Height: 3 to 7 feet.
Habit: A tall, coarse perennial of open habit, with ascending branches and winged stems. The opposite leaves are sessile or decurrent on the stem, ovate to lance-shaped, and pointed at both ends. The flower heads have only one to five yellow rays and flattish yellow disks.
Habitat: Rich woods and thickets. Pennsylvania to Florida and Mississippi; west to Ohio and Illinois. August to October.

WHITE WOODLAND ASTER or MICHAELMAS DAISY
    (*Aster divaricàtus*)   PLATE p. 190
COMPOSITE FAMILY (Compósitae)
Height: 2 to 4 feet.
Habit: A widely branching, slender, erect to zigzag-stemmed perennial with alternate, rough, ovate or lance-shaped leaves, 1 to 6½ inches long, and stalked. The lower leaves are withered at blooming time. The stem is terminated by a flat or rounded inflorescence with numerous small flower heads. Each has five to ten (rarely twelve) spreading white rays, ½ inch long, surrounding the yellow or purplish disk.
Habitat: Clearings; thin, dry woods. New Hampshire to upland Georgia and eastern Alabama; west to Ohio. August to October.

WHITE SNAKEROOT (*Eupatòrium rugòsum*)   PLATE p. 190
COMPOSITE FAMILY (Compósitae)
Height: 2 to 5 feet.
Habit: An erect, smooth perennial with opposite, narrowly to broadly ovate leaves, fine-pointed and smooth above, hairy on the veins beneath. Leaves are progressively smaller and shorter-stalked upward. The inflorescences are in open terminal clusters of bright white, tubular flowers, each $\frac{1}{10}$ to $\frac{1}{5}$ inch long. Each cluster has ten to thirty flower heads.
Habitat: Rich woodlands, thickets, clearings. Quebec to upland Georgia, Alabama, and northern Louisiana; west to northeastern Texas. July to October. A variable widespread species; poisonous to cattle.

TALL BLUE LETTUCE (*Lactùca biénnis*)   PLATE p. 191
COMPOSITE FAMILY (Compósitae)
Height: 5 to 10 feet.
Habit: A tall, nearly smooth, coarse, leafy biennial with variable leaves, some uncut, others with backward-directed lobes and

sharp tips, 4 to 12 inches long. The stem is topped by elongated branches with many lavender blue (sometimes white) flower heads having fifteen to thirty-four (rarely up to fifty-four) ray flowers only. The stem has milky juice.
Habitat: Moist places, waste ground, cultivated fields. Newfoundland to the mountains of North Carolina and Tennessee; west to Idaho and farther west. July to September.

EARLY GOLDENROD (*Solidàgo júncea*)   PLATE p. 191
    COMPOSITE FAMILY (Compósitae)
Height: 2 to 4 feet.
Habit: An erect, rather smooth, leafy, stout-stemmed perennial, solitary or with few stems, and a tuft of persistent basal leaves, 6 to 16 inches long. The alternate stem leaves are progressively smaller upward, narrower, less toothed, and sessile. The dense inflorescence is often as broad as long, with recurved branches. The very small golden flower heads have both a few ray flowers and tiny five-lobed tubular flowers, grouped in compact arching clusters.
Habitat: Open woods, dry, open ground, especially sandy soil. Long Island, Delaware, Maryland, the Piedmont, and upland to Georgia; west to Tennessee and Missouri. June to October. The goldenrods form a large group whose species are often difficult to differentiate. Others in the field will closely resemble the above.

COMMON or BULL THISTLE (*Cirsium vulgàre*)
    COMPOSITE FAMILY (Compósitae)   PLATE p. 192
Height: 3 to 5 feet.
Habit: A tall, stiff, coarse biennial with conspicuously spiny stem leaves, cut and recut into sharp, bristly points. The large, solitary flower heads, 1 to 1½ inches across, have disk flowers only, surrounded by the spiny involucre. The tall stem grows from a rosette of leaves formed the previous year.
Habitat: Pastures, fields, waste ground, roadsides. Throughout our range. June to September. A naturalized, objectionable weed from Europe, now widely established in North America.

PASTURE THISTLE (*Cirsium altissimum*)   PLATE p. 192
    COMPOSITE FAMILY (Compósitae)
Height: 4 to 12 feet.
Habit: A tall, robust, hairy perennial, often branching below, with large, undivided, ovate to narrowly lance-shaped leaves, green above, white-felted beneath. The single to several rosy purple flower heads have disk flowers only, surrounded by the spiny involucre. The tall stem grows from a rosette of spiny leaves formed the previous year.
Habitat: Fields, waste places, open woods, river bottoms. Massa-

chusetts to Florida; west to Texas. July to October. This is an aggressive species that tends to adapt itself to disturbed habitats such as pastures and plowed fields.

BONESET (*Eupatòrium perfoliàtum*)   PLATE p. 193
COMPOSITE FAMILY (Compósitae)
Height: 2 to 5 feet.
Habit: A vigorous, rank-growing, hairy perennial with stout stems and opposite, light green, wrinkled leaves that seem to grow through the blade (perfoliate). They are up to 8 inches long and taper to a delicate tip. The stem is topped by a dull white, flat-topped inflorescence of crowded flower heads, each composed of ten to twenty-three tubular flowers.
Habitat: Low, wet or moist ground. Quebec to Florida; west to Louisiana, Oklahoma, Nebraska, and Minnesota. July to October.

FIREWEED (*Erechtìtes hieracifòlia*)   PLATE p. 193
COMPOSITE FAMILY (Compósitae)
Height: 1 to 10 feet.
Habit: An erect, coarse, slightly succulent, smooth or spreading-hairy annual with large, undivided leaves up to 8 inches long. The lower leaves are obovate and taper to a short stalk; the middle and upper leaves are smaller, elliptic, and sometimes clasping the stem. The broad, flat inflorescence at the top of the stem has numerous small, crowded, dull white flower heads, without rays, surrounded by green bracts. The plants have a rank odor.
Habitat: Variable, dry woodlands to marshes. Newfoundland to Florida; west to Nebraska and Texas. August and September. It is especially abundant after a fire, thus the name Fireweed.

HAWKWEED (*Hieràcium paniculàtum*)   PLATE p. 193
COMPOSITE FAMILY (Compósitae)
Height: 1 to 3 feet.
Habit: A slender perennial with long stems, hairy below and smooth above. The small, undivided leaves, 1 to 3 inches long, are thin and narrowly elliptic; the lowest ones are stalked, but becoming sessile upward. The small flower heads are on long, very slender stalks spreading in all directions. Each small yellow head has ten to twenty ray flowers.
Habitat: Woodland, open woods. Quebec to Georgia; west to Ohio and Michigan. July to September.

ELEPHANT'S-FOOT (*Elephántopus caroliniànus*)
COMPOSITE FAMILY (Compósitae)   PLATE p. 194
Height: 1 to 2 feet.
Habit: A perennial with widely spreading branches and large, uncut, broadly elliptic to obovate leaves, 3 to 8 inches long,

abruptly narrowed at the base or winged along the stalk. The
one to five pinkish lavender flower heads, without rays, are in
leafy bracts at the tips of the branches. The heads, with perfect
tubular flowers, are surrounded by conspicuous triangular to
ovate leafy bracts.   .
Habitat: Dry woods, thickets. New Jersey to Florida; west to
Ohio, Illinois, Kansas, and Texas. August and September.

BLAZING STAR *(Liàtris scariòsa)*   PLATE p. 194
   COMPOSITE FAMILY (Compósitae)
Height: 1 to 3 feet.
Habit: An erect, stout, handsome perennial with narrow,
alternate leaves, 2½ to 7 inches long, becoming progressively
smaller and sessile up the stem. The showy flower heads, up to
⅞ inch across, are magenta purple to pale violet, with small,
perfect, tubular flowers.
Habitat: Dry woods, roadsides, fields, mountains. Southern
Pennsylvania to northern Georgia. August and September.

NODDING POGONIA *(Tríphora trianthóphora)*
   ORCHID FAMILY (Orchidàceae)   PLATE p. 194
Height: 3 to 8 inches.
Habit: A fragile plant with small ovate leaves clasping the stem,
½ to ¾ inch long, alternate, sometimes very close and appear-
ing opposite. The long-stalked, nodding flowers have rose
purple petals and sepals, colored alike, with a white "eye"; a
lower petal is bearded.
Habitat: Rich soil of hardwood forests. Found very locally in
southwestern Maine, New Hampshire, Vermont, New York,
Ohio, Michigan, southern Wisconsin, and Iowa. August and
September.

TICK-TREFOIL *(Desmòdium laevigàtum)*   PLATE p. 195
   PULSE OR BEAN FAMILY (Leguminòsae)
Height: 2 to 4 feet.
Habit: An erect, smooth, simple to much-branched leafy perennial. The compound leaves, 1¼ to 3 inches long, have three
thin, ovate, stalked leaflets, the terminal one largest. Small pea-
shaped flowers, deep rose to purple, are ¼ to ⅓ inch long, in
simple or branched racemes. Later, seedpods are produced sep-
arating into one-seeded joints with hooked hairs.
Habitat: Borders of woods; dry, waste ground; clearings. New
York to Florida; west to Indiana, Tennessee, Louisiana, and
Texas. July and August. The mature seedpods easily cling to
human clothing and fur, a way of widely distributing the seed.

TICK-TREFOIL *(Desmòdium cuspidàtum)*   PLATE p. 195
   PULSE OR BEAN FAMILY (Leguminòsae)
Height: 2 to 4 feet.

Habit: A tall, erect, leafy, stout-stemmed perennial with three-divided, stalked leaflets about equal in size, 1¾ to 3 inches long. The pea-shaped flowers, in a loose raceme, are pale to rose pink and later produce jointed seedpods with hooked hairs.

Habitat: Dry woods, thickets, wooded banks. Massachusetts and Vermont to Georgia; west to Michigan, Wisconsin, and Oklahoma. July and August. Similar to *D. laevigatum* except for slight differences in leaves and flowers. Tick-trefoils are weedy plants distinguished by the characteristic seedpods.

BUSH-CLOVER *(Lespedèza hírta)*   PLATE p. 196
   PULSE OR BEAN FAMILY (Leguminòsae)
Height: 1 to 3 feet.
Habit: A usually unbranched, erect or ascending leafy perennial with one to a few hairy stems, and three divided leaves with ovate leaflets, ½ to 1¼ inches long and nearly as wide. Each leaflet has a small, bristly tip. Small, dense spikes of flowers, from the upper leaf axils, have yellowish white flowers spotted with purple.
Habitat: Dry soil, hillsides. Ontario to Georgia and Alabama; west to Arkansas and eastern Texas. July to October.

BUSH-CLOVER *(Lespedèza virgínica)*   PLATE p. 196
   PULSE OR BEAN FAMILY (Leguminòsae)
Height: 1 to 4 feet.
Habit: An erect, smooth-stemmed perennial, simple or branched above. The narrow, stalked, erect or ascending leaves have three narrowly oblong leaflets, each ⅞ to 1 inch long. The small, pea-shaped, purplish flowers are crowded in racemes from the upper leaf axils and at the top of the plant.
Habitat: Dry, open woods. Massachusetts to Georgia; west to Wisconsin, Kansas, and Texas. August and September.

WILD or HOG-PEANUT *(Amphicárpa bracteàta)*
   PULSE OR BEAN FAMILY (Leguminòsae)   PLATE p. 196
Height: Up to 3½ feet.
Habit: A delicate twining vine with the leaves three divided into ovate hairy leaflets, each 1¼ to 2 inches long. The small, pale lavender flowers, in crowded racemes extending beyond the leaves, are ½ inch long. They later produce flat pods. Also at the base of the plant are flowers with rudimentary petals that produce fleshy, one-seeded pods, the hog peanuts.
Habitat: Woods, thickets. Quebec to Florida; west to Montana and Texas. August and September. This is a variable species, more abundant eastward.

GROUNDNUT or WILD BEAN *(Ápios americàna)*
   PULSE OR BEAN FAMILY (Leguminòsae)   PLATE p. 197
Height: Up to 5 feet.

Habit: A twining perennial with compound leaves divided into three to nine ovate leaflets, the largest 1½ to 2 inches long. The pea-shaped flowers are in short, branching racemes, from the leaf axils. They vary from white suffused with rose to brown purple and mauve, and have a fragrance resembling the odor of violets. *Habitat:* Woods, thickets, climbing over bushes. Quebec to Florida; west to South Dakota and Texas. July to September.

WILD SENSITIVE-PLANT (*Cássia níctitans*)   PLATE p. 197
    PULSE OR BEAN FAMILY (Leguminòsae)
Height: 2 to 5 feet.
Habit: A tall, smooth to slightly hairy, erect annual with leaves divided into ten to twenty pairs of oblong-linear leaflets, each ¼ to ⅓ inch long. The bright yellow to greenish yellow flowers are solitary or in groups of two or three at the base of the leaf, each producing a straight, flat pod with black seeds. *Habitat:* Dry and sandy soil, roadsides, waste ground. Vermont and Massachusetts to Florida; west to Ohio, Kansas, and Texas. July to September. The name refers to the folding of the leaflets at night.

WILD SENNA (*Cássia marilándica*)   PLATE p. 197
    PULSE OR BEAN FAMILY (Leguminòsae)
Height: 4 to 8 feet.
Habit: A tall, erect, smooth to sparsely hairy perennial with four to eight pairs of oblong or elliptic leaflets, each ⅘ to 1½ inches long, and stalked. The light golden yellow flowers, in branched racemes, have five slightly unequal spreading petals and conspicuous brown anthers. *Habitat:* Stream banks, roadsides, open woods. Pennsylvania to Florida; west to Iowa, Kansas, and Texas. July and August.

ROUND-LEAVED PYROLA (*Pýrola rotundifòlia* var.
    americàna)   PLATE p. 198
    PYROLA FAMILY (Pyrolàceae)
Height: 6 to 12 inches.
Habit: A small perennial with roundish, evergreen, thick, leathery, lustrous, dark green leaves, 1 to 3½ inches long and as wide; stalks often as long as the blades. The fragrant, white, waxy, nodding flowers have five thin, rounded, rather cuplike petals, with an extremely long drooping pistil, recurved at the tip. The three to thirteen flowers, in a raceme, top the nearly naked stalk. *Habitat:* Damp sandy or gravelly thickets, woods, clearings. Quebec to North Carolina; west to Kentucky, Indiana, Michigan, Wisconsin, and Minnesota. July to mid-August.

SPREADING DOGBANE (*Apócynum androsaemifòlium*)
    DOGBANE FAMILY (Apocynàceae)   PLATE p. 198
Height: 2 to 24 inches.

HARBINGER-OF-SPRING
Érigenìa bulbòsa

p. 8

GOLDEN SAXIFRAGE
Chrysosplènium americànum

p. 8

COMMON CHICKWEED
Stellària mèdia

p. 8

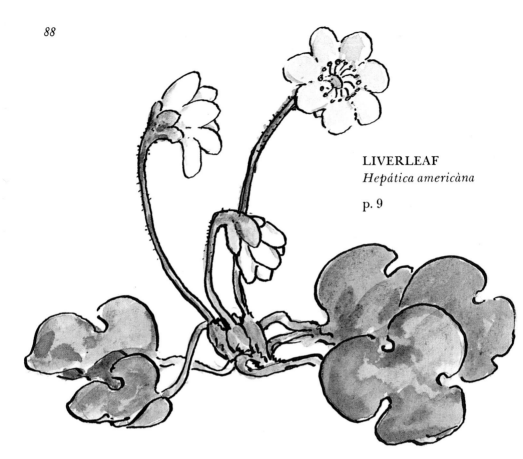

LIVERLEAF
Hepática americàna

p. 9

TRAILING ARBUTUS
Epigaèa rèpens

p. 9

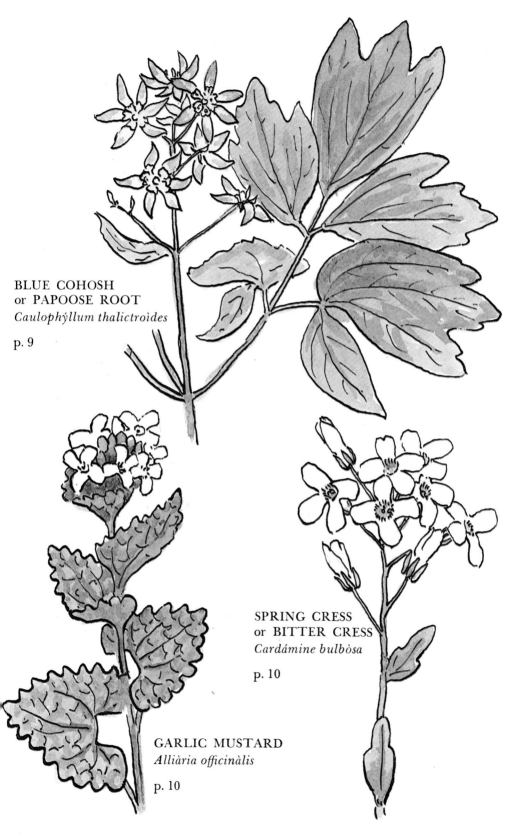

BLUE COHOSH
or PAPOOSE ROOT
Caulophýllum thalictroìdes

p. 9

SPRING CRESS
or BITTER CRESS
Cardámine bulbòsa

p. 10

GARLIC MUSTARD
Alliària officinàlis

p. 10

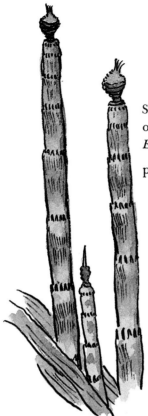

SCOURING RUSH
or HORSETAIL
Equisètum hyemàle

p. 10

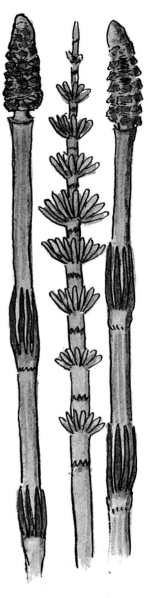

HENBIT
Làmium amplexicaùle

p. 11

HORSETAIL
Equisètum arvénse

p. 10

VIRGINIA BLUEBELLS
Merténsia virgínica

p. 11

BLOODROOT
Sanguinària canadénsis

p. 11

DOG'S-TOOTH VIOLET or TROUT LILY
Erythrònium americànum
and *Erythrònium álbidum*

p. 11

GRAPE-HYACINTH
Muscàri racemòsum

p. 12

PURPLE TRILLIUM
Tríllium séssile

p. 12

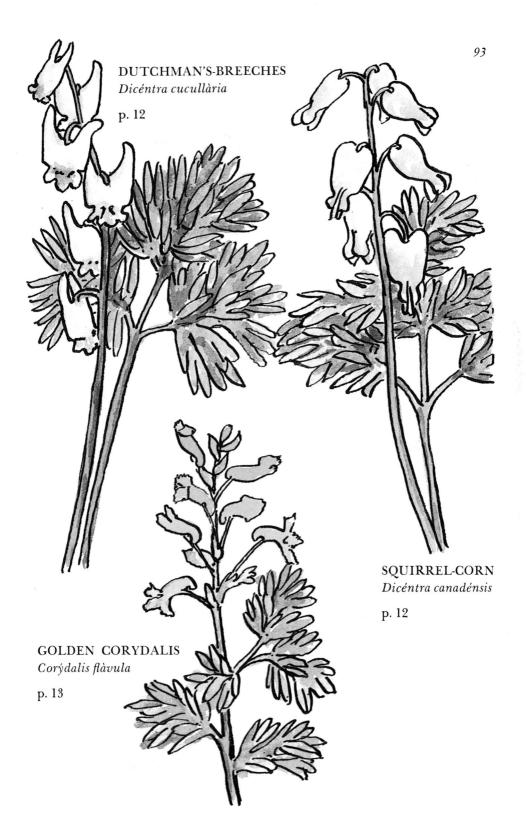

DUTCHMAN'S-BREECHES
Dicéntra cucullària

p. 12

SQUIRREL-CORN
Dicéntra canadénsis

p. 12

GOLDEN CORYDALIS
Corýdalis flàvula

p. 13

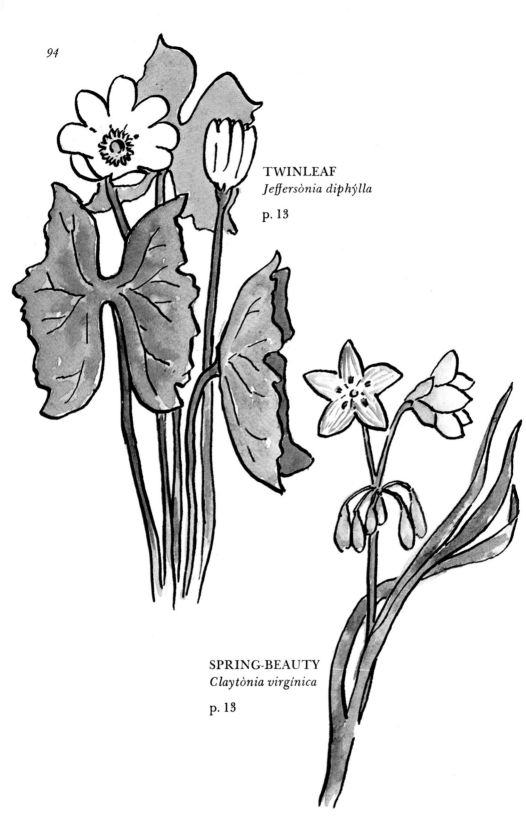

TWINLEAF
Jeffersònia diphýlla

p. 13

SPRING-BEAUTY
Claytònia virgínica

p. 13

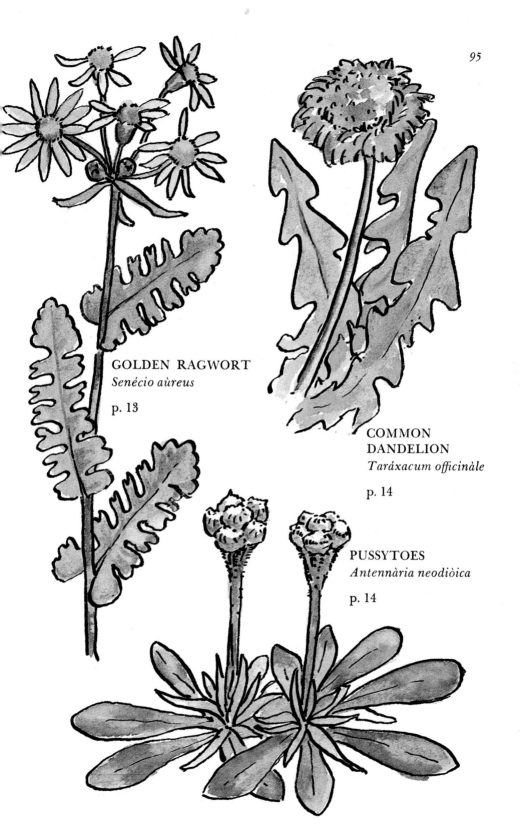

GOLDEN RAGWORT
Senécio aùreus

p. 13

COMMON
DANDELION
Taráxacum officinàle

p. 14

PUSSYTOES
Antennària neodiòica

p. 14

GROUND-IVY
Glechòma hederàcea

p. 14

RED DEAD-NETTLE
Làmium purpùreum

p. 14

EARLY SAXIFRAGE
Saxifraga virginiénsis

p. 15

SWAMP BUTTERCUP
Ranùnculus septentrionàlis

p. 15

COLUMBINE
Aquilègia canadénsis

p. 15

SMALL-FLOWERED CROWFOOT
Ranùnculus abortìvus

p. 15

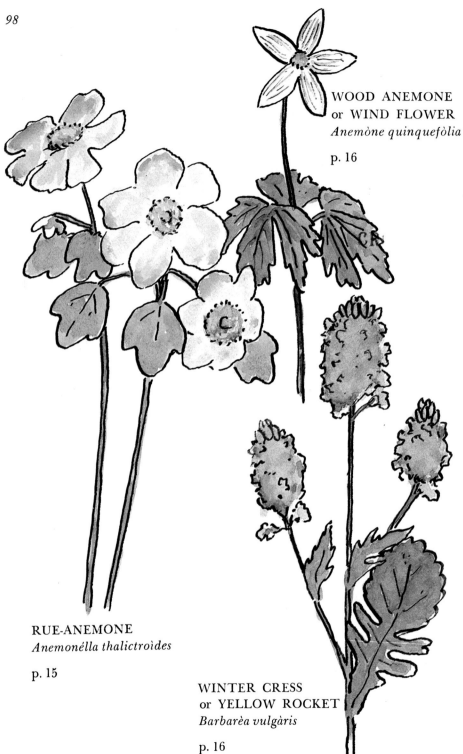

WOOD ANEMONE
or WIND FLOWER
Anemòne quinquefòlia

p. 16

RUE-ANEMONE
Anemonélla thalictroìdes

p. 15

WINTER CRESS
or YELLOW ROCKET
Barbarèa vulgàris

p. 16

CUT-LEAVED TOOTHWORT
Dentària laciniàta

p. 16

CRINKLEROOT
Dentària diphỳlla

p. 16

ROCK CRESS
Árabis lyràta

p. 17

**SMALL
BITTER CRESS**
*Cardámine
pensylvánica*

p. 17

**SHEPHERD'S
PURSE**
*Capsélla
búrsa-pastòris*

p. 17

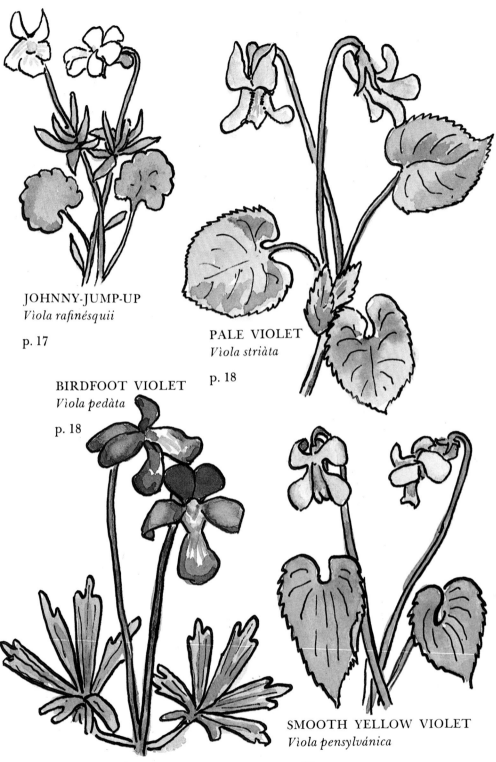

JOHNNY-JUMP-UP
Vìola rafinésquii

p. 17

PALE VIOLET
Vìola striàta

p. 18

BIRDFOOT VIOLET
Vìola pedàta

p. 18

SMOOTH YELLOW VIOLET
Vìola pensylvánica

p. 18

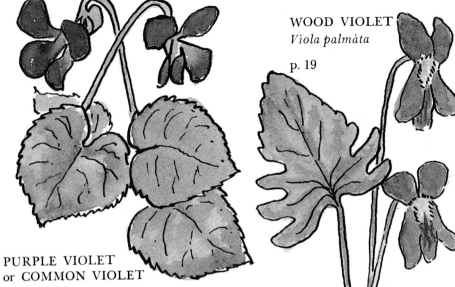

WOOD VIOLET
Vìola palmàta

p. 19

PURPLE VIOLET
or COMMON VIOLET
Vìola papilionàcea

p. 18

BLUETS or QUAKER-LADIES
Houstònia caerùlea

p. 19

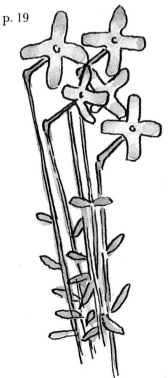

PENNYWORT
Obolària virgínica

p. 19

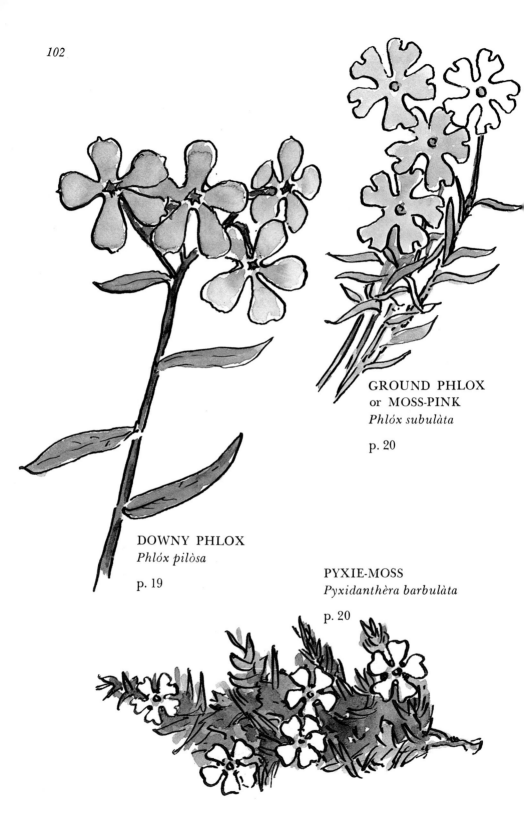

GROUND PHLOX
or MOSS-PINK
Phlóx subulàta

p. 20

DOWNY PHLOX
Phlóx pilòsa

p. 19

PYXIE-MOSS
Pyxidanthèra barbulàta

p. 20

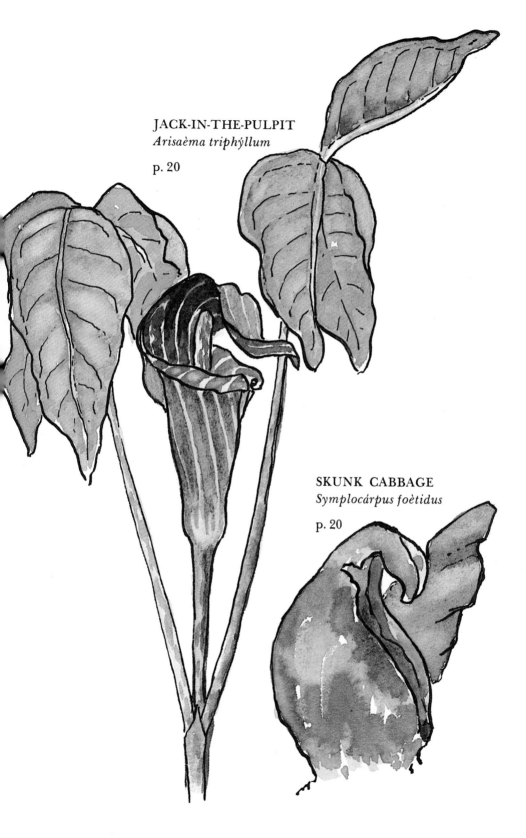

JACK-IN-THE-PULPIT
Arisaèma triphýllum

p. 20

SKUNK CABBAGE
Symplocárpus foètidus

p. 20

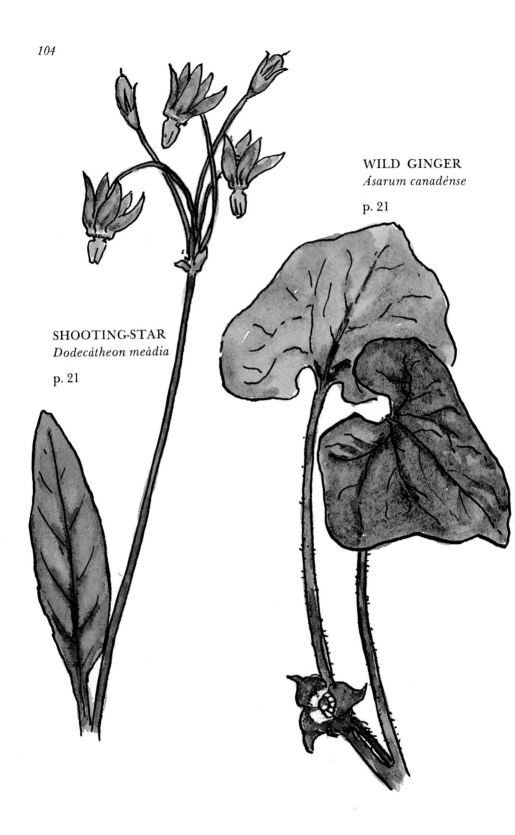

104

WILD GINGER
Ásarum canadénse

p. 21

SHOOTING-STAR
Dodecátheon meàdia

p. 21

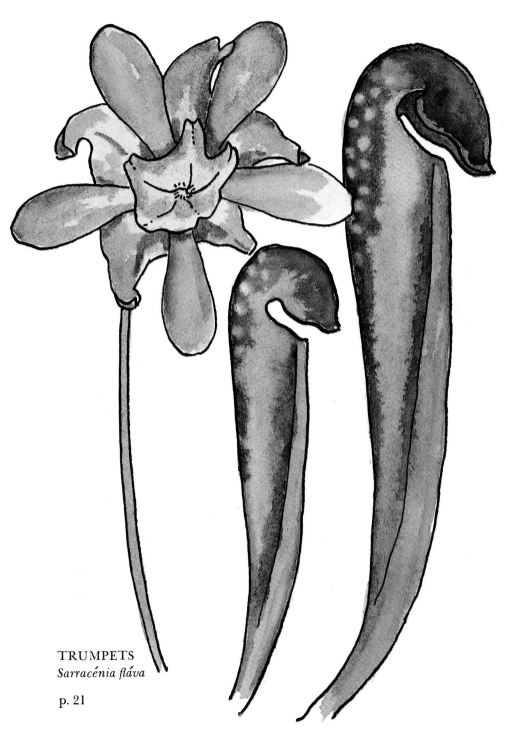

TRUMPETS
Sarracénia fláva

p. 21

ROCK CRESS
Àrabis laevigàta

p. 21

EARLY MEADOW PARSNIP
or GOLDEN ALEXANDERS
Zizia aùrea

p. 22

LARKSPUR
Delphinium tricórne

p. 22

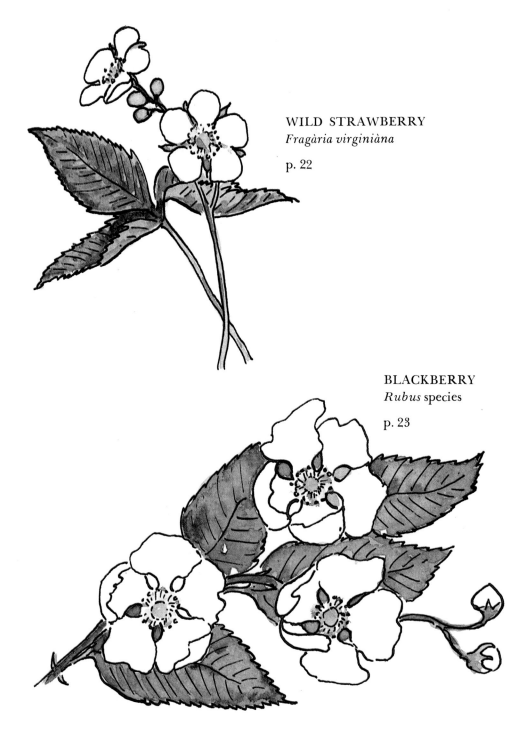

WILD STRAWBERRY
Fragària virginiàna

p. 22

BLACKBERRY
Rubus species

p. 23

CINQUEFOIL
Potentílla canadénsis

p. 23

FLOWERING RASPBERRY
or THIMBLEBERRY
Rùbus odoràtus

p. 23

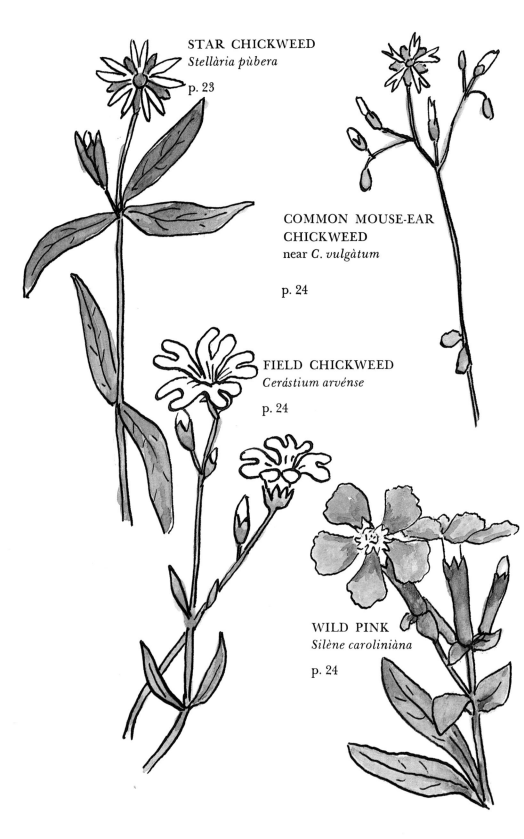

STAR CHICKWEED
Stellària pùbera

p. 23

COMMON MOUSE-EAR CHICKWEED
near *C. vulgàtum*

p. 24

FIELD CHICKWEED
Ceràstium arvénse

p. 24

WILD PINK
Silène caroliniàna

p. 24

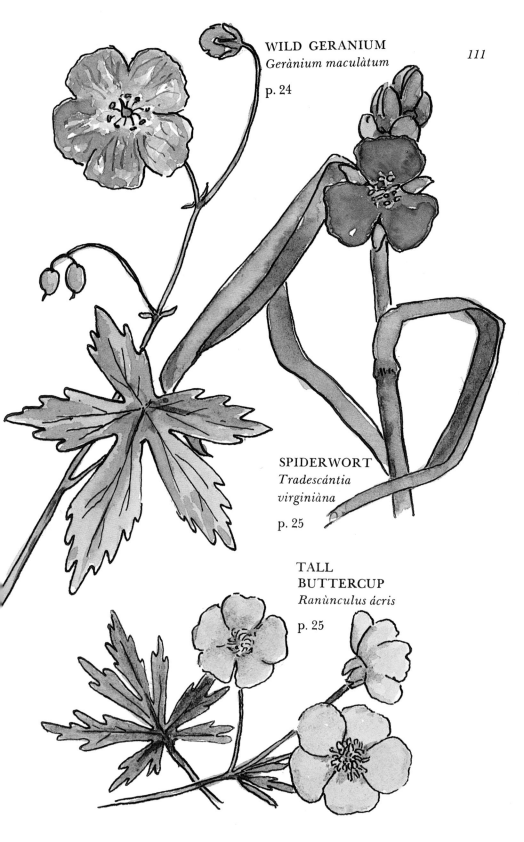

WILD GERANIUM
Geràcium maculàtum

p. 24

SPIDERWORT
Tradescántia
virginiàna

p. 25

TALL
BUTTERCUP
Ranùnculus ácris

p. 25

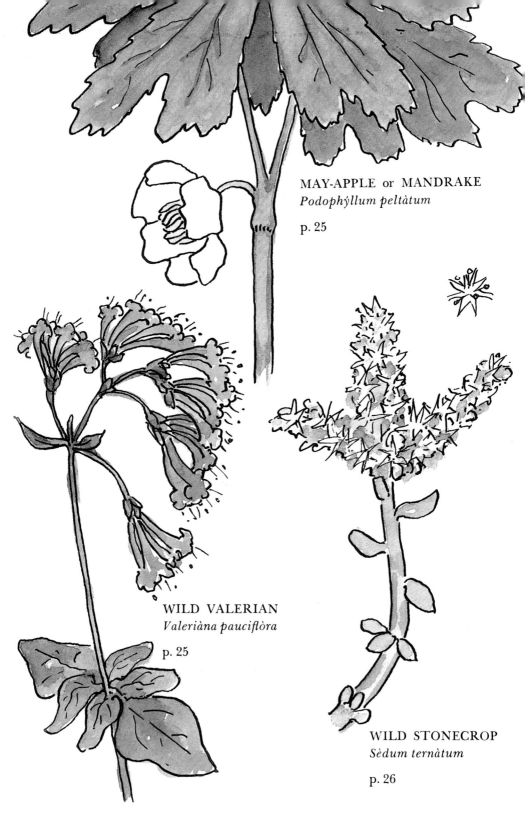

MAY-APPLE or MANDRAKE
Podophýllum peltàtum

p. 25

WILD VALERIAN
Valeriàna pauciflòra

p. 25

WILD STONECROP
Sèdum ternàtum

p. 26

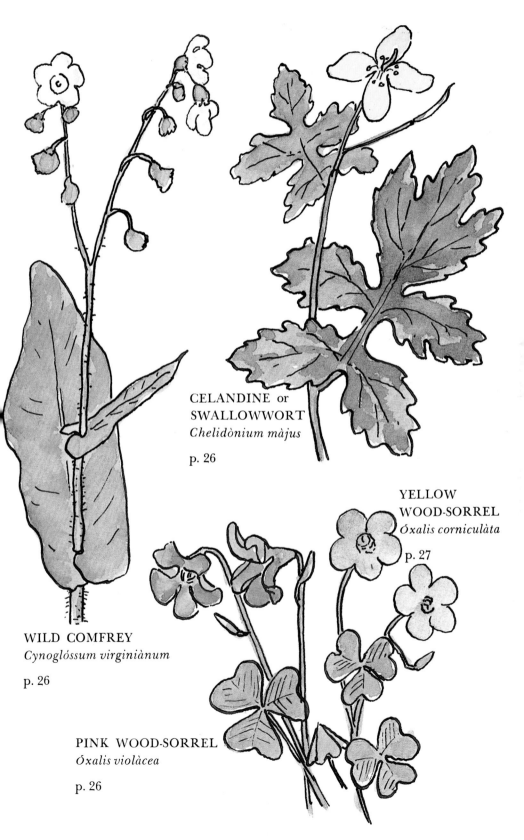

CELANDINE or
SWALLOWWORT
Chelidònium màjus

p. 26

YELLOW
WOOD-SORREL
Óxalis corniculàta

p. 27

WILD COMFREY
Cynoglóssum virginiànum

p. 26

PINK WOOD-SORREL
Óxalis violàcea

p. 26

RATTLESNAKE-WEED
Hieràcium venòsum

p. 27

DWARF DANDELION
Krigia virginica

p. 27

ROBIN'S PLANTAIN
Erígeron pulchéllus

p. 28

FIELD DAISY
Leucánthemum vulgáre

p. 27

GOLDENSTAR
*Chrysógonum
virginiànum*

p. 28

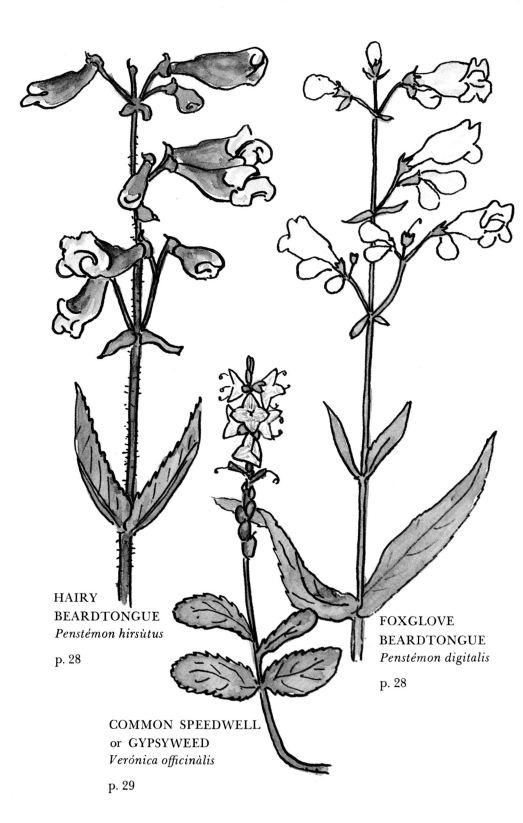

HAIRY
BEARDTONGUE
Penstémon hirsùtus

p. 28

COMMON SPEEDWELL
or GYPSYWEED
Verónica officinàlis

p. 29

FOXGLOVE
BEARDTONGUE
Penstémon digitalis

p. 28

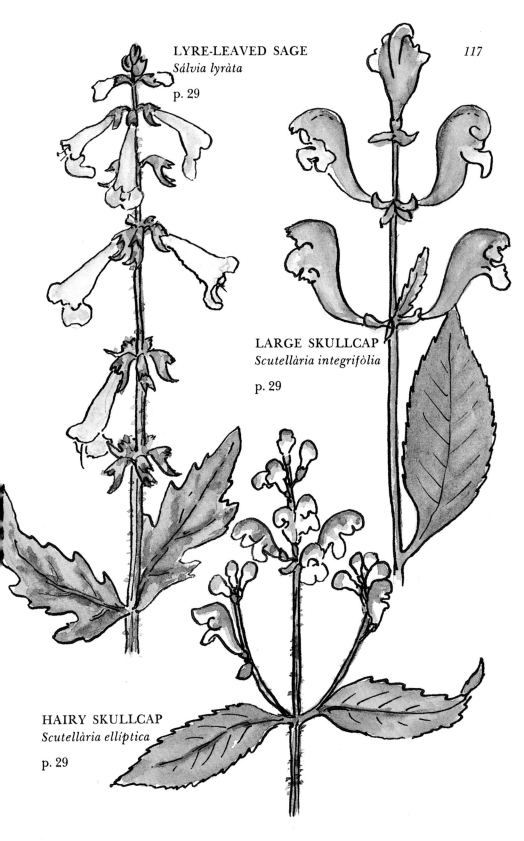

LYRE-LEAVED SAGE
Sálvia lyràta

p. 29

LARGE SKULLCAP
Scutellària integrifòlia

p. 29

HAIRY SKULLCAP
Scutellària ellíptica

p. 29

FALSE SPIKENARD
Smilacìna racemòsa

p. 30

BELLWORT
Uvulària perfoliàta

p. 30

SOLOMON'S-SEAL
Polygónatum biflòrum

p. 30

STAR-OF-BETHLEHEM
Ornithógalum umbellàtum

p. 31

INDIAN CUCUMBER
Medèola virginiàna

p. 30

STARRY FALSE SOLOMON'S-SEAL
Smilacìna stellàta

p. 31

SHOWY ORCHIS
Órchis spectábilis

p. 31

LARGE TWAYBLADE
Líparis lilifòlia

p. 31

ROSEBUD ORCHID
Cleìstes divaricàta

p. 32

PUTTYROOT
Apléctrum hyemàle

p. 32

**SMALL YELLOW
LADY'S-SLIPPER**
Cypripèdium calcèolus
var. *parviflòrum*

p. 33

**YELLOW
LADY'S-SLIPPER**
Cypripèdium calcèolus

p. 32

123

PINK LADY'S-SLIPPER
or MOCCASIN-FLOWER
Cypripèdium acaùle

p. 33

SHOWY LADY'S SLIPPER
Cypripèdium regìnae

p. 33

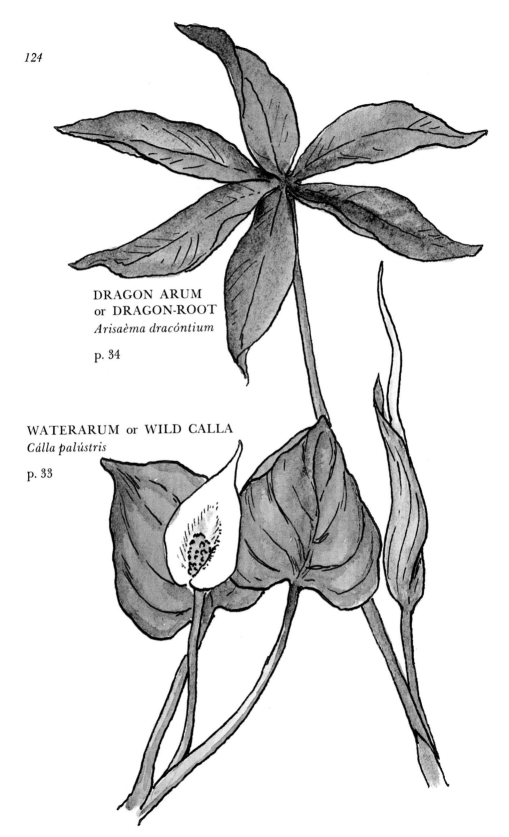

DRAGON ARUM
or DRAGON-ROOT
Arisaèma dracóntium

p. 34

WATERARUM or WILD CALLA
Cálla palústris

p. 33

BLUE FLAG or WILD IRIS
Iris versicolor

p. 34

VIPER'S BUGLOSS
or BLUEWEED
Échium vulgàre

p. 34

PASSIONFLOWER or MAYPOPS

Passiflòra incarnàta

p. 35

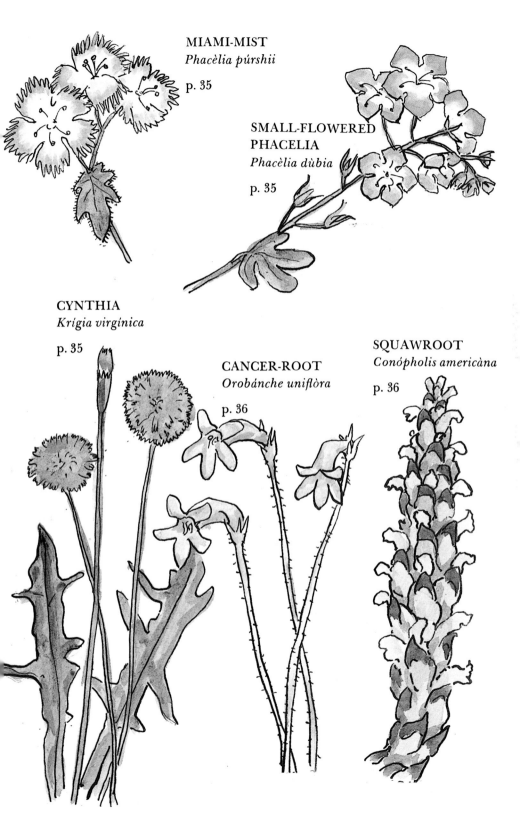

MIAMI-MIST
Phacèlia púrshii

p. 35

**SMALL-FLOWERED
PHACELIA**
Phacèlia dùbia

p. 35

CYNTHIA
Krígia virgínica

p. 35

CANCER-ROOT
Orobánche uniflòra

p. 36

SQUAWROOT
Conópholis americàna

p. 36

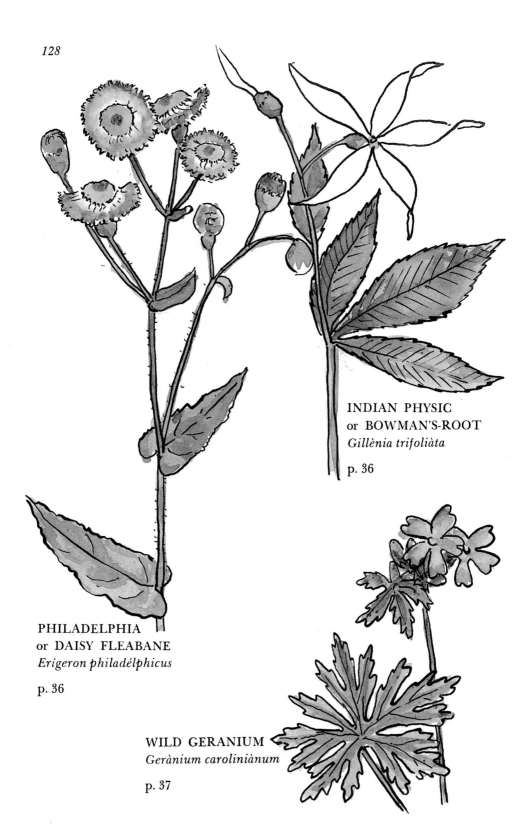

INDIAN PHYSIC
or BOWMAN'S-ROOT
Gillènia trifoliàta

p. 36

PHILADELPHIA
or DAISY FLEABANE
Erígeron philadélphicus

p. 36

WILD GERANIUM
Geràium caroliniànum

p. 37

YELLOW JESSAMINE
Gelsèmium sempérvirens

p. 37

FRINGED MILKWORT
Polýgala paucifòlia

p. 37

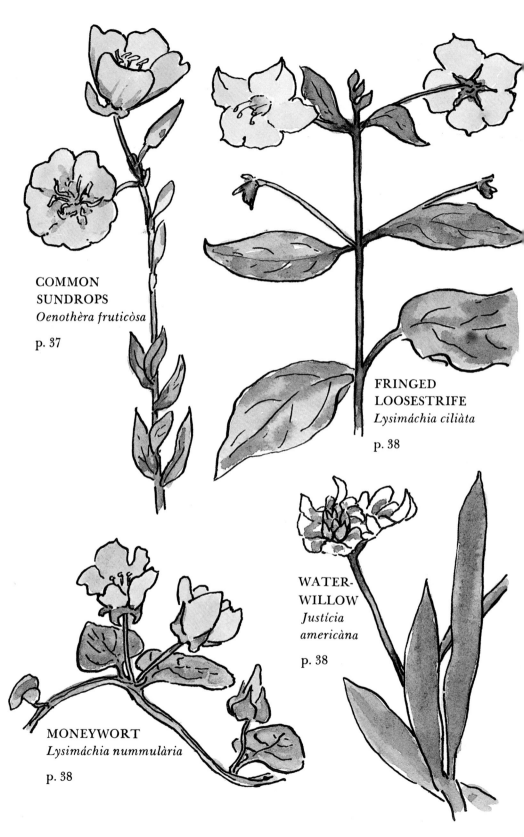

COMMON
SUNDROPS
Oenothèra fruticòsa

p. 37

FRINGED
LOOSESTRIFE
Lysimáchia ciliàta

p. 38

WATER-
WILLOW
*Justícia
americàna*

p. 38

MONEYWORT
Lysimáchia nummulària

p. 38

BLUE FALSE INDIGO
Baptisia austràlis

p. 38

COMMON VETCH
Vicia angustifòlia

p. 39

WOOD-VETCH
Vicia caroliniàna

p. 39

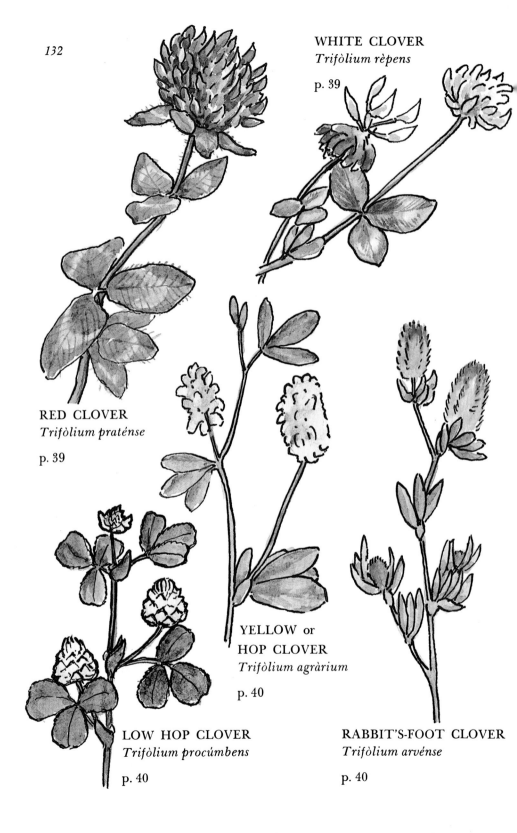

132

WHITE CLOVER
Trifòlium règpens

p. 39

RED CLOVER
Trifòlium praténse

p. 39

YELLOW or
HOP CLOVER
Trifòlium agràrium

p. 40

LOW HOP CLOVER
Trifòlium procúmbens

p. 40

RABBIT'S-FOOT CLOVER
Trifòlium arvénse

p. 40

BLACK-EYED SUSAN
Rudbéckia hírta

p. 41

TICKSEED
Coreópsis verticillàta

p. 41

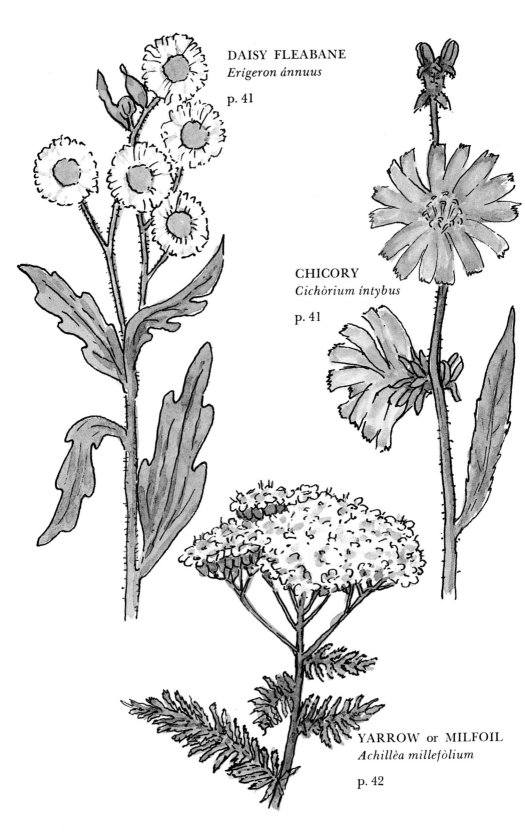

DAISY FLEABANE
Erigeron ánnuus

p. 41

CHICORY
Cichòrium intybus

p. 41

YARROW or MILFOIL
Achillèa millefòlium

p. 42

TALL BELLFLOWER
Campánula americàna

p. 42

VENUS'S LOOKING-GLASS
Speculària perfoliàta

p. 42

BLUE-EYED
GRASS
*Sisyrinchium
angustifòlium*

p. 42

GOLD-EYED GRASS or
YELLOW STARGRASS
Hypóxis hirsùta

p. 43

WATERLEAF
Hydrophýllum canadénse

p. 43

GOAT'S-BEARD
Arúncus dioìcus

p. 43

PASTURE ROSE
Ròsa carolìna

p. 44

SWEETBRIAR ROSE
Ròsa rubiginòsa

p. 44

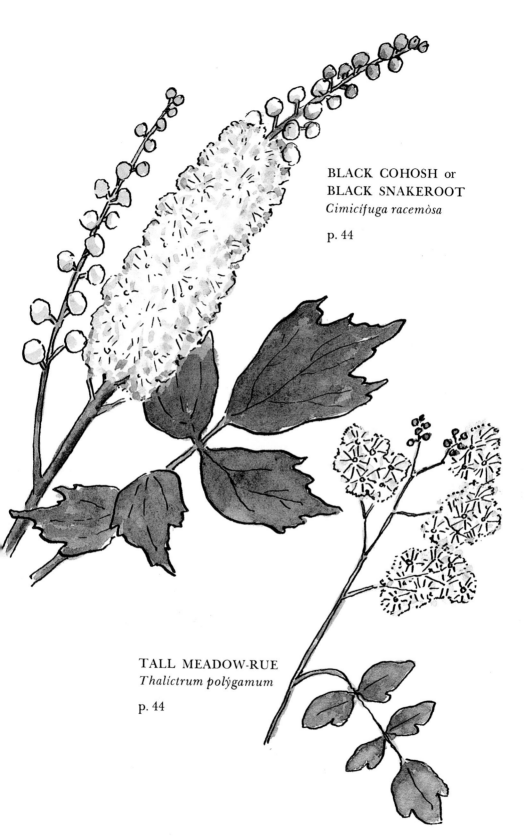

BLACK COHOSH or
BLACK SNAKEROOT
Cimicifuga racemòsa

p. 44

TALL MEADOW-RUE
Thalictrum polýgamum

p. 44

LEATHER-FLOWER
Clématis viórna

p. 45

THIMBLEWEED
Anemòne ripària

p. 45

WHITE AVENS
Gèum canadénse

p. 45

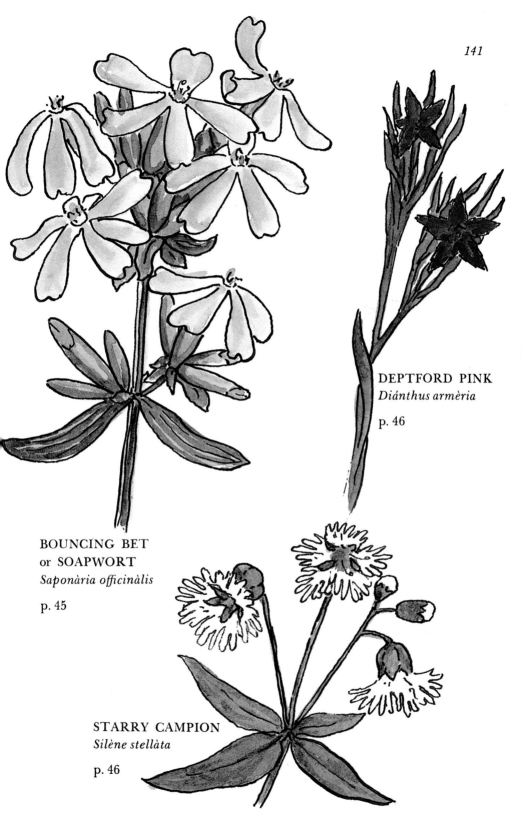

DEPTFORD PINK
Diánthus arméria

p. 46

BOUNCING BET
or SOAPWORT
Saponària officinàlis

p. 45

STARRY CAMPION
Silène stellàta

p. 46

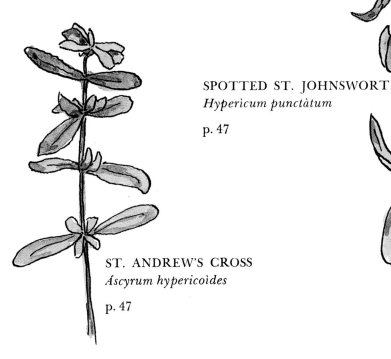

142

GOLDEN ST. JOHNSWORT
Hypericum kalmiànum

p. 46

COMMON ST. JOHNSWORT
Hypericum perforàtum

p. 46

SPOTTED ST. JOHNSWORT
Hypericum punctàtum

p. 47

ST. ANDREW'S CROSS
Áscyrum hypericoìdes

p. 47

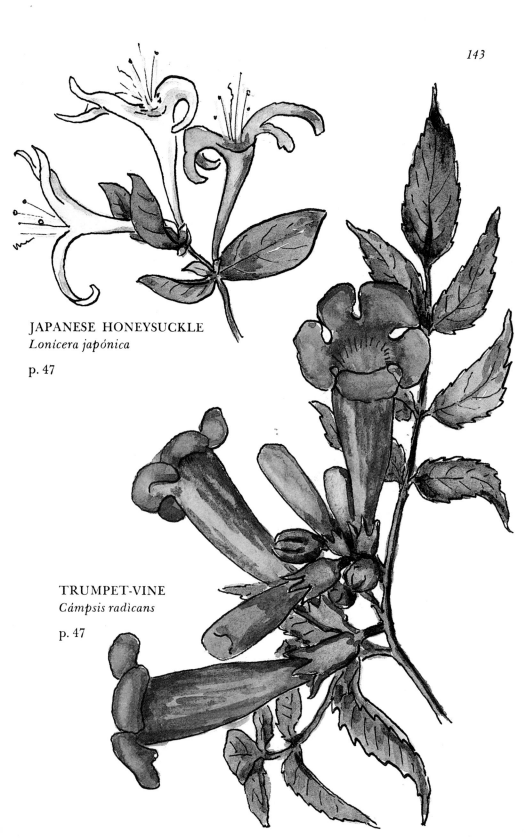

JAPANESE HONEYSUCKLE
Lonicera japónica

p. 47

TRUMPET-VINE
Cámpsis radìcans

p. 47

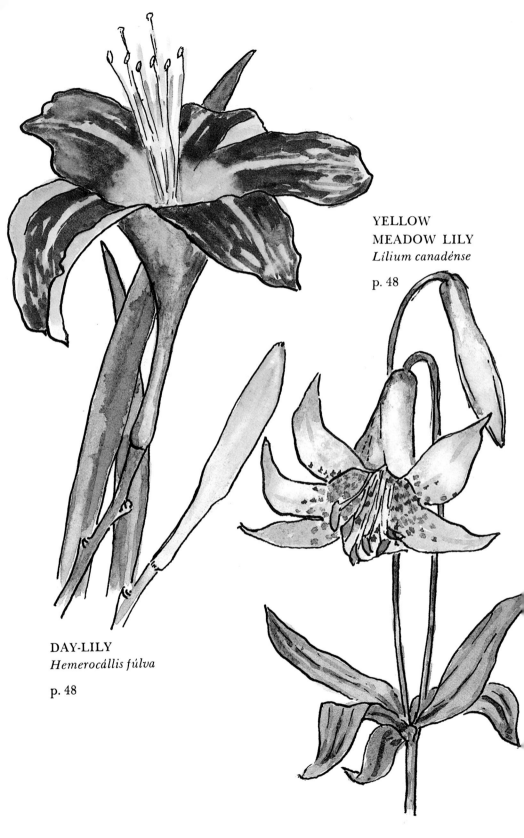

YELLOW
MEADOW LILY
Lilium canadénse

p. 48

DAY-LILY
Hemerocállis fúlva

p. 48

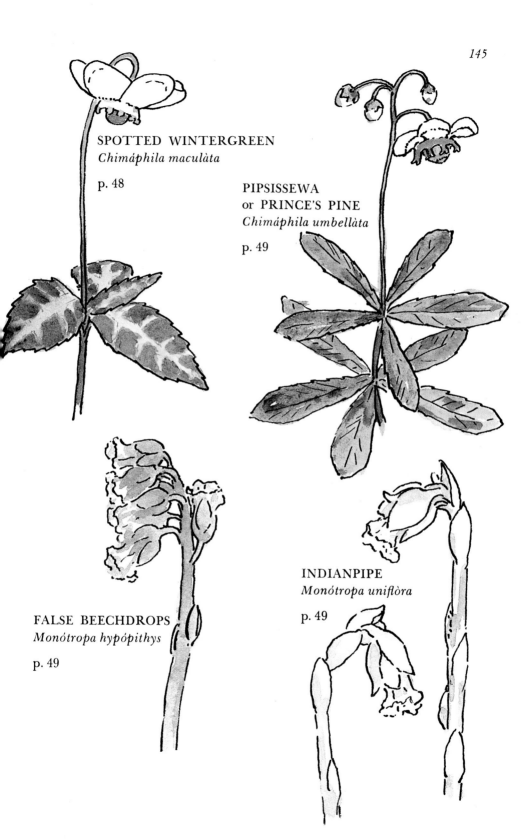

145

SPOTTED WINTERGREEN
Chimáphila maculàta

p. 48

PIPSISSEWA
or PRINCE'S PINE
Chimáphila umbellàta

p. 49

FALSE BEECHDROPS
Monótropa hypópithys

p. 49

INDIANPIPE
Monótropa uniflòra

p. 49

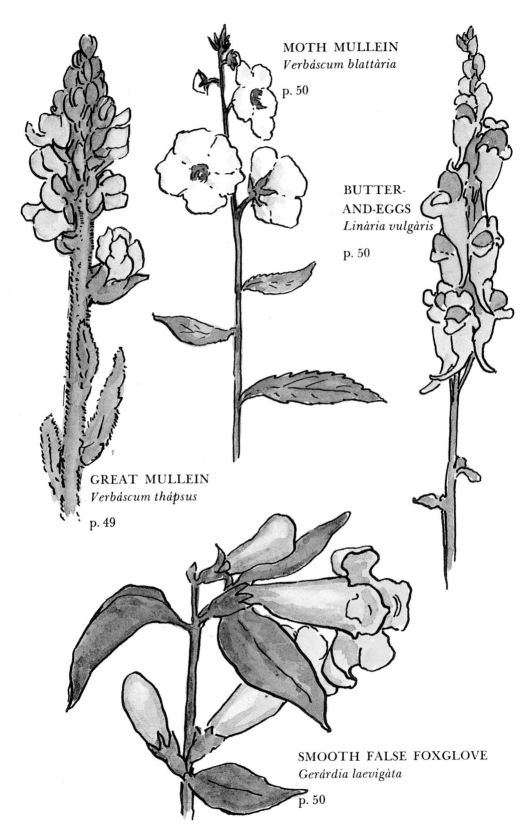

MOTH MULLEIN
Verbáscum blattària

p. 50

BUTTER-
AND-EGGS
Linària vulgàris

p. 50

GREAT MULLEIN
Verbáscum thápsus

p. 49

SMOOTH FALSE FOXGLOVE
Gerárdia laevigàta

p. 50

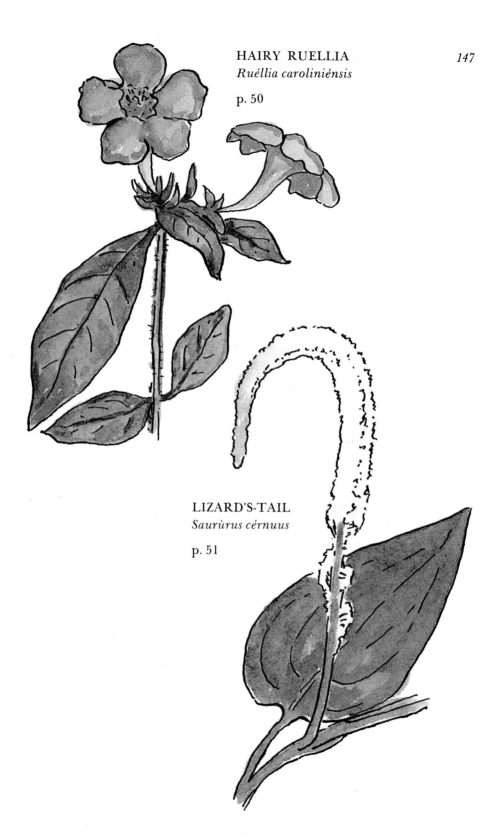

Ruéllia caroliniénsis

p. 50

LIZARD'S-TAIL
Saurùrus cérnuus

p. 51

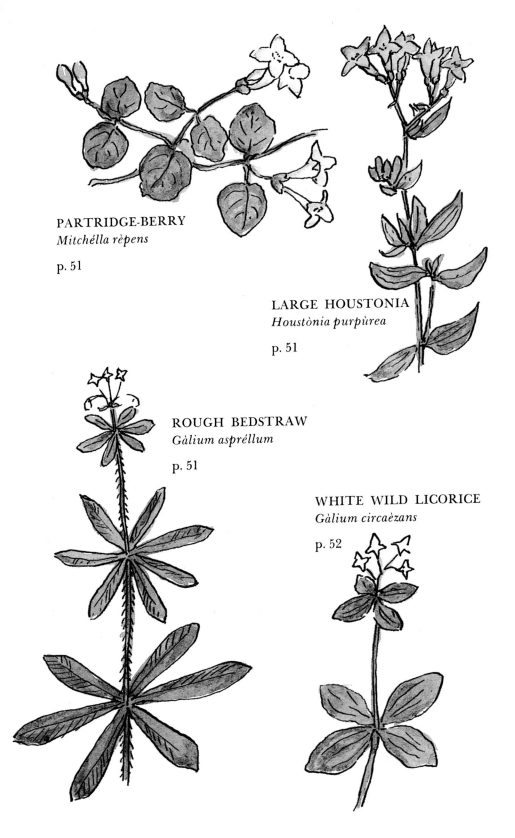

PARTRIDGE-BERRY
Mitchélla rèpens

p. 51

LARGE HOUSTONIA
Houstònia purpùrea

p. 51

ROUGH BEDSTRAW
Gàlium aspréllum

p. 51

WHITE WILD LICORICE
Gàlium circaèzans

p. 52

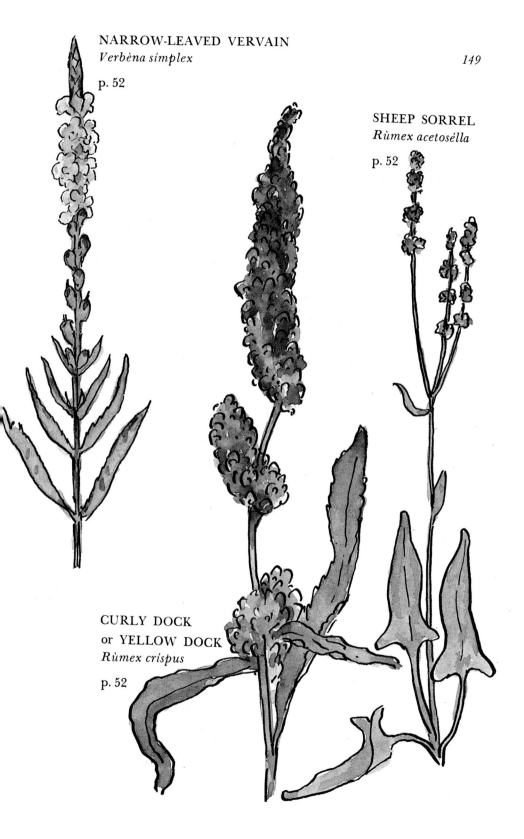

NARROW-LEAVED VERVAIN
Verbèna simplex

p. 52

SHEEP SORREL
Rùmex acetosélla

p. 52

CURLY DOCK
or YELLOW DOCK
Rùmex crispus

p. 52

QUEEN ANNE'S LACE
Daùcus caròta

p. 53

HORSENETTLE
Solànum carolinénse

p. 53

GRASS-OF-PARNASSUS
Parnássia glaùca

p. 53

WOOD-BETONY or
COMMON LOUSEWORT
Pediculàris canadénsis

p. 53

SENECA SNAKEROOT
Polýgala sénega

p. 54

ROSE POGONIA
Pogònia ophioglossoìdes

p. 54

YELLOW MILKWORT
Polýgala lùtea

p. 54

GRASS-PINK
Calopògon pulchéllus

p. 54

LARGE PURPLE-
FRINGED ORCHIS
Habenària fimbriàta

p. 55

**NARROWLEAF
PLANTAIN**
Plantàgo lanceolàta

p. 55

COMMON MALLOW
Málva neglécta

p. 55

BLUE LUPINE
Lupìnus perénnis

p. 55

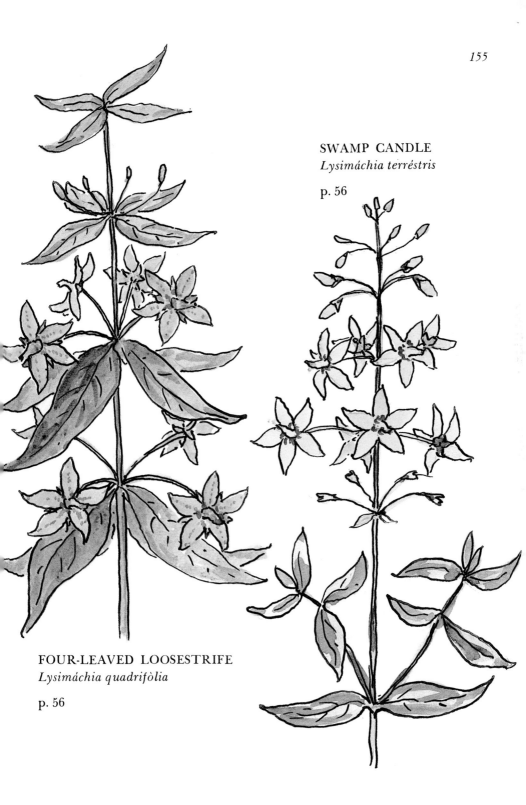

SWAMP CANDLE
Lysimáchia terréstris

p. 56

FOUR-LEAVED LOOSESTRIFE
Lysimáchia quadrifòlia

p. 56

BUTTERFLY-WEED
Asclèpias tuberòsa

p. 56

SWAMP MILKWEED
Asclèpias incarnàta

p. 56

COMMON MILKWEED
Asclèpias syrìaca

p. 57

HEDGE BINDWEED or **WILD MORNING-GLORY**
Convólvulus sèpium

p. 57

COMMON DODDER
Cuscùta gronòvii

p. 58

MORNING-GLORY
Ipomoèa hederàcea

p. 57

158

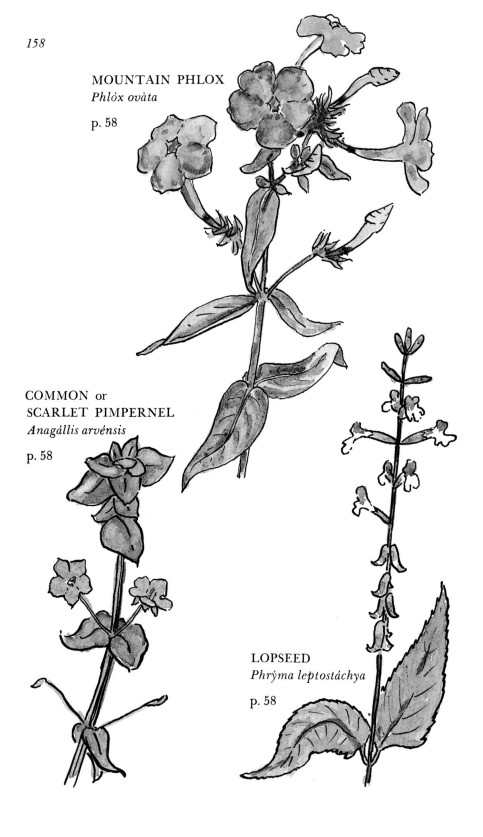

MOUNTAIN PHLOX
Phlóx ovàta

p. 58

COMMON or
SCARLET PIMPERNEL
Anagállis arvénsis

p. 58

LOPSEED
Phrýma leptostáchya

p. 58

WHORLED ROSINWEED
Sílphium trifoliàtum

p. 59

**SHARP-LEAVED
GOLDENROD**
Solidàgo argùta

p. 59

DROPSEED
Galinsòga parviflòra

p. 59

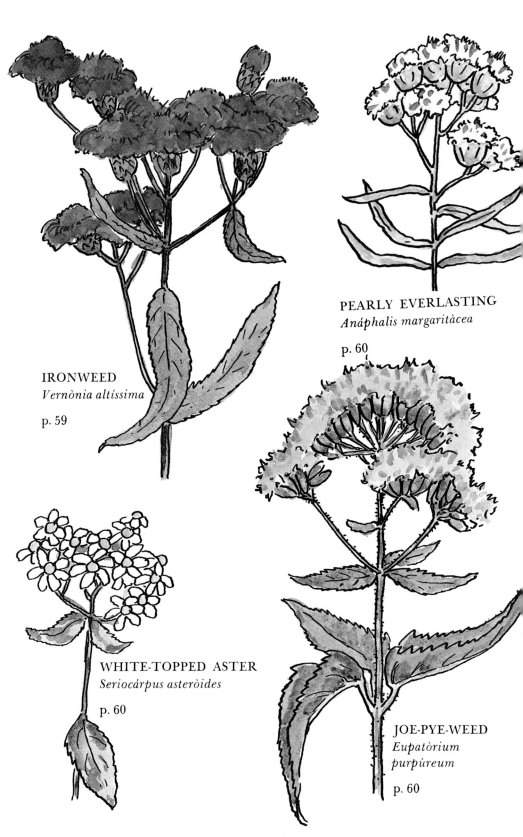

IRONWEED
Vernònia altíssima

p. 59

PEARLY EVERLASTING
Anáphalis margaritàcea

p. 60

WHITE-TOPPED ASTER
Seriocárpus asteròides

p. 60

JOE-PYE-WEED
Eupatòrium
purpùreum

p. 60

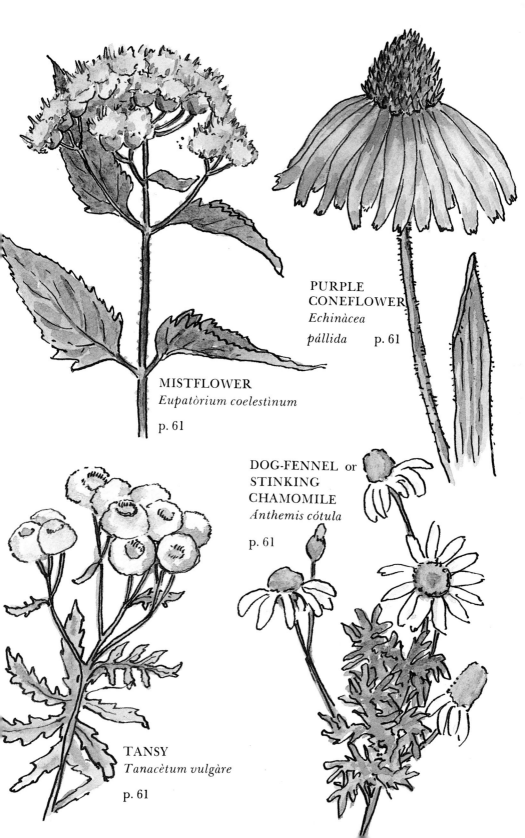

PURPLE
CONEFLOWER
Echinàcea
pállida p. 61

MISTFLOWER
Eupatòrium coelestìnum

p. 61

DOG-FENNEL or
STINKING
CHAMOMILE
Ánthemis cótula

p. 61

TANSY
Tanacètum vulgàre

p. 61

BLACK MUSTARD
Brássica nìgra

p. 62

ENCHANTER'S NIGHTSHADE
Circaèa quadrisulcàta var. *canadénsis*

p. 62

WINTERGREEN or **CHECKERBERRY**
Gaulthèria procùmbens

p. 62

POKEBERRY
Phytolácca americàna

p. 63

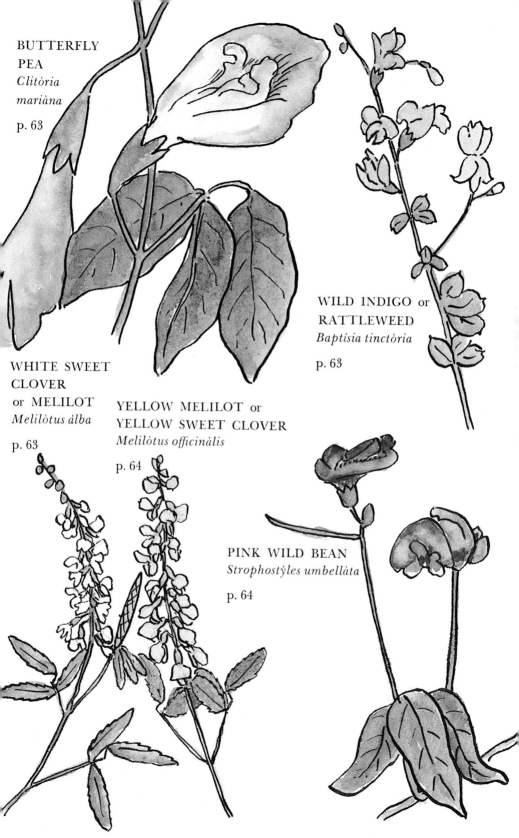

BUTTERFLY
PEA
*Clitòria
mariàna*

p. 63

WILD INDIGO or
RATTLEWEED
Baptísia tinctòria

p. 63

WHITE SWEET
CLOVER
or MELILOT
Melilòtus álba

p. 63

YELLOW MELILOT or
YELLOW SWEET CLOVER
Melilòtus officinàlis

p. 64

PINK WILD BEAN
Strophostýles umbellàta

p. 64

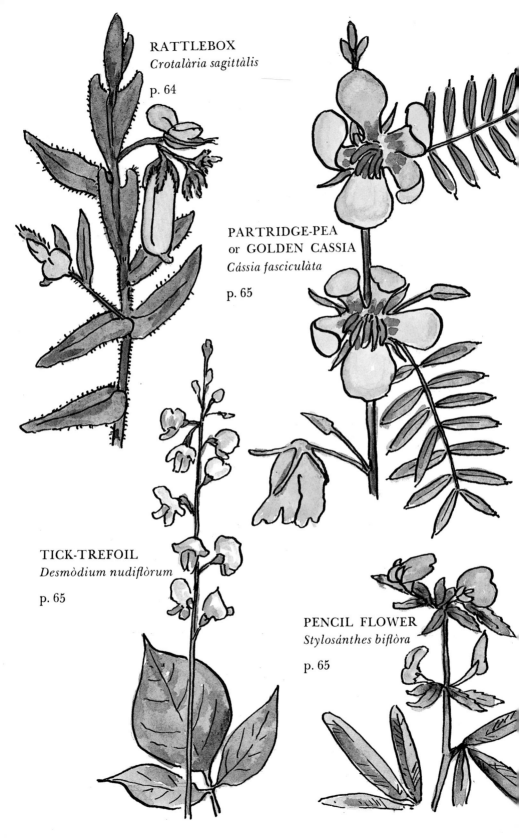

RATTLEBOX
Crotalària sagittàlis

p. 64

PARTRIDGE-PEA
or **GOLDEN CASSIA**
Cássia fasciculàta

p. 65

TICK-TREFOIL
Desmòdium nudiflòrum

p. 65

PENCIL FLOWER
Stylosánthes biflòra

p. 65

FALSE DRAGONHEAD
Physostégia virginiàna

p. 65

AMERICAN
GERMANDER
or WOOD-SAGE
Teùcrium canadénse

p. 66

BASIL
Saturèja vulgàris

p. 66

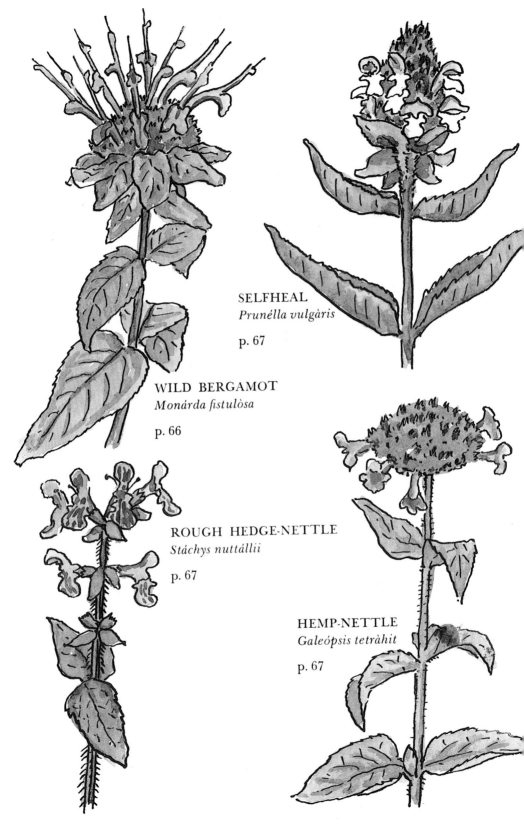

SELFHEAL
Prunélla vulgàris

p. 67

WILD BERGAMOT
Monárda fistulòsa

p. 66

ROUGH HEDGE-NETTLE
Stáchys nuttállii

p. 67

HEMP-NETTLE
Galeópsis tetràhit

p. 67

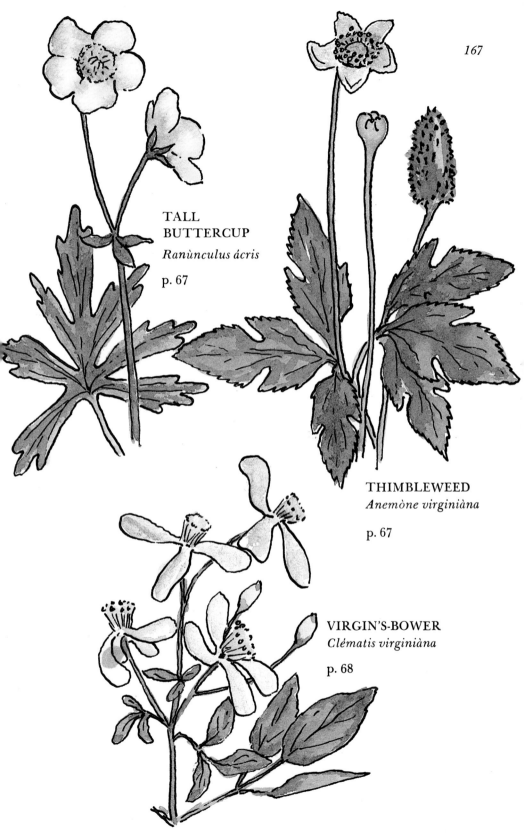

TALL
BUTTERCUP
Ranùnculus ácris

p. 67

THIMBLEWEED
Anemòne virginiàna

p. 67

VIRGIN'S-BOWER
Clématis virginiàna

p. 68

168

MONKEY-FLOWER
Mímulus alàtus

p. 68

CULVER'S-ROOT
Veronicástrum virginicum

p. 68

FALSE PIMPERNEL
Lindérnia dùbia

p. 68

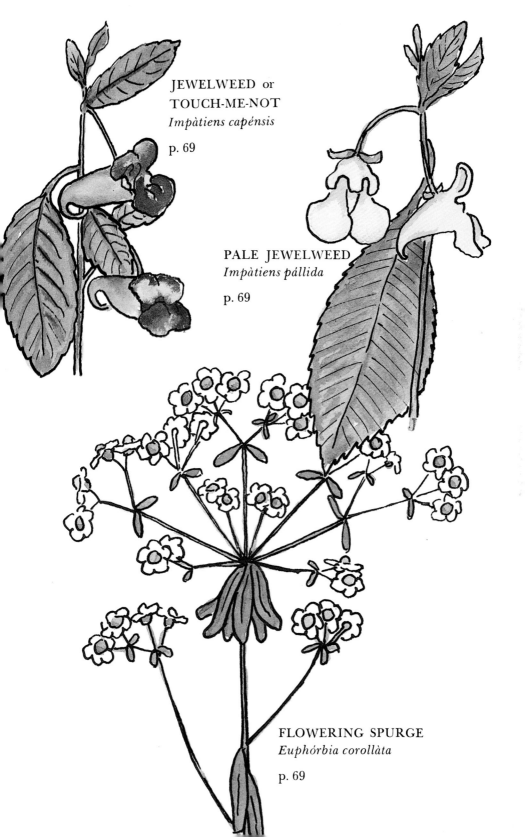

JEWELWEED or
TOUCH-ME-NOT
Impàtiens capénsis

p. 69

PALE JEWELWEED
Impàtiens pállida

p. 69

FLOWERING SPURGE
Euphórbia corollàta

p. 69

WATER-PARSNIP
Sìum suàve

p. 69

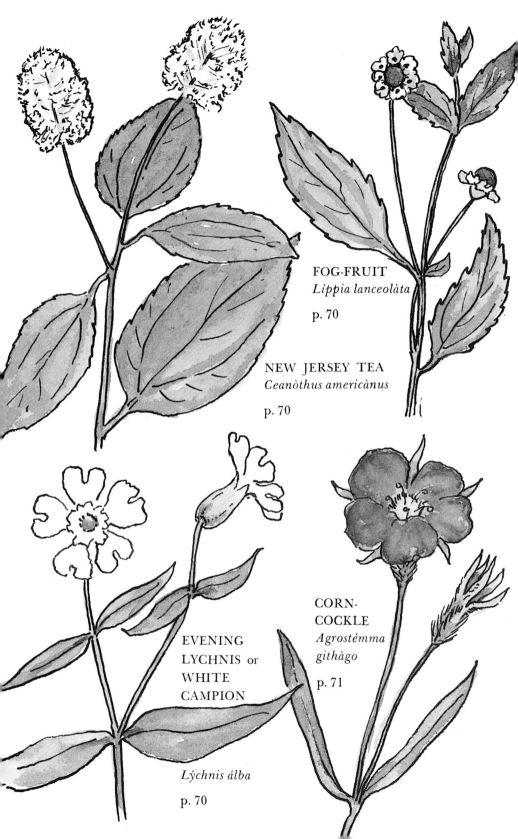

FOG-FRUIT
Lippia lanceolàta

p. 70

NEW JERSEY TEA
Ceanòthus americànus

p. 70

EVENING
LYCHNIS or
WHITE
CAMPION

Lýchnis álba

p. 70

CORN-
COCKLE
*Agrostémma
githàgo*

p. 71

WILD GARLIC
Állium canadénse

p. 71

NODDING WILD ONION
Állium cérnuum

p. 71

WOOD LILY
Lilium philadélphicum

p. 71

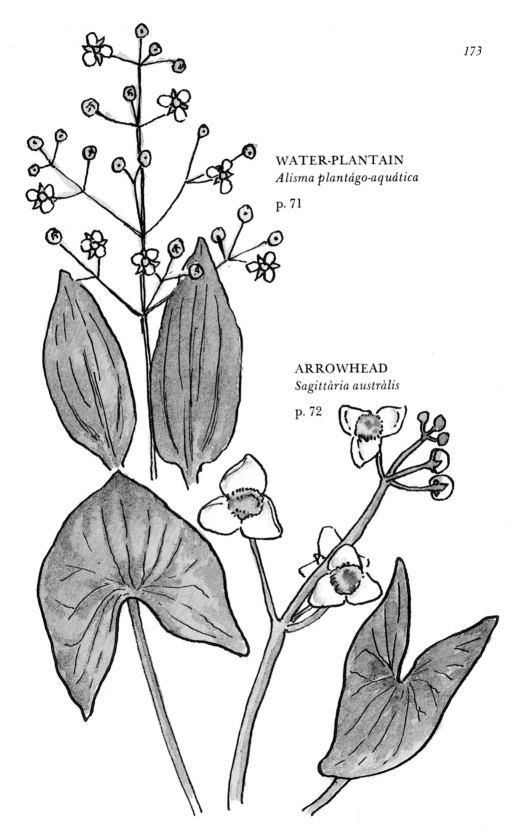

WATER-PLANTAIN
Alísma plantágo-aquática

p. 71

ARROWHEAD
Sagittària austràlis

p. 72

ARROWHEAD
Saggittària rigida

p. 72

ARROWHEAD
Sagittària latifòlia

p. 72

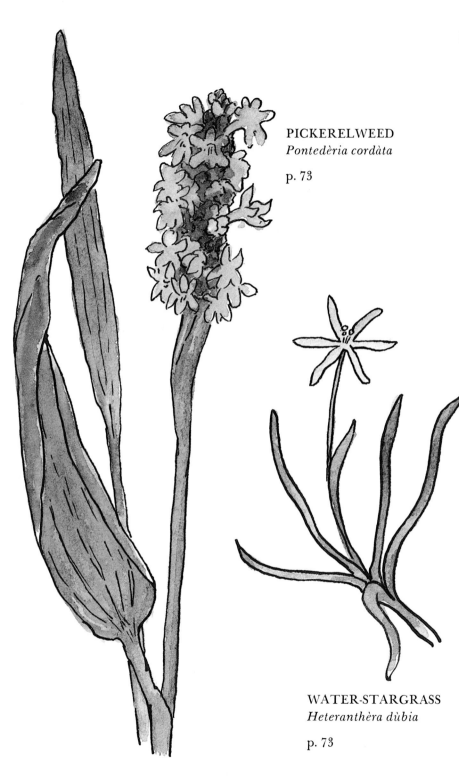

PICKERELWEED
Pontedèria cordàta

p. 73

WATER-STARGRASS
Heteranthèra dùbia

p. 73

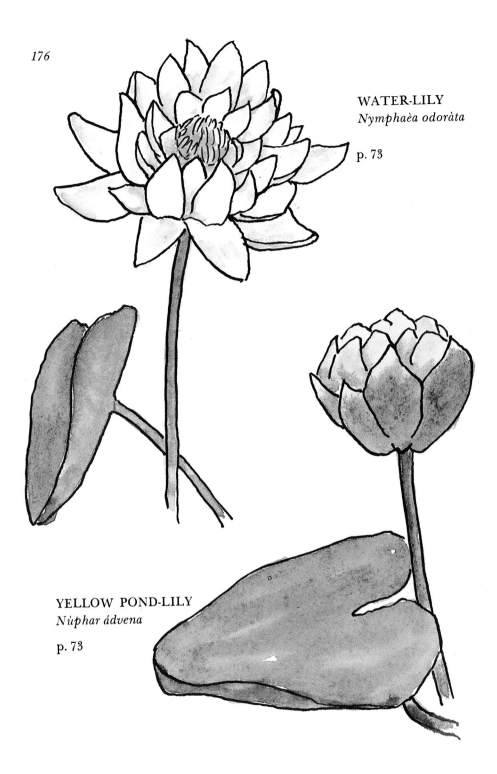

WATER-LILY
Nymphaèa odoràta

p. 73

YELLOW POND-LILY
Nùphar ádvena

p. 73

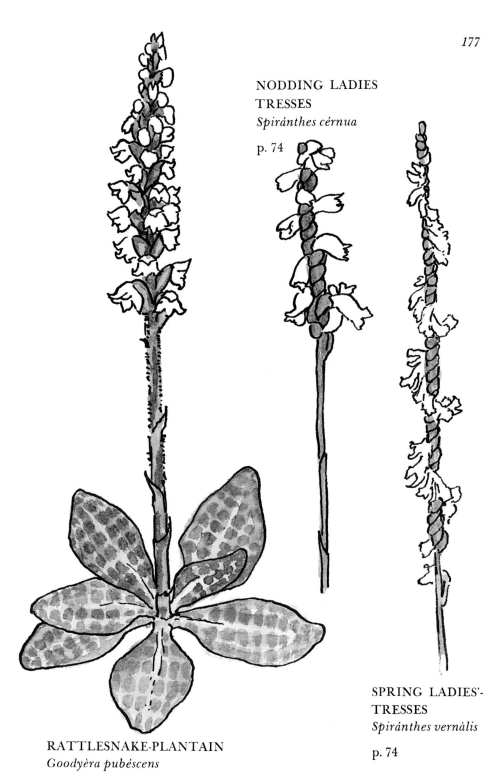

NODDING LADIES
TRESSES
Spiránthes cérnua

p. 74

SPRING LADIES'-
TRESSES
Spiránthes vernàlis

p. 74

RATTLESNAKE-PLANTAIN
Goodyèra pubéscens

p. 74

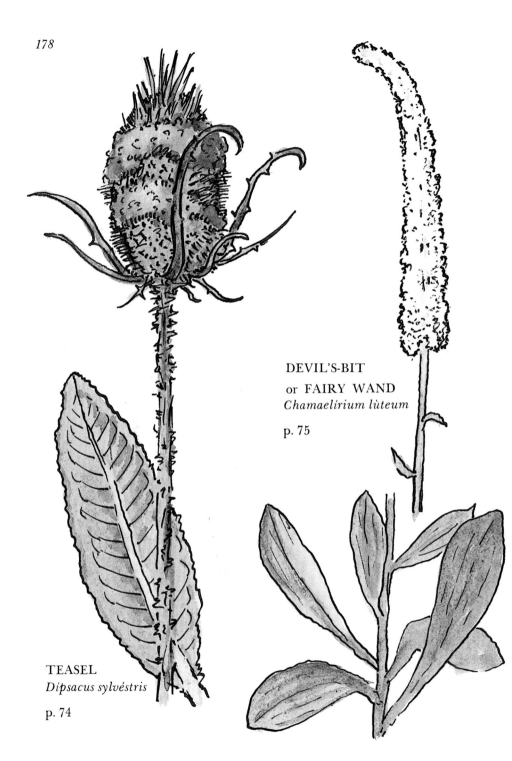

DEVIL'S-BIT
or FAIRY WAND
Chamaelirium lùteum

p. 75

TEASEL
Dipsacus sylvéstris

p. 74

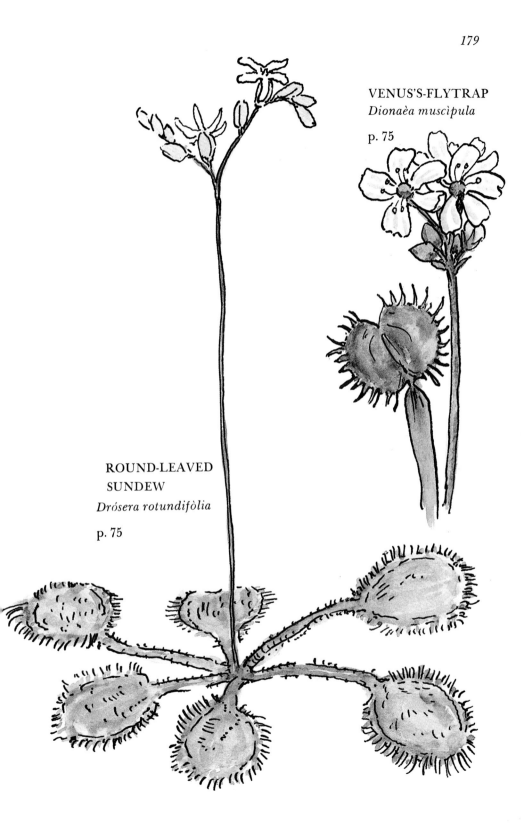

VENUS'S-FLYTRAP
Dionaèa muscìpula

p. 75

**ROUND-LEAVED
SUNDEW**
Drósera rotundifòlia

p. 75

BLACKBERRY-LILY
Belamcánda chinénsis

p. 76

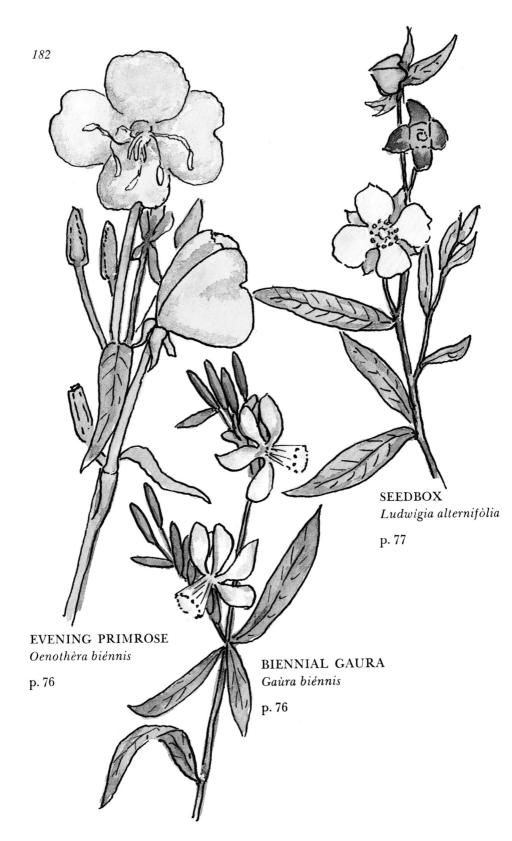

SEEDBOX
Ludwigia alternifòlia

p. 77

EVENING PRIMROSE
Oenothèra biénnis

p. 76

BIENNIAL GAURA
Gaùra biénnis

p. 76

MARSH MALLOW
Hibíscus militàris

p. 77

CRIMSON-EYE ROSE-MALLOW
Hibiscus moscheùtos

p. 78

MUSK MALLOW
Málva moschàta

p. 77

JERUSALEM ARTICHOKE
Heliánthus tuberòsus

p. 78

SNEEZEWEED
Helénium autumnàle

p. 78

TALL CONEFLOWER
Rudbéckia laciniàta

p. 78

TALL TICKSEED
Coreópsis tripteris

p. 79

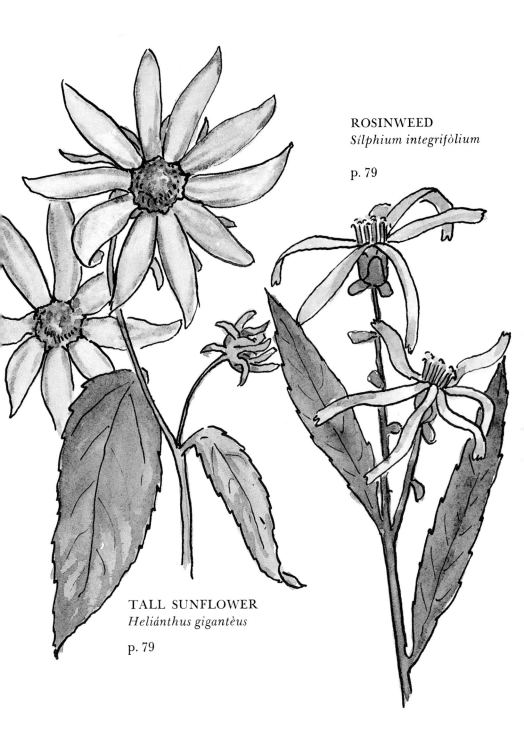

ROSINWEED
Silphium integrifòlium

p. 79

TALL SUNFLOWER
Heliánthus gigantèus

p. 79

**TICKSEED-
SUNFLOWER**
Bìdens aristòsa

p. 80

LEAFCUP
Polýmnia uvedàlia

p. 79

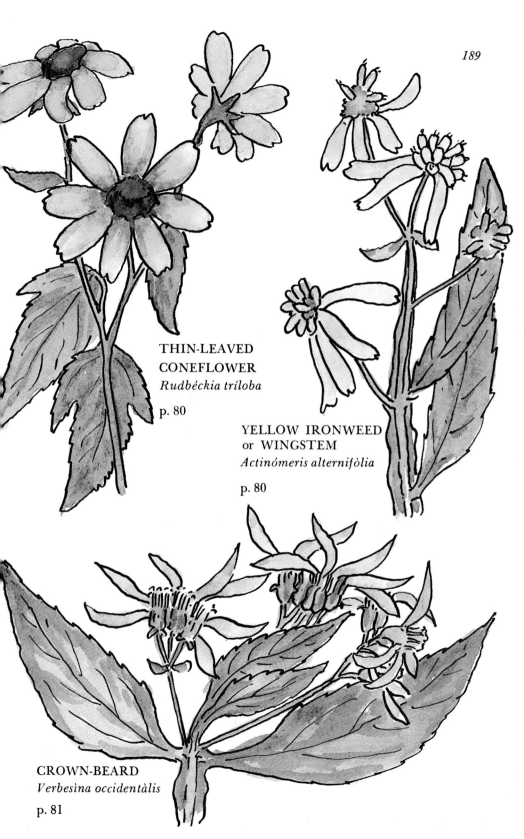

**THIN-LEAVED
CONEFLOWER**
Rudbéckia tríloba

p. 80

**YELLOW IRONWEED
or WINGSTEM**
Actinómeris alternifòlia

p. 80

CROWN-BEARD
Verbesìna occidentàlis

p. 81

WHITE WOODLAND ASTER or
MICHAELMAS DAISY
Aster divaricàtus

p. 81

WHITE SNAKEROOT
Eupatòrium rugòsum

p. 81

TALL BLUE LETTUCE
Lactùca biénnis

p. 81

EARLY GOLDENROD
Solidàgo júncea

p. 82

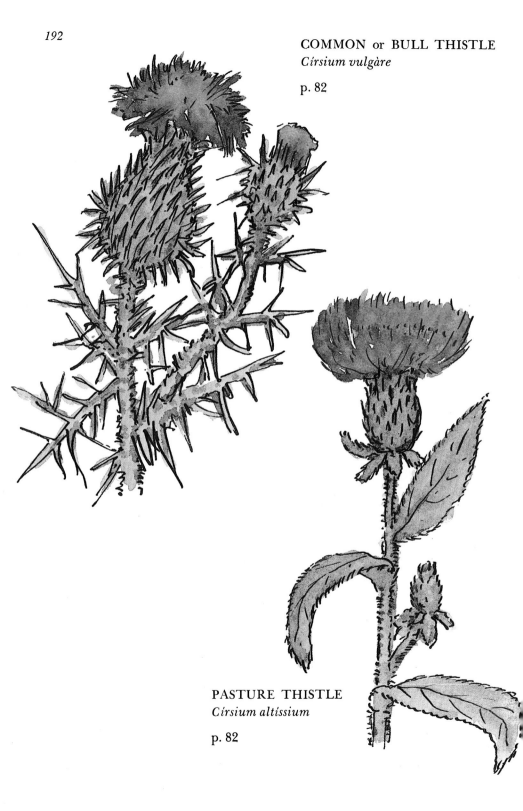

COMMON or BULL THISTLE
Círsium vulgàre

p. 82

PASTURE THISTLE
Círsium altíssium

p. 82

BONESET
Eupatòrium perfoliàtum

p. 83

FIREWEED
Erechtìtes hieracifòlia

p. 83

HAWKWEED
Hieràcium paniculàtum

p. 83

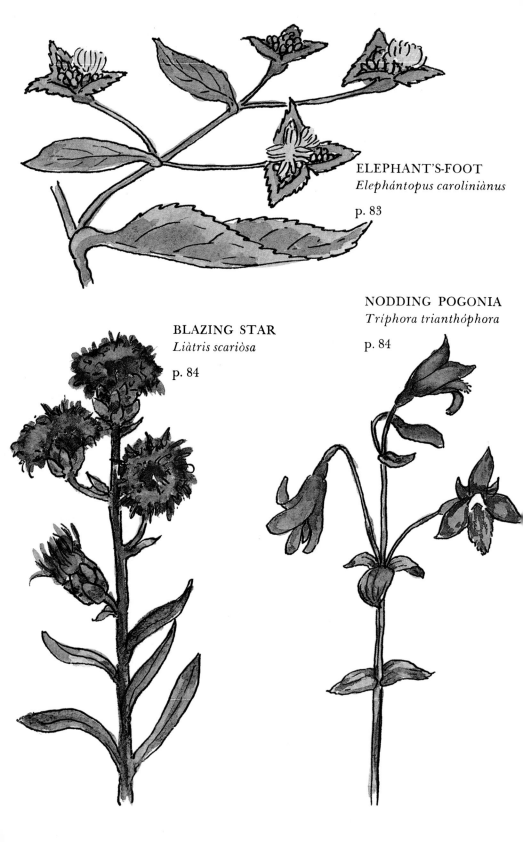

ELEPHANT'S-FOOT
Elephántopus caroliniànus

p. 83

NODDING POGONIA
Tríphora trianthóphora

p. 84

BLAZING STAR
Liàtris scariòsa

p. 84

TICK-TREFOIL
Desmòdium cuspidàtum

p. 84

TICK-TREFOIL
Desmòdium laevigàtum

p. 84

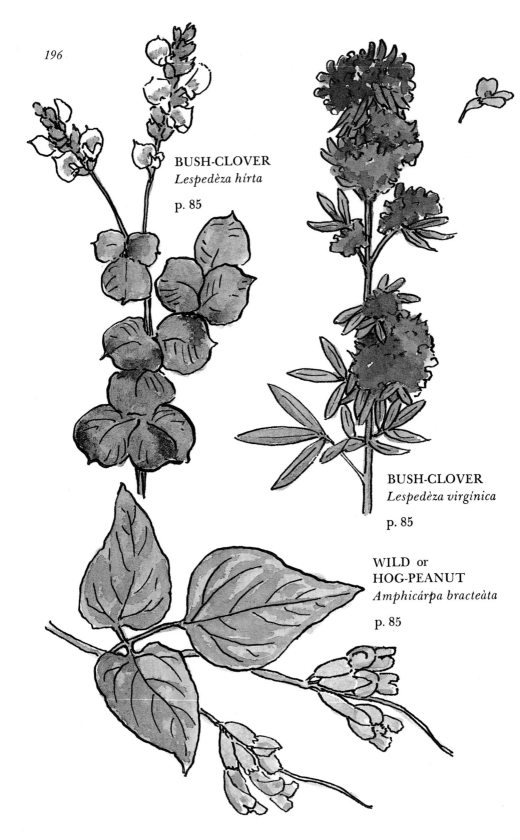

BUSH-CLOVER
Lespedèza hírta

p. 85

BUSH-CLOVER
Lespedèza virgínica

p. 85

WILD or
HOG-PEANUT
Amphicárpa bracteàta

p. 85

GROUNDNUT
or WILD BEAN
Ápios americàna

p. 85

WILD SENSITIVE-
PLANT
Cássia nictitans

p. 86

WILD SENNA
Cássia marilándica

p. 86

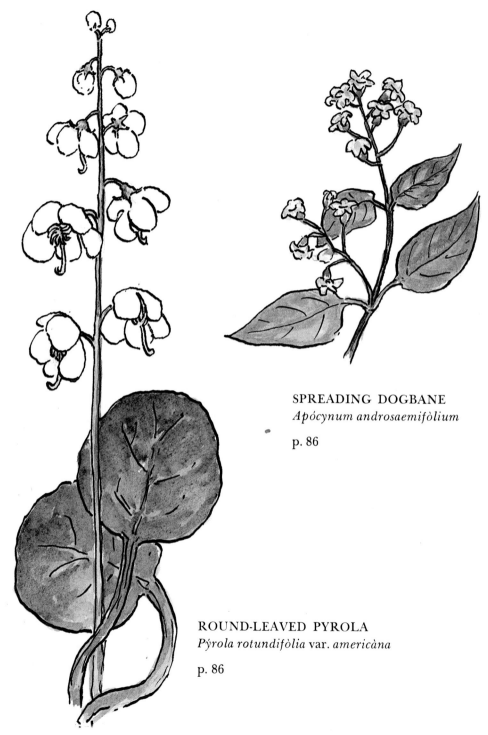

SPREADING DOGBANE
Apócynum androsaemifòlium

p. 86

ROUND-LEAVED PYROLA
Pýrola rotundifòlia var. *americàna*

p. 86

BLUE VERVAIN
Verbèna hastàta

p. 231

WHITE VERVAIN
Verbèna urticifòlia

p. 231

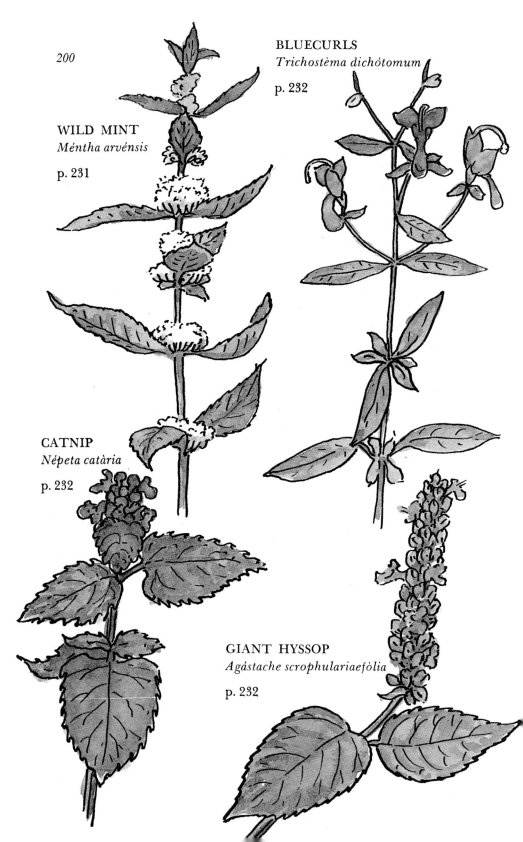

200

WILD MINT
Méntha arvénsis

p. 231

BLUECURLS
Trichostèma dichótomum

p. 232

CATNIP
Népeta catària

p. 232

GIANT HYSSOP
Agástache scrophulariaefòlia

p. 232

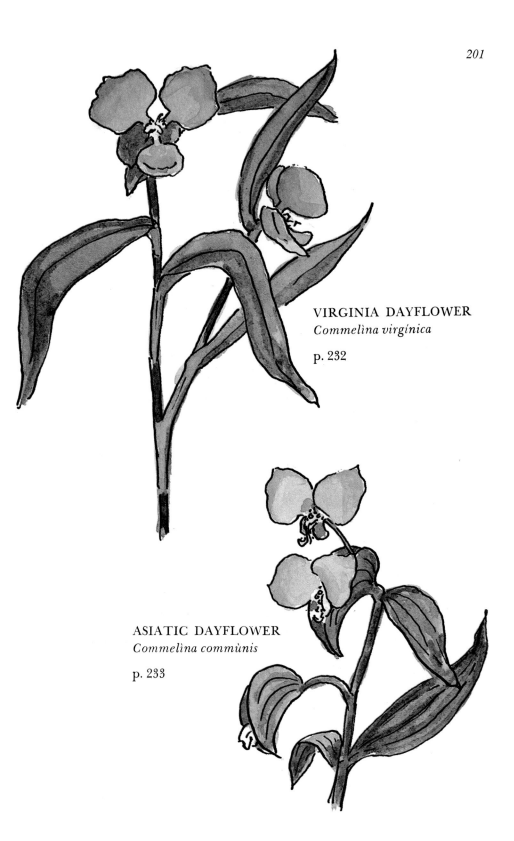

VIRGINIA DAYFLOWER
Commelìna virgínica

p. 232

ASIATIC DAYFLOWER
Commelìna commùnis

p. 233

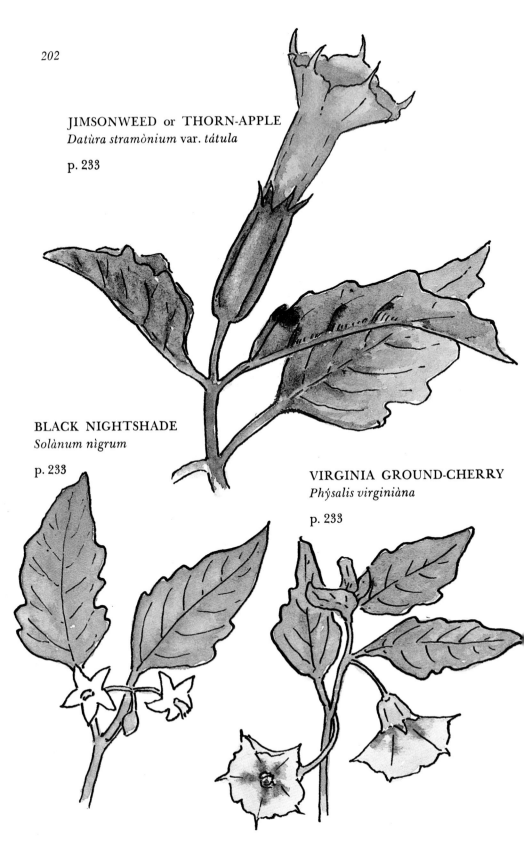

JIMSONWEED or THORN-APPLE
Datùra stramònium var. *tátula*

p. 233

BLACK NIGHTSHADE
Solànum nìgrum

p. 233

VIRGINIA GROUND-CHERRY
Phýsalis virginiàna

p. 233

GREAT LOBELIA
Lobèlia siphilítica

p. 234

PALE-SPIKED LOBELIA
Lobèlia spicàta

p. 234

CARDINAL LOBELIA
Lobèlia cardinàlis

p. 235

INDIAN-TOBACCO
Lobèlia inflàta

p. 234

SAND VINE
Ampélamus álbidus

p. 235

WILD or PRICKLY CUCUMBER
Echinocýstis lobàta

p. 235

206

SWAMP LOOSESTRIFE
or WATER-WILLOW
Décodon verticillàtus

p. 235

CLAMMY CUPHEA
or BLUE WAXWEED
Cùphea petiolàta

p. 236

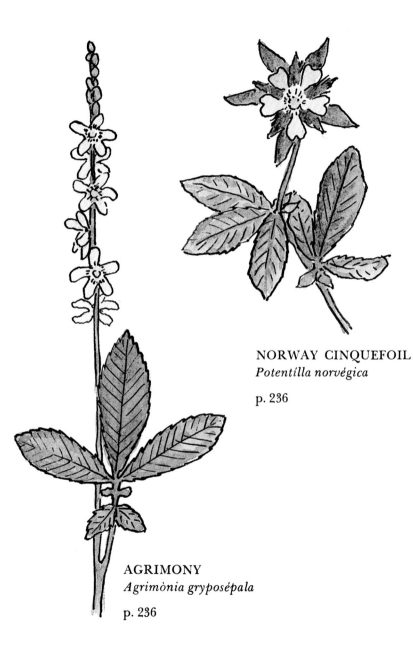

NORWAY CINQUEFOIL
Potentílla norvégica

p. 236

AGRIMONY
Agrimònia gryposépala

p. 236

DITTANY
Cunìla origanoìdes

p. 237

BUTTONWEED
Dìódia tères

p. 237

ROSE-GENTIAN or ROSE-PINK
Sabàtia angulàris

p. 237

BOTTLE or CLOSED GENTIAN
Gentiàna andrèwsii

p. 238

CLOSED GENTIAN
Gentiàna villòsa

p. 238

PRINCE'S FEATHER
or WATER SMARTWEED
Polýgonum coccineum

p. 238

JUMPSEED
Tovàra virginiàna

p. 239

LADY'S-THUMB
Polýgonum persicària

p. 239

**HALBERD-LEAVED
TEARTHUMB**
Polýgonum arifòlium

p. 239

**COMMON SMARTWEED
or MILD WATER-PEPPER**
Polýgonum hydropiperoìdes

p. 239

YELLOW FALSE FOXGLOVE
Gerárdia flàva

p. 240

SLENDER-LEAVED GERARDIA
Gerárdia tenuifòlia

p. 240

TURTLEHEAD
Chelòne glàbra

p. 240

PURPLE GERARDIA
Gerárdia purpùrea

p. 240

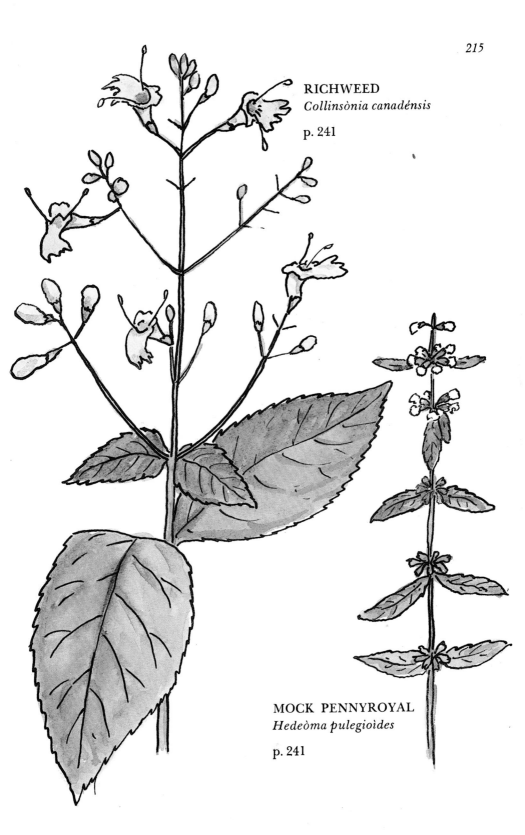

RICHWEED
Collinsònia canadénsis

p. 241

MOCK PENNYROYAL
Hedeòma pulegioìdes

p. 241

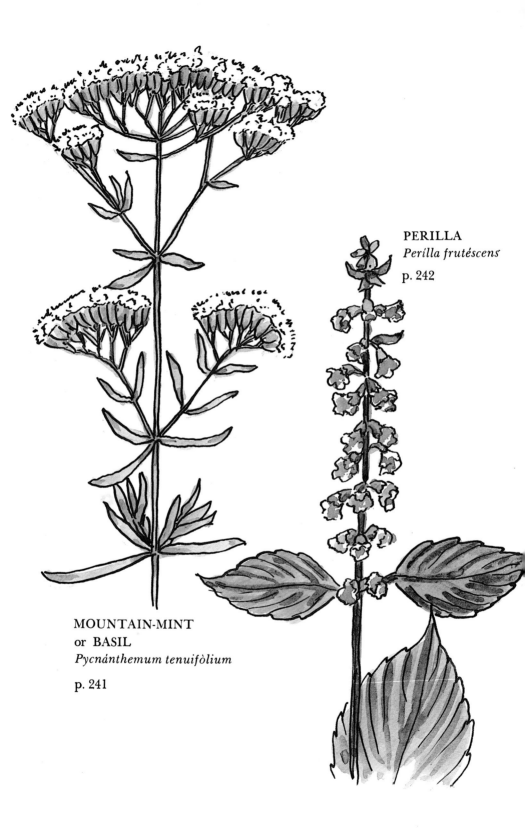

PERILLA
Perilla frutéscens
p. 242

MOUNTAIN-MINT
or BASIL
Pycnánthemum tenuifòlium

p. 241

NEW ENGLAND ASTER
Aster nòvae-ángliae

p. 242

GOLDEN-ASTER or
MARYLAND GOLDEN-ASTER
Chrysópsis mariàna

p. 242

SPREADING ASTER
Aster pàtens

p. 243

WAVY-LEAVED ASTER
Aster undulàtus

p. 243

BRISTLE-LEAVED ASTER
Aster linariifòlius

p. 243

WHITE ASTER
Aster simplex

p. 244

SMALL WHITE ASTER
Aster patèrnus

p. 243

SMOOTH
ASTER
Aster laèvis

p. 244

CROOKED-STEMMED ASTER
Aster prenanthoìdes

p. 244

LARGE-
FLOWERED
ASTER
Aster grandiflòrus

p. 244

HEART-LEAVED ASTER
Aster cordifòlius

p. 245

BUSHY ASTER
Aster dumòsus

p. 245

WHITE HEATH ASTER
Aster ericoìdes

p. 245

LARGER BUR-MARIGOLD
Bìdens laèvis

p. 246

SPANISH NEEDLES
Bìdens bipinnàta

p. 246

BEGGAR-TICKS
Bìdens frondòsa

p. 246

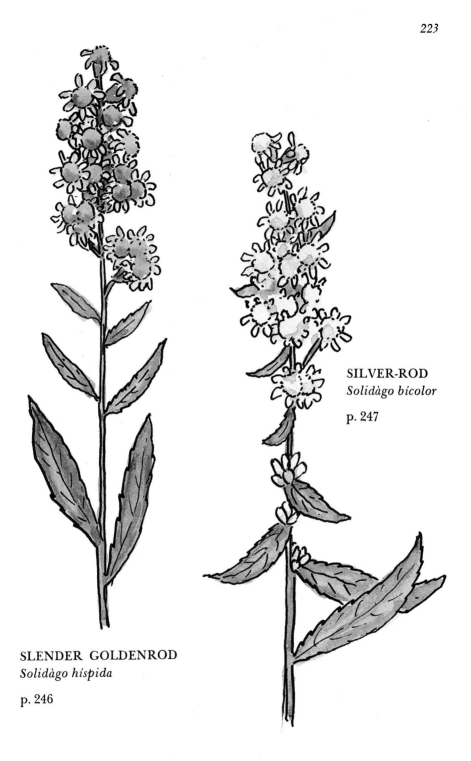

SILVER-ROD
Solidàgo bicolor

p. 247

SLENDER GOLDENROD
Solidàgo hispida

p. 246

BLUE-STEMMED GOLDENROD
Solidàgo caèsia

p. 247

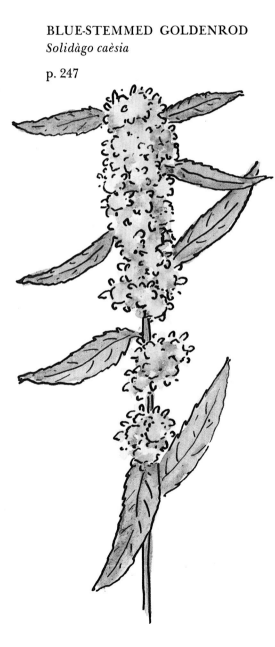

STOUT GOLDENROD
Solidàgo squarròsa

p. 247

SPREADING GOLDENROD
Solidàgo flexicaùlis

p. 247

CATFOOT or CUDWEED
Gnaphàlium obtusifòlium

p. 248

RATTLESNAKE-ROOT
Prenánthes álba

p. 248

CONEFLOWER
Rudbéckia fúlgida

p. 248

HARDHACK
Spiraèa tomentòsa

p. 248

ELECAMPANE
Ínula helénium

p. 249

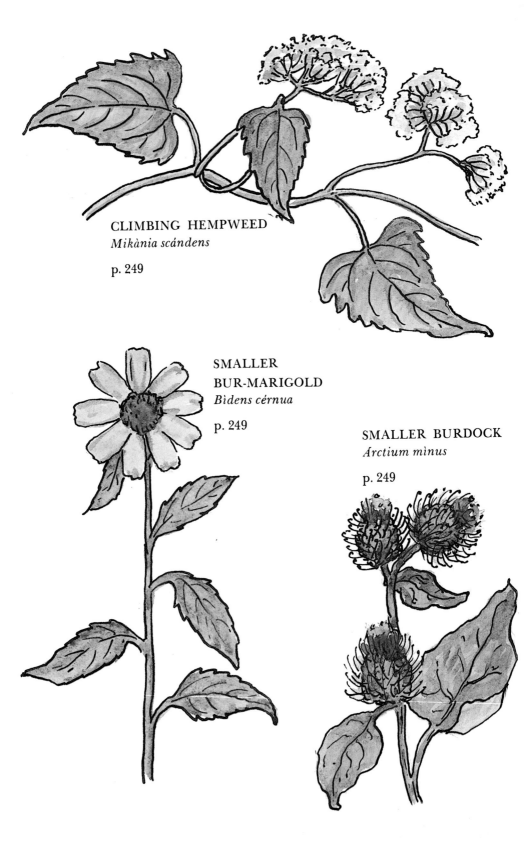

CLIMBING HEMPWEED
Mikània scándens

p. 249

SMALLER
BUR-MARIGOLD
Bìdens cérnua

p. 249

SMALLER BURDOCK
Árctium mìnus

p. 249

LIVE-FOREVER
Sèdum telephioìdes

p. 250

CLIMBING FALSE
BUCKWHEAT
Polýgonum scándens

p. 250

Habit: A much-branched, shrublike perennial with rather reddish stems and opposite, ovate leaves, 1 to 3 inches long. Small clusters of delicate, pale pink, bell-shaped flowers are striped inside with deeper pink and have five outward-curving lobes. The flowers are both terminal and in the upper leaf axils. The plant has a milky juice.

Habitat: Dry thickets, borders of woods, occasionally fields and roadsides. Newfoundland to Georgia; west to Arkansas, Indiana, and Nebraska. June to August.

BLUE VERVAIN (*Verbèna hastàta*)   PLATE p. 199
VERVAIN FAMILY (Verbenàceae)
Height: 1 to 5 feet.
Habit: A tall, erect, coarse-stemmed perennial, open-branched above, with opposite, oblong to lance-shaped leaves, $1\frac{1}{2}$ to 6 inches long, with pointed tips and coarsely toothed margins. Occasionally the lower leaves have two short, pointed lobes near the base. Numerous dense flower spikes, with whorls of tiny, deep blue to bright lavender, tubular flowers, have the upper lobes smaller than the lower outer lobes. The flowers bloom upward along the spike, in small whorls.
Habitat: Rich, sandy soil; low ground; marshes, swamps, stream sides. Nova Scotia to Florida; west to Tennessee, Texas, and Missouri. July to September.

WHITE VERVAIN (*Verbèna urticifòlia*)   PLATE p. 199
VERVAIN FAMILY (Verbenàceae)
Height: 3 to 5 feet.
Habit: A coarse, erect, weedy perennial with a slightly hairy stem and sparingly branched. The opposite, oblong to ovate leaves, $2\frac{1}{2}$ to 6 inches long, have pointed tips, coarsely toothed margins, and are stiff-hairy beneath. Threadlike terminal spikes have scattered small, white, tubular flowers, $\frac{1}{2}$ inch across, that bloom irregularly up the spike from the base.
Habitat: River banks, edges of woods, fields, waste places. Quebec to Florida; west to Texas and South Dakota. June to September.

WILD MINT (*Méntha arvénsis*)   PLATE p. 200
MINT FAMILY (Labiàtae)
Height: 2 to 3 feet.
Habit: A tall, leafy, erect, stout, square-stemmed perennial, simple or branching, with opposite, lance-shaped to broadly ovate, stalked or nearly sessile leaves, 1 to $2\frac{1}{4}$ inches long. The tiny, bell-shaped, lilac pink, violet, or white flowers, $\frac{1}{8}$ to $\frac{1}{4}$ inch long, are in dense whorls in the leaf axils. The plant has a minty odor.
Habitat: Wet or damp open soil, low woods. Labrador to Vir-

ginia; west to Kentucky and Missouri. July to September. Our only native species.

BLUECURLS (Trichostèma dichótomum)   PLATE p. 200
   MINT FAMILY (Labiàtae)
Height: 6 to 18 inches.
Habit: A small, erect, sticky-hairy, much-branched annual with uncut, pointed leaves, ⅘ to 2 inches long. The long-stalked, blue, tubular flowers arise from the upper axils of greatly reduced bracteal leaves. A distinguishing characteristic is the shape of the four long stamens that extend beyond the petal lobes and curve downward.
Habitat: Dry soil, upland woods, old fields. Maine to Florida; west to Michigan, Missouri, and Texas. August and September.

CATNIP (*Népeta catària*)   PLATE p. 200
   MINT FAMILY (Labiàtae)
Height: 1 to 3 feet.
Habit: An erect, robust, much-branched, downy perennial with stalked, broadly triangular, toothed leaves, 1 to 2½ inches long. The flowers are pale lavender or white, spotted with pink, and crowded at the tips of the branches.
Habitat: A weed of gardens, roadsides, waste places. Throughout our range and beyond. June to September. Naturalized from Europe. A strongly aromatic plant cats enjoy.

GIANT HYSSOP (*Agástache scrophulariaefòlia*) PLATE p. 200
   MINT FAMILY (Labiàtae)
Height: 1 to 3 feet.
Habit: A tall, erect perennial with square stems branched above and opposite, lance-shaped to ovate, coarsely toothed leaves, 2 to 6 inches long. The pale pink or purplish, tubular flowers are crowded in cylindrical spikes, 4 to 10 inches long, tapering a little at the top.
Habitat: Upland forests and rich woods, thickets. Vermont to North Carolina; west to Kentucky, Missouri, and Kansas. July to September.

VIRGINIA DAYFLOWER (*Commelìna virgínica*)
   SPIDERWORT OR DAYFLOWER FAMILY (Commelinàceae)
Height: 1 to 3 feet.   PLATE p. 201
Habit: A stout perennial with succulent stems, erect to ascending, often widely branched, and long, lance-shaped, tapering leaves, 4 to 6 inches long. The showy, ephemeral, clear blue flowers have three roundish petals (the two upper ones stalked, the lower one slightly smaller) with golden stamens. Each flower blooms for only a morning.
Habitat: Moist to wet woodlands, thickets, clearings. New Jer-

sey to Florida; west to Indiana, Missouri, and Texas. July to
October.

ASIATIC DAYFLOWER *(Commelìna commùnis)*

SPIDERWORT OR DAYFLOWER FAMILY (Commelinàceae)

Height: 1 to 2 feet. PLATE p. 201

Habit: An annual with succulent stems, erect at first, later
spreading in all directions and rooting at the nodes. The ovate
to lance-shaped, sessile leaves are 2 to 4 inches long and ½ to ¾
inch wide. Pure blue to lavender flowers, opening from enfold-
ing bracts, have two erect, rather oval upper petals and a smaller,
nearly white lower one. Each blooms for only a morning.

Habitat: Often a garden weed, moist or shaded ground. Massachusetts to Alabama; west to Arkansas and Wisconsin. June to
October. An immigrant from eastern Asia.

JIMSONWEED or THORN-APPLE *(Datùra stramònium var. tátula)*

NIGHTSHADE FAMILY (Solanàceae) PLATE p. 202

Height: 1 to 5 feet.

Habit: A coarse, hollow-stemmed, stout, much-branched annual
with large, thin, ovate leaves, 2 to 7 inches long, and coarsely
notched or toothed near the stalk. The stalk and midrib may be
slightly purplish. Large, trumpet-shaped, lavender flowers, 2 to
4 inches long, flare out with five distinct points. The green,
angled calyx is also tubular. Later, an ovoid spiny capsule, 2
inches long, is produced.

Habitat: Waste ground. Throughout our area and beyond. July
to October. A dangerously poisonous plant with an unpleasant
odor. Naturalized from Asia.

BLACK NIGHTSHADE *(Solànum nìgrum)* PLATE p. 202

NIGHTSHADE FAMILY (Solanàceae)

Height: 1 to 3 feet.

Habit: A tall, smooth, erect to widely branching annual with
thin, long-stalked, large, ovate, irregularly toothed leaves, widest near the base. The white or pale lavender flowers have five
widely flaring, pointed lobes and yellow stamens, which surround the pistil in a tiny projecting cone. The flowers are in
few-flowered umbels, later producing round black berries.

Habitat: Waste ground, thickets, dry woods, roadsides. Maine to
Florida; west to North Dakota and Texas. June to November.
The unripe berries are poisonous and the plant often referred
to as deadly nightshade.

VIRGINIA GROUND-CHERRY *(Phýsalis virginiàna)*

NIGHTSHADE FAMILY (Solanàceae) PLATE p. 202

Height: 1 to 3 feet.

Habit: A perennial with somewhat hairy stems that later become reclining and spreading, with forked ascending branches. The ovate to lance-shaped leaves are irregularly and shallowly toothed and taper to both ends. Long-stalked, greenish to dull yellow flowers with tubular, wide-flaring corollas have five brownish or purplish markings deep in the throat. Later, a red berry is produced.
Habitat: Rocky or sandy woods, openings, clearings. Connecticut to Florida; west to Michigan, Wisconsin, and Minnesota. May to August.

GREAT LOBELIA (*Lobèlia siphilítica*)   Plate p. 203
    Lobelia Family (Lobeliàceae)
Height: 1 to 3 feet.
Habit: A perennial with a stout simple stem, slightly hairy in the upper part, and alternate, thin, narrowly oblong to lance-shaped leaves, $2\frac{1}{2}$ to 6 inches long, pointed and narrowed to a sessile base. The stem is topped by a long raceme of crowded flowers in leafy bracts. Bluish to purplish tubular flowers, split to the base and up to 1 inch long, have an upper lip with two erect lobes and a lower lip with three spreading lobes.
Habitat: Wet, rich, low ground; swamps. Rarely in Maine, to upland North Carolina, Alabama, and Mississippi; west to Missouri and Kansas. August and September. Plants spread by basal offshoots and many may be clustered together making a beautiful display.

PALE-SPIKED LOBELIA (*Lobèlia spicàta*)   Plate p. 203
    Lobelia Family (Lobeliàceae)
Height: 8 to 24 inches.
Habit: A low plant with a simple, erect stem, densely short-hairy at the base and smooth above, and with short-stalked, spatulate lower leaves and nearly linear upper leaves, all uncut and ascending. The stem is terminated by a slender raceme of small, white or pale blue, tubular flowers, each $\frac{1}{8}$ inch long.
Habitat: Rich meadows, fields, thickets. Canada to Georgia; west to Arkansas and Minnesota. June to August. It is often a weed.

INDIAN-TOBACCO (*Lobèlia inflàta*)   Plate p. 204
    Lobelia Family (Lobeliàceae)
Height: 6 to 36 inches.
Habit: An erect, simple or branching annual with a slightly hairy stem and thin, ovate to lance-shaped leaves, 2 to $3\frac{1}{2}$ inches long. The lower leaves are short-stalked, but become sessile upward. The stem is topped by a slender raceme of tiny, light blue to white, tubular flowers, $\frac{1}{4}$ to $\frac{1}{3}$ inch long, in the axils of leafy bracts. Later, an inflated pod is produced.

Habitat: Moist or dry ground, open woods. Prince Edward Island to Georgia and Mississippi; west to Minnesota. July to October. Often a weed in gardens and lawns. It is poisonous. This is the commonest species.

CARDINAL LOBELIA (*Lobèlia cardinàlis*) PLATE p. 204
LOBELIA FAMILY (Lobeliàceae)

Height: 2 to 4 feet.

Habit: An erect, leafy, stout, smooth-stemmed perennial, usually unbranched, with thin, lance-shaped to oblong leaves, sharp-pointed and slightly toothed, up to 4 inches long. The lower leaves are short-stalked, but become sessile upward. The tubular flowers are in a loose raceme, 3 to 15 inches long; they are brilliant scarlet with narrow, pointed lobes, 1 to 1½ inches long, very colorful and showy.

Habitat: Wet soil, damp shores, swamps. Quebec to Florida; west to eastern Texas, Michigan, Wisconsin, and Minnesota. One of our most beautiful wildflowers, easily grown from seeds.

SAND VINE (*Ampélamus álbidus*) PLATE p. 205
MILKWEED FAMILY (Asclepiadàceae)

Height: Up to 7 feet.

Habit: A twining vine with large, heart-shaped, conspicuous, long-stalked leaves, up to 3 inches long, deeply indented at the base, and pointed. Clusters of small, whitish, tubular flowers, ¼ inch long, are in umbels or short racemes, in the leaf axils.

Habitat: Low, moist woods or fields; sandy thickets. Pennsylvania to Georgia; west to Indiana, Missouri, Kansas, and Texas. July and August. This plant is often a troublesome weed.

WILD or PRICKLY CUCUMBER (*Echinocýstis lobàta*)
GOURD OR CUCUMBER FAMILY (Cucurbitàceae) PLATE p. 205

Height: 15 to 20 feet.

Habit: A vigorous, rapid-growing, smooth annual vine, climbing by branched tendrils over small trees and bushes. The large, alternate, angular leaves, 2½ to 3 inches long, usually have five (sometimes three to seven) sharp-pointed lobes, indented at the base and long-stalked. The staminate flowers are in erect racemes, each long-stalked, with six white petals nearly cleft to the base; one or two pistillate flowers droop from the same leaf axil. Later, an oval prickly fruit, 1 to 1½ inches long, is produced.

Habitat: Moist ground and thickets. Throughout our entire range. July to September.

SWAMP LOOSESTRIFE or WATER-WILLOW
(*Décodon verticillàtus*) PLATE p. 206
LOOSESTRIFE FAMILY (Lythràceae)

Height: Aerial stems 1 to 2 feet.

Habit: A leafy perennial with slender, reclining or recurved, angled stems, 2½ to 10 feet long, and nearly stalkless, lance-shaped leaves, opposite or in whorls of three or four, each 1½ to 4½ inches long. Dense clusters of small, magenta, tubular flowers, ⅓ to ½ inch long, with five pointed petals and ten stamens (five long, five short) are in the upper leaf axils.

Habitat: Swamps or shallow pools. Maine to Florida and Louisiana; west to Illinois and Indiana. July and August. Arching branches root at the tips, enabling the plant to spread rapidly. The submersed stem is thickened and spongy.

CLAMMY CUPHEA or BLUE WAXWEED (*Cùphea petiolàta*)   PLATE p. 206
LOOSESTRIFE FAMILY (Lythràceae)

Height: 1 to 2 feet.

Habit: A very sticky-hairy, erect, branching annual with small, ovate to lance-shaped, mostly opposite leaves, ½ to 1 inch long, stalked and with pointed tips. The small, reddish purple, tubular flowers, ¼ inch long, with two larger upper petals and four smaller lower ones, may be solitary or paired, from the upper leaf axils.

Habitat: Dry, open soil. New Hampshire to Georgia and Louisiana; west to Illinois and Kansas. July to September. Small insects may be trapped on the sticky stem.

AGRIMONY (*Agrimònia gryposépala*)   PLATE p. 207
ROSE FAMILY (Rosàceae)

Height: 2 to 6 feet.

Habit: A tall, weedy perennial with a stout, sticky-hairy stem. The numerous alternate, compound leaves, pinnately divided, with up to seven ovate, coarsely toothed leaflets, are interspersed with two or more tiny leaflets. The stem is topped by a spikelike raceme of small, bright yellow flowers, ¼ to ⅓ inch across, with five yellow petals and orange anthers. The seedpod has tiny, hooked bristles.

Habitat: Roadsides, moist or dry open woods. Maine to the mountains of Tennessee; west to Michigan, Indiana, Missouri, and New Mexico. July and August.

NORWAY CINQUEFOIL (*Potentílla norvégica*)
ROSE FAMILY (Rosàceae)   PLATE p. 207

Height: 1 to 2 feet.

Habit: An erect or ascending, stout-stemmed, stiff, branched, very hairy annual. The compound leaf has three elliptic, hairy, coarsely toothed leaflets, each up to 2¼ inches long, and often two smaller rudimentary leaflets. The few to numerous small yellow flowers, less than ½ inch across, with five widely spaced rounded and indented petals, are surrounded by longer green sepals and bracts.

Habitat: Thickets, clearings, roadsides, waste places. Greenland to North Carolina; west to Texas and Arizona. June to August. Often a weed.

BUTTONWEED (*Diódia tères*)   PLATE p. 208
MADDER FAMILY (Rubiàceae)

Height: 5 to 10 inches.

Habit: A low annual with hairy, prostrate, spreading or ascending stems and numerous, mostly opposite, small, narrow, stiff leaves, ¾ to 1 inch long, with bristlelike pointed tips and sessile at the base. There are bristlelike stipules at the nodes. The small, sessile, tubular flowers, ¼ to ⅓ inch long, may be pale purple, pink, or white, with four equal lobes. Later, a small, hairy fruit is produced.

Habitat: Dry, sandy, poor ground. Rhode Island to Florida; west to Michigan, Iowa, and Texas. July to September. Often a troublesome weed.

DITTANY (*Cunìla origanoìdes*)   PLATE p. 208
MINT FAMILY (Labiàtae)

Height: 1 to 2 feet.

Habit: A freely branched perennial with stems woody at the base and opposite, ovate, finely toothed leaves, ¾ to 1 inch long, widest near the base, and almost sessile. The tiny, lavender (rarely white), tubular flowers have a notched upper lip, a three-cleft lower lip, and projecting stamens. The flowers are clustered in the upper leaf axils and at the tips of the branches. The plant has a minty fragrance.

Habitat: Thickets; dry, open woods; clearings. Southeastern New York, eastern Pennsylvania, West Virginia; west to Ohio, Indiana, Missouri, Oklahoma, and Texas. July to October. Once known, the plant can be identified by its characteristic aromatic fragrance.

ROSE-GENTIAN or ROSE-PINK (*Sabàtia angulàris*)
GENTIAN FAMILY (Gentianàceae)   PLATE p. 209

Height: 2 to 3 feet.

Habit: An erect, stout, square-stemmed biennial with numerous opposite upper branches. It grows from a persistent rosette of basal spatulate leaves. The opposite, ovate stem leaves, ½ to 1½ inches long, are broadly clasping at the base. The attractive fragrant, shining, pink, tubular flowers are in spreading clusters at the tips of the branches; each has five equal petals and is marked in the center with a yellowish green star.

Habitat: Moist meadows, peaty soil, damp woods. Connecticut to Florida and Louisiana; west to Michigan, Kansas, and Oklahoma. July to September.

CLOSED GENTIAN (*Gentiàna villòsa*)   PLATE p. 210
GENTIAN FAMILY (Gentianàceae)
Height: 10 to 40 inches.
Habit: A perennial with a smooth, slender stem and large, opposite, obovate to oblong leaves, 1½ to 3½ inches long, usually widest beyond the middle toward the blunt tip and tapering to a sessile base. The closed, greenish to white, club-shaped corollas, 1¼ to 1½ inches long, are erect or ascending. The stamens and anthers are united into a tube. Fertilization takes place within the closed flowers. Flowers are mostly in terminal clusters.
Habitat: Open woods, pine lands. New Jersey to Florida and Louisiana; west to Ohio and Indiana. September and October.

BOTTLE or CLOSED GENTIAN (*Gentiàna andrèwsii*)
GENTIAN FAMILY (Gentianàceae)   PLATE p. 210
Height: 1 to 2 feet.
Habit: A showy and beautiful perennial with a smooth, stout stem, usually unbranched, and large, opposite, lance-shaped to ovate leaves, narrowed at the base. The large, erect corollas, 1¼ inch long, are greenish at the base and intense blue at the tightly closed top. The flowers are mostly in a dense terminal cluster, with a few in the upper leaf axils. Fertilization takes place within the closed flowers.
Habitat: Moist woods and thickets, meadows, low ground. Quebec to eastern Massachusetts and the mountains of North Carolina to Georgia and Arkansas; west to Missouri and Nebraska. August to October.

PRINCE'S FEATHER or WATER SMARTWEED
(*Polýgonum coccíneum*)   PLATE p. 211
BUCKWHEAT OR SMARTWEED FAMILY (Polygonàceae)
Height: 2 to 4 feet.
Habit: A perennial of two forms; terrestrial or aquatic. In the terrestrial form the stems are usually branched and sheathed at the joints, and there are large alternate, lance-shaped to ovate leaves, 3 to 7 inches long. In the aquatic form the stems are floating or conspicuously inflated when submersed, with longer stalks and rounded bases. Tiny pinkish red flowers are in a dense spike at the top of the stem. These are in two forms on different plants: (1) stamens are short and inconspicuous, (2) stamens project conspicuously.
Habitat: Edges of ponds, river banks. Quebec to North Carolina; west to Arkansas, Kentucky, and Texas. July to September.

The terrestrial and aquatic forms may change with a change in water level.

JUMPSEED (*Tovàra virginiàna*) PLATE p. 211
BUCKWHEAT OR SMARTWEED FAMILY (Polygonàceae)
Height: 1 to 3 feet.
Habit: A tall, slender, erect, unbranched perennial with large, alternate, ovate to broadly lance-shaped leaves, up to 6 inches long, and tapering at both ends, the base sheathed. Very small, widely separated white flowers, less than $\frac{1}{4}$ inch long, are in an elongated raceme at the top of the stem. Flowers bloom from the base of the raceme upward, the lower ones soon drooping.
Habitat: Moist, rich woods; thickets. New Hampshire to Florida; west to Minnesota and Texas. August and September. At maturity, pressure on the seed causes it to be thrown 3 to 6 feet.

LADY'S-THUMB (*Polýgonum persicària*) PLATE p. 212
BUCKWHEAT OR SMARTWEED FAMILY (Polygonàceae)
Height: 2 to 4 feet.
Habit: An erect or ascending, simple or commonly branched annual with long, narrow, alternate leaves, $1\frac{1}{2}$ to 2 inches long, often blotched with purple above and with a sheath at the base. Dense slender spikes of inconspicuous pink to purplish and green flowers, $\frac{1}{12}$ to $\frac{1}{10}$ inch long, terminate the stem and upper leaf axils.
Habitat: Damp clearings, roadsides, shores, cultivated ground. Throughout our range. Spring through fall. A common weed naturalized from Europe.

COMMON SMARTWEED or MILD WATER-PEPPER
(*Polýgonum hydropiperoìdes*) PLATE p. 212
BUCKWHEAT OR SMARTWEED FAMILY (Polygonàceae)
Height: 1 to 3 feet.
Habit: A perennial with branching stems that may be prostrate, ascending, or erect. The leaves are smooth, narrow, lance-shaped, and ascending, sheathed around the stem at the leaf axil. Tiny pink (rarely greenish white) flowers are in slender, erect racemes at the tips of the branches.
Habitat: Wet shores, shallow water, flooded bottomlands. Quebec to Florida; west to Texas, Michigan, Wisconsin, Minnesota, and Nebraska. June to November.

HALBERD-LEAVED TEARTHUMB (*Polýgonum arifòlium*) PLATE p. 212
BUCKWHEAT OR SMARTWEED FAMILY (Polygonàceae)
Height: 2 to 5 feet.
Habit: A perennial having long, slender, angled stems, with reflexed prickles, erect when young, later reclining on other

plants. Its large, arrow-shaped leaves are up to 7¾ inches long,
and progressively shorter-stalked above. The upper leaves may
be unlobed. The few-flowered racemes, in leaf axils, bear tiny
rose pink to greenish flowers on glandular, bristly stalks.
Habitat: Wet meadows, tidal marshes, swamps. Delaware to
Florida; west to Minnesota and Missouri. August and September.

YELLOW FALSE FOXGLOVE *(Gerárdia flàva)*
FIGWORT OR SNAPDRAGON FAMILY (Scrophulariàceae)
Height: 3 to 6 feet.   PLATE p. 213
Habit: A tall, smooth, stout-stemmed, leafy perennial with
stems ascending and branched above. The large lower leaves,
2 to 4 inches long, are deeply cut almost to the midrib; the
upper ones are less lobed, the uppermost becoming bracts. The
large bright yellow flowers are axillary in the bracts. The corolla
tube, 1½ to 2 inches long, is smooth outside and densely hairy
in the throat, with five equal lobes.
Habitat: Dry upland woods and thickets. Maine to Florida; west
to Minnesota and Illinois. July to September.

SLENDER-LEAVED GERARDIA *(Gerárdia tenuifòlia)*
FIGWORT OR SNAPDRAGON FAMILY (Scrophulariàceae)
Height: 1 to 2 feet.   PLATE p. 213
Habit: A smooth, slender, many-branched plant with opposite,
small, narrow, pointed leaves, ½ to 1½ inches long, spreading
to ascending. The showy, bell-like, nodding corollas, pink to
light rose purple, are ½ to 1 inch long. They are borne singly
on long, slender stalks or in few-flowered racemes from the leaf
axils.
Habitat: Dry fields, thickets, roadsides. Maine to Georgia and
Alabama, but inward from the coastal plains; west to Mississippi, Louisiana, and Michigan. August to October.

PURPLE GERARDIA *(Gerárdia purpùrea)*   PLATE p. 214
FIGWORT OR SNAPDRAGON FAMILY (Scrophulariàceae)
Height: 6 inches to 3 feet.
Habit: A smooth, slender annual, simple to much-branched.
The very narrow, opposite, sessile leaves are 1 to 1½ inches
long. The showy, bell-shaped, more or less hairy corollas are
pinkish to lavender, with five oval lobes, 1 to 1½ inches long,
and four stamens with large yellow anthers.
Habitat: Damp meadows; moist, sandy, acid soil; bogs; shores.
New England to Florida; west to Texas, Michigan, Wisconsin,
and Minnesota. Late July to September.

TURTLEHEAD *(Chelòne glàbra)*   PLATE p. 214
FIGWORT OR SNAPDRAGON FAMILY (Scrophulariàceae)
Height: 2 to 4 feet.

Habit: A simple or sparingly branched, smooth-stemmed perennial with large, opposite, ovate, lance-shaped leaves, up to 5¾ inches long, scarcely reduced in size upward. Leaves are coarsely or finely toothed with pointed tips and are short-stalked to sessile. The stem is topped by a dense spike of flowers with large corollas, ⅘ to 1½ inches long, white or tinged with pink or purple (rarely greenish yellow). The two lips do not open widely, the upper lip hoods over the straight lower lip, and the stamens are woolly.

Habitat: Damp, acid soil; wet woods and meadows, beside streams. Newfoundland to Alabama; west to Minnesota. Late July to October.

RICHWEED *(Collinsònia canadénsis)*　　　Plate p. 215
　Mint Family (Labiàtae)
Height: 1 to 4 feet.
Habit: A tall, coarse, leafy perennial, branched above and with opposite, ovate, blunt-tipped, and sharply toothed leaves. The lower leaves, 4 to 8 inches long, have slender stalks; the upper ones are progressively shorter-stalked to sessile. The inflorescences are in several loose racemes of small, ½-inch long, dull yellow, lemon-scented flowers. The corollas are obliquely bell-shaped, with four equal lobes and a larger, fringed, slightly drooping fifth lobe, a prominent pistil, and two long, projecting stamens.
Habitat: Rich, damp woodlands. Quebec to Florida; west to Mississippi, Arkansas, and Michigan. July to September.

MOCK PENNYROYAL *(Hedeòma pulegioìdes)* Plate p. 215
　Mint Family (Labiàtae)
Height: 6 to 12 inches.
Habit: A strongly scented, erect, aromatic annual, usually branched. It has opposite, lance-shaped or elliptic leaves, very short-stalked or sessile. The small, lavender or bluish white, tubular flowers with a three-lobed lower lip, are about ⅛ inch long, in whorls, in the upper leaf axils.
Habitat: Dry soil. Quebec to Florida; west to Tennessee, Arkansas, Kansas, and Minnesota. July to September. This is not true Pennyroyal, which is a European plant *(Mentha pulegium)*.

MOUNTAIN-MINT or BASIL *(Pycnánthemum*
　　tenuifòlium)　　　　　　　　　　Plate p. 216
　Mint Family (Labiàtae)
Height: 1 to 3 feet.
Habit: A stiff, erect perennial with slightly hairy, angled stems and simple or forked branches. The opposite leaves are very narrow, ¼ inch wide and up to 2 inches long, smooth and sessile. Small whitish flowers are in crowded and branched, con-

vex to flat-topped clusters, with many bracts. Each tiny corolla has an undivided upper lip, a three-lobed lower lip, and projecting stamens.

Habitat: Sandy to clay soil, open ground, thickets, bogs. Ontario to Georgia; west to Ohio, Michigan, Wisconsin, Minnesota, and Texas. June to September. The common name is a misnomer, as the plant grows in lowlands.

PERILLA *(Perílla frutéscens)*   PLATE p. 216
  MINT FAMILY (Labiàtae)
Height: 1 to 3 feet.
Habit: A coarse, erect, branching, aromatic annual, often purple or suffused with purple. The broadly ovate, stalked leaves, 3 to 4½ inches long, are coarsely toothed or sometimes slightly slashed. The plant is topped by spikelike, one-sided racemes of small purple to white flowers. Each small corolla has five equal, broadly rounded lobes.
Habitat: Roadsides, waste places. New York to Florida; west to Ohio, Missouri, Kansas, and Texas. August to October. Introduced from eastern Asia. Cultivated for its attractive folliage, but often escapes and may become a troublesome weed.

NEW ENGLAND ASTER *(Aster nòvae-ángliae)*
  COMPOSITE FAMILY (Compósitae)   PLATE p. 217
Height: 2 to 8 feet.
Habit: A tall, stout, many-stemmed, very leafy, hairy perennial. The small leaves, 1 to 3 inches long, are sessile and clasp the stem at the base. They have ear-shaped lobes and are rough above and soft-hairy beneath, with pointed tips and smooth margins. The large, flat, showy flower heads are at the tips of the upper branches. Each has forty to fifty rays, which may vary from deep purple to pale lavender or even pink or white, and a yellow disk.
Habitat: Meadows; thickets; moist, open places. Vermont to Alabama; west to North Dakota, Wyoming, and New Mexico. August to October. One of our most beautiful wild asters; many color forms are cultivated in gardens.

GOLDEN-ASTER or MARYLAND GOLDEN-ASTER
  (Chrysópsis mariàna)   PLATE p. 217
  COMPOSITE FAMILY (Compósitae)
Height: 1 to 3 feet.
Habit: A perennial with one or more erect or arched-ascending stems, at first silky-hairy, later smooth. The lower leaves are spatulate and taper to a stalk up to 7 inches long; middle and upper leaves are lance-shaped to elliptic and sessile. Both disk and ray flowers are golden yellow.

Habitat: Dry, sandy fields; pine woods. New York to Florida and Louisiana; west to Ohio and Kentucky. August to October.

WAVY-LEAVED ASTER *(Aster undulàtus)* PLATE p. 218
COMPOSITE FAMILY (Compósitae)
Height: 1 to 3 feet.
Habit: A tall perennial with stiff ascending stems covered with dense, spreading hairs. The lower leaves have long, broad stalks, indented at the base, with wavy margins, 1½ to 5½ inches long, progressively shorter-stalked upward and partly clasping the stem. The flowers have eight to fifteen blue or lilac rays and yellow disks.
Habitat: Dry, open woods; thickets; clearings. Maine to northern Florida; west to southeastern Indiana, Tennessee, and eastern Mississippi. August to October.

SPREADING ASTER *(Aster pàtens)* PLATE p. 218
COMPOSITE FAMILY (Compósitae)
Height: 1 to 2 feet.
Habit: A perennial with rather slender, brittle stems covered with short, scattered hairs. The leaves are 1 to 6 inches long, rough, rather thick, firm, ovate to oblong, and nearly encircle the stem. The branches have reduced bracteal leaves. Showy lavender to purple flowers are mostly single on short branches; each has fifteen to thirty ray flowers and a yellow disk.
Habitat: Open, dry woods and clearings. Maine to Florida and Alabama; west to Mississippi, Louisiana, and Texas. August to October. Similar to *A. laevis,* which is smooth and with persistent lower leaves. *A patens* is hairy and its lower leaves shrivel and turn brown when the plant blooms.

BRISTLE-LEAVED ASTER *(Aster linariifòlius)* PLATE p. 219
COMPOSITE FAMILY (Compósitae)
Height: 1 to 2 feet.
Habit: A perennial with several fine-hairy, wiry stems and numerous narrow, firm, linear leaves with smooth margins, ¾ to 1½ inches long. The lower leaves soon die off. Flower heads are solitary, with ten to twenty lavender rays and a yellow disk.
Habitat: Sandy soil, open woods, dry ground. Quebec to Florida; west to Wisconsin, Oklahoma, and Texas. Less common westward. July to October.

SMALL WHITE ASTER *(Aster patèrnus)* PLATE p. 219
COMPOSITE FAMILY (Compósitae)
Height: 1 to 2 feet.
Habit: A perennial with one to several fine-hairy, wiry stems. The persistent lower leaves are up to 4 inches long and broadly oblanceolate to obovate. The upper leaves are progressively re-

duced, the uppermost sessile. The stem is topped by a cluster of flower heads, each with four to eight small white (rarely pink) rays and a yellow disk.

Habitat: Dry woods. Maine to Florida and eastern Alabama; west to Ohio and Kentucky. June to September.

WHITE ASTER (*Aster símplex*)   PLATE p. 219
COMPOSITE FAMILY (Compósitae)

Height: 2 to 5 feet.

Habit: A perennial with stout, smooth stems and narrow, linear to lance-shaped leaves, 3 to 6 inches long, tapering to a stalklike base, and sometimes slightly clasping the stem. The white flower heads are ¾ inch across, each with twenty to forty rays, sometimes tinged with lavender, and a yellow disk. The flowers are borne in loose clusters.

Habitat: Low, moist places; damp thickets; meadows and shores. Newfoundland to upland North Carolina and West Virginia; west to Kentucky, Missouri, and Kansas. August to October.

SMOOTH ASTER (*Aster laèvis*)   PLATE p. 220
COMPOSITE FAMILY (Compósitae)

Height: 1 to 4 feet.

Habit: A tall, smooth-stemmed perennial with thick, firm leaves, sometimes toothed. The lower leaves taper to winged stalks; the upper ones are sessile and clasping the stem; the uppermost are bractlike and widest at the base. Light violet to white flower heads, about 1 inch across, have fifteen to twenty-five rays and a yellow disk.

Habitat: Dry, open places; borders of woods. Maine to Georgia and Alabama; west to Oregon, Utah, and New Mexico. August to October. Plant differs from *A. patens* in being smooth; the lower leaves have winged stalks and are persistent.

CROOKED-STEMMED ASTER (*Aster prenanthoìdes*)
COMPOSITE FAMILY (Compósitae)   PLATE p. 220

Height: 8 to 40 inches.

Habit: A perennial easily distinguished by the leaves, with blades rather abruptly contracted near the base, ending in enlarged lobes, clasping the stem, which is slightly zigzag. Each of the lavender or occasionally white flower heads has twenty to thirty-five rays.

Habitat: Damp thickets, stream banks, wet edges of swamps. New York to Tennessee; west to Minnesota and Iowa. August to October. A northern species.

LARGE-FLOWERED ASTER (*Aster grandiflòrus*)
COMPOSITE FAMILY (Compósitae)   PLATE p. 220

Height: 1 to 3 feet.

Habit: An open-branched perennial with stiff, erect stems and numerous small, firm, rough, sessile leaves with smooth margins and numerous upper bracts. Each of the showy lavender to purple violet flower heads has twenty to forty-five rays and a yellow disk.

Habitat: Open pine or oak woods, thickets and clearings on or near the costal plain. Eastern Virginia to Florida. Late September to early November.

HEART-LEAVED ASTER *(Aster cordifòlius)* PLATE p. 221
COMPOSITE FAMILY (Compósitae)
Height: 1 to 4 feet.
Habit: A slender, smooth, much-branched perennial with variable leaves, usually heart-shaped and pointed, with large sharp teeth; the upper leaves are short-stalked to sessile and ovate to lance-shaped. The flower heads are small; the rays are lavender, pale blue, or white; the yellow disk turns red with age.
Habitat: Open woods, clearings, thickets. Quebec to Georgia and Alabama; west to Missouri and Wisconsin. August to October.

BUSHY ASTER *(Aster dumòsus)* PLATE p. 221
COMPOSITE FAMILY (Compósitae)
Height: 1 to 3 feet.
Habit: A perennial with slender stems and spreading to ascending branches and branchlets. The narrow, linear, sessile leaves are rough above and smooth beneath; the uppermost are numerous, small, and bractlike. Each of the many small, lavender to blue, sometimes white, flower heads has thirteen to thirty very short rays and a pale yellow to brownish disk.
Habitat: Wet or dry sandy ground, thickets, shores. Common on or near the coastal plain. Massachusetts to Florida and Louisiana; west to Arkansas, Kentucky, Ohio, and Michigan. August to October.

WHITE HEATH ASTER *(Aster ericoìdes)* PLATE p. 221
COMPOSITE FAMILY (Compósitae)
Height: 1 to 3 feet.
Habit: A bushy-branched perennial with divergent to ascending crowded branches. The numerous rough, linear, sessile leaves are rarely 1 inch long; the uppermost are reduced to bracts. Tiny white flower heads, each with eight to twenty rays, are crowded at the tips of the branches.
Habitat: Dry, open places; thickets. Maine to Georgia and Alabama; west to Mississippi, Arkansas, Oklahoma, and Texas. July to October. One of the commonest of the small white-flowered asters and one of the latest to bloom.

LARGER BUR-MARIGOLD *(Bìdens laèvis)*   PLATE p. 222
COMPOSITE FAMILY (Compósitae)
Height: 1 to 3½ feet.
Habit: A smooth-stemmed annual, simple or with ascending middle and upper branches. The narrow, opposite, lance-shaped leaves are coarsely toothed. Light golden yellow flower heads may be 2 inches across and showy.
Habitat: Marshes, stream banks. New Hampshire to Florida; west to Indiana. August to October.

SPANISH NEEDLES *(Bìdens bipinnàta)*   PLATE p. 222
COMPOSITE FAMILY (Compósitae)
Height: 1 to 6 feet.
Habit: A tall, smooth annual with opposite, divided and re-divided leaves, varying in length from 1½ to 8 inches. The flower heads may be without rays. The narrow disks produce long, four-angled seeds, with two to four spines, at the tip—the Spanish needles.
Habitat: Waste ground, fields, open woods, roadsides. Massachusetts to Florida; west to Ohio, Indiana, Illinois, Missouri, and Kansas. August to October. The spiny seeds fasten themselves to the passerby and so gain a wide distribution.

BEGGAR-TICKS *(Bìdens frondòsa)*   PLATE p. 222
COMPOSITE FAMILY (Compósitae)
Height: 1 to 6 feet.
Habit: A tall, smooth, weedy, branched, unattractive annual. It has large, opposite, long-stalked, cut leaves, with three to five leaflets, the terminal one largest. The flowers are without rays. The orange yellow disks later produce narrow, flat, wedge-shaped, blackish seeds (achenes), each with two barbed awns.
Habitat: Damp places, wasteland. Newfoundland to Virginia, West Virginia, and Louisiana. June to October. An objectionable weed.

SLENDER GOLDENROD *(Solidàgo híspida)*   PLATE p. 223
COMPOSITE FAMILY (Compósitae)
Height: 1 to 2 feet.
Habit: A stiff-hairy perennial with one to a few erect or ascending branches. The hairy basal leaves are oblanceolate to obovate and long-stalked; the stem leaves are lance-shaped, sessile, and spreading-hairy, becoming smaller upward. Orange yellow disk flowers, ¼ to ⅓ inch across, with shorter rays, are in a loose inflorescence in the axils of upper leaves and bracts.
Habitat: Dry or moist rocky places, peaty ground. Quebec to Georgia; west to Tennessee, Arkansas, and South Dakota. July to October. Plant variable in size.

SILVER-ROD (*Solidàgo bicolor*)   PLATE p. 223
COMPOSITE FAMILY (Compósitae)
Height: 1 to 3 feet.
Habit: A perennial with one to few stems, covered with a whitish down. The basal leaves are 3½ to 7 inches long and narrowed to a short stalk. The alternate, sessile, finely toothed stem leaves decrease in size upward. The plant is topped by a long, narrow inflorescence of whitish to cream-colored flower heads, each having seven to nine short rays and a disk, ¼ to ⅓ inch across.
Habitat: Dry, poor, open soil; thin woods. Quebec to Georgia; west to Arkansas. July to October.

BLUE-STEMMED GOLDENROD (*Solidàgo caèsia*)
COMPOSITE FAMILY (Compósitae)   PLATE p. 224
Height: 8 to 40 inches.
Habit: A smooth, slender perennial with a purplish green stem covered with a whitish bloom. The narrow, alternate leaves, lance-shaped to elliptic, are nearly uniform in size, 1¾ to 4½ inches long, pointed, with finely cut margins. The small golden heads, with three to four rays, are in loose to compact clusters, in the upper leaf axils.
Habitat: Rich or open woods, thickets, clearings. Quebec to Florida; west to Wisconsin and Texas. August to October.

STOUT GOLDENROD (*Solidàgo squarròsa*)   PLATE p. 224
COMPOSITE FAMILY (Compósitae)
Height: 2 to 5 feet.
Habit: A coarse perennial with a conspicuous rosette of large basal leaves, 3 to 8 inches long and ¼ to 4 inches wide. The stem leaves are alternate, ovate, much smaller, with pointed tips and slightly toothed. The small golden flowers with twelve to sixteen rays are in the upper leaf axils.
Habitat: Rich, dry, or rocky open woods; thickets and clearings. Quebec to Maryland, uplands of West Virginia, North Carolina, and Kentucky. August to early October.

SPREADING GOLDENROD (*Solidàgo flexicaùlis*)
COMPOSITE FAMILY (Compósitae)   PLATE p. 225
Height: 8 to 40 inches.
Habit: A strongly ascending, somewhat zigzag-stemmed perennial with nearly smooth stems. The alternate, ovate stem leaves are large, 2 to 6 inches long and 1 to 3 inches wide, thin and abruptly narrowed to a winged stalk, pointed, and irregularly toothed. The small golden flower heads, with three to four small rays, are clustered in the upper leaf axils or at the top of the stem.

Habitat: Rich woods, thickets. Quebec to North Carolina; west to Tennessee, Kansas, and Iowa. July to October.

CATFOOT or CUDWEED (*Gnaphàlium obtusifòlium*)
COMPOSITE FAMILY (Compósitae)   PLATE p. 225
Height: 1 to 2 feet.
Habit: A very leafy biennial, the stems covered with close, white, feltlike, downy hairs. The lower branches may fork in well-developed plants. Smooth or slightly woolly sessile leaves are distributed evenly along the stem. Fragrant whitish flower heads, in clusters from the upper leaf axils, are surrounded by dry bracts.
Habitat: Clearings, borders of woods and fields. Ontario to Florida, Alabama, and Louisiana; west to Texas. August to November.

RATTLESNAKE-ROOT (*Prenánthes álba*)   PLATE p. 226
COMPOSITE FAMILY (Compósitae)
Height: 2 to 5 feet.
Habit: An erect perennial with milky juice. The lower leaves are long-stalked and few-lobed, to merely coarsely toothed; the upper ones are smaller, almost sessile, less cut to entire. Fragrant, greenish or yellowish white, nodding flower heads, in the upper leaf axils and the top of the plant, are surrounded by smooth purplish bracts covered with a white bloom.
Habitat: Rich woods and thickets. Quebec to Georgia; west to Tennessee, Missouri, and South Dakota. August and September.

CONEFLOWER (*Rudbéckia fúlgida*)   PLATE p. 226
COMPOSITE FAMILY (Compósitae)
Height: 10 to 40 inches.
Habit: A tall, hairy-stemmed perennial with the basal and lower stem leaves oblanceolate to heart-shaped, with long stalks. The middle and upper stem leaves are alternate, mostly linear-oblong to broadly ovate, and progressively shorter-stalked to sessile. The plant is topped by large yellow to orange flower heads, 2 to 3 inches across, each with eight to twenty rays and a dark purplish brown ovoid disk.
Habitat: Dry or moist, open or shaded places. New Jersey and Pennsylvania to Florida; west to Texas, Missouri, and Michigan. July to October.

HARDHACK (*Spiraèa tomentòsa*)   PLATE p. 227
ROSE FAMILY (Rosàceae)
Height: 3 to 4 feet.
Habit: A much-branched, many-stemmed, very leafy shrub. The leaves are alternate, ovate, irregularly toothed, woolly beneath, and short-stalked. Small rose-colored flowers, in crowded termi-

nal panicles, have five petals and numerous stamens. The panicles bloom from the top downward.
Habitat: Poor, low ground and pastures. Quebec to Georgia; west to Tennessee and Arkansas. July to September.

ELECAMPANE (*Ínula helénium*)   PLATE p. 227
   COMPOSITE FAMILY (Compósitae)
Height: 3 to 5 feet.
Habit: A stout, coarse, open-branched perennial, with stalked lower leaves up to 20 inches long and 9 inches wide. The upper leaves are progressively smaller and partly clasp the stem. All leaves are white-veined, rough above and fine-hairy beneath, lance-shaped, pointed, and finely toothed. The large yellow flower heads, 1 to 2 inches across, have many conspicuous, long, narrow, irregularly arranged rays.
Habitat: Roadsides, fence rows, rich ground. Quebec and south beyond our range. July to September. Introduced from Europe, naturalized in the United States.

CLIMBING HEMPWEED (*Mikània scándens*)   PLATE p. 228
   COMPOSITE FAMILY (Compósitae)
Height: 15 feet or more.
Habit: A twining perennial vine with many opposite, ovate leaves, toothed at the base of the blade and with long tips and stalks. The compact clusters of small, pale lavender to flesh-colored flower heads are on long stalks from the leaf axils.
Habitat: Thickets, swamps, hedgerows. Maine to Florida; west to Texas, Missouri, and Michigan. July to October. The only vine of the Composite Family in our area.

SMALLER BUR-MARIGOLD (*Bìdens cérnua*)   PLATE p. 228
   COMPOSITE FAMILY (Compósitae)
Height: 1 to 6 feet.
Habit: An annual with a simple or freely branched stout stem and opposite, smooth, narrow, coarsely toothed, lance-shaped leaves, narrowed at the base. The nodding flower disks, $\frac{1}{2}$ to 1 inch across, may have short yellow rays, $\frac{3}{5}$ inch long, or rays may be lacking. The achenes are convex at the top, usually with four awns, barbed downward.
Habitat: Springs, shores, sloughs. Canada to Maryland and western North Carolina; west to Tennessee, Missouri, South Dakota, Wyoming, and westward. August to October. The leaves are opposite, except occasionally those on the uppermost part of the stem (as in the illustration).

SMALLER BURDOCK (*Árctium mìnus*)   PLATE p. 228
   COMPOSITE FAMILY (Compósitae)
Height: 2 to 5 feet.

Habit: A coarse, weedy, much-branched biennial. The lower leaves are broadly ovate, up to 15 inches long and 12 inches wide, nearly smooth above, sparsely white-hairy beneath, becoming smaller and shorter-stalked upward. Tiny, pink to purplish, tubular flowers are surrounded by a globular head with numerous stiff, hooked, pointed bracts.

Habitat: Waste places, roadsides. Newfoundland to Virginia; west to Indiana, Missouri, and Texas. July to October. A native of Eurasia, now well-established in this country.

LIVE-FOREVER (*Sèdum telephioìdes*)   PLATE p. 229
  ORPINE OR SEDUM FAMILY (Crassulàceae)
Height: 6 to 30 inches.

Habit: A perennial with light green, fleshy, smooth, succulent leaves, tapering to very short stalks or sessile. Frequently the stem is purplish. The plant is topped by showy clusters of very small white to pink flowers, pointed and nearly square in form, broader than long.

Habitat: Cliffs and knobs. New York, especially in the mountains, to Georgia; west to Illinois. August and September.

CLIMBING FALSE BUCKWHEAT (*Polýgonum scándens*)
  BUCKWHEAT OR SMARTWEED FAMILY (Polygonàceae)
Height: Up to 15 feet.   PLATE p. 230

Habit: A twining, smooth perennial clambering over other plants. The leaves are oblong, heart-shaped, 1 to 4 inches long. Inconspicuous greenish white or pale pink flowers have four to six petallike sepals, the outer three broadly winged. The flowers are in racemes from the upper leaf axils.

Habitat: Moist woods, thickets, roadsides, shores. Quebec to Florida; west to Oklahoma and Texas. Late August to November.

Flower Families

Families of the flowers are subdivided into genera (singular, genus). The Rose Family, for example, includes the genera *Rosa* (the rose), *Rubus* (the wild raspberry and blackberry), *Fragaria* (the strawberry), and scores of others. Each genus has its own species, rarely only one, usually several to many. The genus *Rosa* includes the species *carolina* (Pasture Rose); *Rubus* includes the species *odoratus* (Flowering Raspberry); and *Fragaria* includes the species *virginiana* (Wild Strawberry).

In more technical works the plant families are usually arranged in an evolutionary sequence, from the most primitive to the most advanced.

But as the flowers in this book are grouped according to time of blooming—spring, summer, and autumn, for ease of identification—the families are alphabetized and group likenesses are ignored.

Only those families illustrated in the book are described here.

ACANTHUS FAMILY (Acanthaceae)

Mostly herbs with opposite, simple leaves and tubular flowers, usually with a two-lobed upper lip and a three-lobed lower lip, but the lobes may be regular and equal in size. A large family, mostly tropical, with only a few genera in our range. About 175 genera in all and 2500 species.

AMARYLLIS FAMILY (Amaryllidaceae)

Mostly herbs from bulbs, corms, or rhizomes, with narrow grasslike leaves, having six equal divisions of the flower, petals and sepals colored alike. Differ from the lilies in that flower divisions are inserted on top of the ovary. Very few native species. About 80 genera and 1250 species, worldwide, but mainly in the tropics and subtropics. A family largely of bulbous plants.

ARUM FAMILY (Araceae)

Herbs, often with acrid or pungent juice. Leaves simple or compound. Flowers very tiny and crowded on a clublike spadix, staminate flowers above, pistillate below (or on different plants) sheathed by the hood or spathe. Fruit usually fleshy berries. A large family, worldwide, chiefly tropical, with about 100 genera and 2000 species, mostly herbaceous. Only a few genera in our area.

BARBERRY FAMILY (Berberidaceae)

Shrubs and herbs with perfect flowers having one pistil and usually as many stamens as petals and opposite them. Fruit a berry or capsule. A small family, widely distributed in the north temperate zone, with a few genera in our area. In all, only about 20 genera and 200 species.

BELLFLOWER FAMILY (Campanulaceae)

Herbs with alternate leaves and usually milky juice. Perfect flowers, bell-shaped corolla of united petals, sometimes flat and circular, 5 stamens and a two- to five-lobed stigma. Distributed worldwide. About 35 genera and 600 species, but mostly in the temperate zone.

BIGNONIA FAMILY (Bignoniaceae)

Shrubs or trees with simple or compond leaves, opposite, rarely alternate. Showy tubular flowers, five-lobed and somewhat irregular, or two-lipped with the lower lobe largest. Stamens are attached to the corolla. Produces beanlike pods. Mostly tropical, about 100 genera but a few extending into the temperate zone; 3 genera in our area.

BIRTHWORT FAMILY (Aristolochiaceae)

Herbs or twining shrubs with large, heart-shaped, stalked leaves and perfect flowers, a pistil and six or more stamens. The flower has three triangular, flaring petallike sepals that form a cup united with the ovary (petals absent). A small family of tropical and temperate zones; 2 genera and about 400 species.

BORAGE OR FORGET-ME-NOT FAMILY (Boraginaceae)

Annual or perennial herbs in our range, with rough-hairy stems and usually alternate leaves. The perfect flowers are convolute or coiled in bud and straighten as the flower opens, often in one-sided spikes. A rather large family of nonpoisonous, slightly bitter, sticky plants. Worldwide, most numerous in the Rocky Mountain states and West Coast. About 900 genera and 1700 species.

BROOM-RAPE FAMILY (Orobanchaceae)

Small, fleshy, parasitic herbs with leaves reduced to scales and without green coloring matter. Perfect irregular flowers with two-lipped corollas usually crowded in a conelike cluster or solitary. Worldwide, about 150 species, mostly in the north temperate zone. Only one species is widely distributed in our range.

BUCKTHORN FAMILY (Rhamnaceae)

Shrubs or small trees with simple, mostly alternate leaves, small regular flowers, petals folded inward in the bud (or may be without petals). Flowers often pistillate and staminate on the same or different plants. Worldwide. About 45 genera and 600 species.

BUCKWHEAT or SMARTWEED FAMILY (Polygonaceae)

Herbs, sometimes shrubs, often with zigzag stems having swollen joints or sheaths at the points of leaf attachments. The tiny flowers have petallike sepals, four to twelve stamens, and are usually in a cluster or head. Mostly objectionable weeds. Worldwide, but mostly in the northern hemisphere; 30 genera and over 900 species.

COMPOSITE FAMILY (Compositae)

Characterized by flowers borne on a disk in a dense head, surrounded by the involucre. Each tiny disk flower has a united corolla with five lobes. Many are surrounded by ray flowers; in others, rays are absent. The heads of some (e.g., chicory) have strap-shaped rays. One of the largest families of flowering plants—the largest in most parts of the temperate zone—with more than 15,000 species, worldwide in distribution.

CONVOLVULUS or MORNING-GLORY FAMILY (Convolvulaceae)

Herbs (in our range) with twining stems, alternate leaves, perfect flowers in fours or fives, and a tubular, flaring corolla. Mostly tropical, but widely distributed in warm to temperate regions. About 40 genera and 1200 species.

CROWFOOT or BUTTERCUP FAMILY (Ranunculaceae)

A large family of herbs or sometimes woody plants, characterized by numerous stamens surrounding a central ovary. Sometimes staminate and pistillate flowers on different plants. Two to fifteen petals (sometimes absent); three to fifteen sepals, often petallike. Leaves often dissected, mostly alternate, sometimes opposite. Family includes some acrid narcotic poisons. About 40 genera and at least 1500 species, widely distributed but most abundant in the north temperate zone.

DIAPENSIA FAMILY (Diapensiaceae)

Low, evergreen perennial herbs with simple, alternate leaves and perfect flowers, the stamens attached to the corolla with five-parted lobes and a three-lobed stigma. There are about 6 genera and 10 species in the cool and arctic regions of the north temperate zone.

DOGBANE FAMILY (Apocynaceae)

Our species are herbs or twining, woody vines with alternate or opposite leaves. Flowers are perfect, convolute (rolled up in bud), with a united corolla with five lobes, and five stamens. Plant has acrid, poisonous milky juice. Mostly tropical, with about 140 genera and 1500 species, a few in the temperate zone. Oleander is in this family.

EVENING-PRIMROSE FAMILY (Onagraceae)

Mostly herbs with perfect flowers, usually in fours: four petals, four sepals, and four or eight stamens, stigma with four lobes forming a cross. Ovary is inferior. Mostly showy flowers. Simple leaves are alternate or opposite. Worldwide distribution, especially in the temperate regions of America. About 30 genera and 600 species.

FIGWORT OR SNAPDRAGON FAMILY (Scrophulariaceae)

Mostly herbs with iregular flowers, corolla with an upper lip with two lobes and a lower lip with three lobes (sometimes lobes are more regular), and two sets of stamens, longer and shorter. Leaves are alternate, opposite, or rarely whorled. A large family of rather bitter plants, some of them narcotic and poisonous. Worldwide distribution. About 175 genera and possibly up to 4000 species.

GENTIAN FAMILY (Gentianaceae)

Herbs (in our area) having flowers with tubular or wheel-shaped corollas, four to twelve lobes, and an equal number of stamens joined to them. Leaves usually undivided, stalkless, and opposite. Plants have a colorless, bitter juice. Most abundant in the north temperate zone. In all, about 70 genera and 800 species.

GERANIUM FAMILY (Geraniaceae)

Herbs (in our region) with perfect symmetrical flowers with five sepals, five petals, and five to fifteen stamens. The pistil forms a characteristic beaklike "cranes' bill." The leaves are alternate or opposite, compound or simple. North temperate zone and subtropical regions of both hemispheres. About 11 genera and 850 species.

GOURD or CUCUMBER FAMILY (Cucurbitaceae)
Mostly herbaceous vines, climbing by tendrils, with alternate lobed leaves. Flowers are staminate and pistillate on the same or different plants. Worldwide, abundant in the southwestern United States and Mexico. About 90 genera and 900 species.

HEATH FAMILY (Ericaceae)
Shrubs, rarely trailing (in our area), with simple leaves mostly alternate, sometimes opposite or whorled. The corolla with four or five lobes, a single pistil, and eight or ten stamens. Others in this family are rhododendrons, azaleas, blueberries, huckleberries. Widely distributed in acid soil in temperate regions of the northern and southern hemispheres. Few in the tropics. About 70 genera and 1900 species.

HONEYSUCKLE FAMILY (Caprifoliaceae)
Shrubs and vines with simple, opposite leaves and perfect flowers, tubular corollas with three to five lobes, irregular, or wheel-shaped and more or less regular, and stamens as many, or rarely fewer, than the lobes. Mainly of the north temperate zone, a few tropical. About 12 genera and 400 species.

HORSETAIL FAMILY (Equisetaceae)
Flowerless herbs from rhizomes, with jointed stems simple or branched, cylindrical, ridged, and banded, rough to the touch. Internodes usually hollow. Fruiting cones are usually at the top of the stalks or on separate fertile stalks. This is an ancient genus, related to ferns, much more prominent in earlier geological periods. Only 1 genus and about 25 species. Worldwide, except Australia and New Zealand.

IRIS FAMILY (Iridaceae)
Herbs having flat, sword-shaped leaves overlapping each other at the base, from a horizontal rhizome, bulb, or corm. The showy flowers are perfect, regular or irregular, with three sepals and three petals alike, three stamens and three styles. Worldwide, especially abundant in South Africa. About 58 genera and 1500 species; only a few native in our area.

JEWELWEED or TOUCH-ME-NOT FAMILY (Balsaminaceae)
Juicy-stemmed herbs with thin, soft leaves and perfect, irregular, pendant flowers. Petals and sepals are not easily dis-

tinguished. The spurred, bell-shaped sac is formed from one of the three sepals; the other two are small, green, and lateral. The three petals are in unlike lobes. The ripe seedpod explodes at a touch, coiling and scattering the seed. Most plentiful in Asia and Africa; 2 genera and about 450 species. Only 2 species are native to eastern United States.

LILY FAMILY (Liliaceae)
Mostly perennial herbs (rarely shrubby and treelike), growing from bulbs, corms, or tubers. The leaves are usually parallel-veined. The floral envelope is in threes, some with separate petals, usually perfect, with six stamens and a pistil with a three-lobed stigma. Plants often with showy flowers. Worldwide, about 240 genera and 4000 species.

LIZARD'S-TAIL FAMILY (Saururaceae)
Perennial herbs with jointed stems; alternate, large, coarse, simple leaves; and long, dense spikes or "tails" of tiny flowers, without sepals or petals. A small family, with 3 genera and 6 species in eastern North America, eastern Asia to India, and northern Mexico.

LOBELIA FAMILY (Lobeliaceae)
Perennial herbs, sometimes shrubs, with perfect irregular flowers in which the tubular united corolla opens on the upper side. The flowers are in fives; the upper lip has two lobes and the lower lip three lobes. The stamens are joined in a tube around the style. Leaves are alternate. The plant has a milky or colored juice. Worldwide, but most abundant in the tropics. About 24 genera and 700 species.

LOGANIA FAMILY (Loganiaceae)
Mostly tropical, but a number of species are found in the southeastern United States. Leaves are opposite, joined by a tiny ridge around the stem. Flowers have four or five petals, joined on the tubular corolla, and the same number of stamens. Widely distributed in the tropics, with only a few species in the temperate zones. About 30 genera and 550 species.

LOOSESTRIFE FAMILY (Lythraceae)
Herbs (in our area), woody shrubs, and trees with simple leaves, opposite or whorled. Flowers usually regular, rarely irregular, in fours or fives, petals sometimes absent, and four to fourteen stamens. Most abundant in the American tropics and warm temperate zone. About 32 genera and 800 species, few native in our area. The family produces strychnine and curare poisons.

LOPSEED FAMILY (Phrymaceae)

A perennial herb with simple, opposite, coarsely toothed leaves. The slender flower spike has two-lipped flowers, the lower lip three-lobed. The flowers also are in pairs and after maturity lop down against the stem. This family has only 1 genus and 1 species.

MADDER FAMILY (Rubiaceae)

Herbs (in our area), shrubs, trees, and vines with uncut leaves, opposite or in whorls, and perfect, united or rotate, tubular flowers, usually in fours. Stipules are at the nodes. Largely a tropical family including commercially important plants, such as coffee and cinchona (quinine). Nearly 400 genera and 7000 species.

MALLOW FAMILY (Malvaceae)

Herbs or shrubs characterized by having the stamens form a column around the style. Flowers are usually showy, with five petals, convolute in bud, and five sepals. The calyx is subtended by an involucre. Leaves may be more or less cut or divided. Mucilaginous, nonpoisonous plants, with a tough bark. Worldwide distribution about 50 genera and 1200 species. This is the family of cotton and okra.

MEADOW-BEAUTY or MELASTOMA FAMILY (Melastomataceae)

Herbs (in our region), shrubs, or trees, mostly tropical. Our only genus (*Rhexia*) has opposite leaves and perfect, regular flowers, mostly with four or five petals and sepals, petals convolute in bud. Stamens are twice the number of petals, and the anthers open by terminal spores. Mostly tropical; over 150 genera and 4000 species.

MILKWEED FAMILY (Asclepiadaceae)

Herbs and vines (in our area), shrubs, rarely small trees, sometimes cactuslike, often with poisonous juice. Simple, opposite, or whorled leaves. Complicated flowers in umbels, each flower perfect and regular with a deeply five-parted corolla, usually recurved, five stamens, usually joined to the pistil to produce a column surrounded by the corona. The anthers and stigma are much enlarged and five-lobed, and pollen is in waxlike masses. A pod is produced full of seed, each with long silky hairs. About 220 genera and 2400 species, mostly tropical, but also many warm temperate zone genera.

MILKWORT FAMILY (Polygalaceae)

Herbs (in our area), shrubs, or small trees. Leaves usually alternate, sometimes opposite. Flowers perfect, irregular, with five sepals, two of which are colored and petallike; three petals, two of which are alike, the third often crested; and eight stamens. A two-sided capsule is produced. Worldwide, about 12 genera and 1000 species. *Polygala* is the only genus in our region.

MINT FAMILY (Labiatae)

Mainly herbs (in our area), but also shrubs and rarely trees in the tropics; commonly aromatic. The stems usually square, with opposite to compound leaves. The calyx is tubular, and the tubular corolla more or less two-lipped. Stamens, two or four, on the corolla tube. Worldwide, well represented in our region. About 160 genera and at least 3500 species.

MUSTARD FAMILY (Cruciferae)

A huge family of annual, biennial, and perennial herbs, rarely subshrubs, with a peppery, watery juice. Leaves simple to compound, usually alternate. The small flowers have four petals forming a cross, four sepals that later drop off, one pistil, and six stamens, two of which often shorter than the rest. Flowers in a raceme. Worldwide, primarily in the north temperate zone. About 350 genera and 2500 species.

NIGHTSHADE FAMILY (Solanaceae)

Herbs, rarely shrubs or vines in our area; mostly tropical. Leaves are alternate, simple to compound. Perfect flower parts, basically in fives, united corollas, tubular to rotate, usually with five lobes, and five stamens. This family gives us potato, tomato, and pepper plants, but some species are poisonous. Most numerous in tropical America, but widely distributed in both tropical and temperate zones. About 80 genera and 2500 species.

ORCHID FAMILY (Orchidaceae)

A large family of perennial herbs (in our area), terrestrial, sometimes saprophytic, often epiphytic in the tropics. Perfect, irregular flowers usually in threes, two lateral petals and below these a larger petal often inflated or saclike, the "lip" or "slipper." The stamen column at the base of the lip is composed of one or two stamens united with the style. The anthers, with two cavities, have pollen masses (pollinia). Flowers may be single, in spikes, or in clusters. Leaves are simple and entire, usually parallel-veined. Worldwide, having more than 500 genera and about 20,000 species. Most abundant in the tropics.

ORPINE or SEDUM FAMILY (Crassulaceae)

Succulent annual or perennial herbs (in our area), rarely shrubs, with opposite or alternate, simple or entire leaves.

Clusters of small, perfect, symmetrical flowers have four to thirty sepals and petals (petals distinct) and stamens equal or double the number of petals. Widely distributed, but most plentiful in subtropical zones, particularly dry regions. About 30 genera and 1500 species.

PARSLEY FAMILY (Umbelliferae)

Mostly biennial or perennial herbs (in our region), occasionally shrubby or treelike. A large family, many aromatic, with hollow stems and alternate, usually compound, rarely simple leaves with sheathing. Tiny, perfect, stalked flowers are in flat-topped umbels; each has five separate petals, five stamens, and two styles. Some are poisonous; others are garden vegetables—carrot, parsley, celery, parsnip. A large family distributed worldwide, but most plentiful in drier parts of the temperate zones. About 300 genera and 3000 species.

PASSIONFLOWER FAMILY (Passifloraceae)

Herbs or woody vines, usually climbing by tendrils, with perfect flowers. Five stamens, united, which sheathe the long stalk of the ovary, with large anthers attached at the middle, five sepals united at the base, a corona of double or triple fringes, and five petals. Leaves are alternate, simple or compound. About 11 genera and 400 species, mostly tropical American. The largest genus (*Passiflora*) is represented by 2 species in our region.

PHLOX FAMILY (Polemoniaceae)

Annual, biennial, or perennial herbs, with opposite or alternate leaves, simple to compound. Perfect, regular flowers with a tubular corolla, convoluted in bud, and five flat equal lobes. The five stamens and three-part style are concealed in the tube. Mostly in western United States; about 15 genera and 275 species. The genus *Phlox* is commonest in our area.

PICKERELWEED FAMILY (Pontederiaceae)

Aquatic herbs living in shallow water, with large, glossy leaves floating or emerging from the water. Perfect flowers, more or less irregular, are tightly clustered. Each has a floral envelope of six divisions and forming a tube below with three to six stamens attached. Tropical and subtropical regions. About 8 genera and 25 species.

PINK FAMILY (Caryophyllaceae)

A large family of herbs usually having swollen joints and opposite or whorled, undivided leaves. Perfect, regular flowers have five (sometimes four) notched petals, five sepals, five to ten stamens. Worldwide, but most abundant in the north temperate zone. About 80 genera and 2000 species.

PITCHER-PLANT FAMILY (Sarraceniaceae)

Perennials of bogs, with hollow pitcher- or trumpet-shaped leaves with an arching hood. The perfect, regular flowers have five colored and persistent sepals, five petals, and numerous stamens. Flowers are large and solitary or in few-flowered racemes. Only 3 genera and about 16 species, some restricted to the mountains of Venezuela.

PLANTAIN FAMILY (Plantaginaceae)

Herbs (in our region), rarely shrubs, with mostly basal leaves, prominently parallel-veined, sheathed at the base, and uncut. Tiny, inconspicuous flowers, usually regular and perfect, or may be unisexual, are in fours. The calyx is tubular, the corolla chaffy. Flowers are in heads or spikes on a separate stalk. Widely distributed, with 3 genera and about 260 species. The principal genus (*Plantago*) is worldwide; several species are pernicious weeds.

POKEWEED FAMILY (Phytolaccaceae)

Herbs (in our area), shrubs, or trees with large, thick, juicy stems and large, entire, alternate leaves. Perfect or unisexual flowers have five rounded greenish white sepals, no petals, and five or more stamens. The small flowers, in racemes or spikes, later produce purplish black berries. Mostly in tropical America; 16 genera and about 100 species. Represented in our area by *Phytolacca*, the Pokeberry.

POPPY FAMILY (Papaveraceae)

Herbs (in our area), rarely shrubs, with white, yellow, or red juice. Leaves are alternate, entire to compound. Flowers are perfect, regular, and often showy, with two or three sepals that fall early; four, eight, or twelve separate petals; and many stamens. Mostly of the north temperate zone, common in western United States. At least 26 genera and 428 species; 6 species in our area.

PRIMROSE FAMILY (Primulaceae)

Herbs (in our area) with simple, opposite leaves. Perfect flowers, usually regular, have five petals or corolla lobes; the corolla is tubular or rotate, with stamens as many as petals and opposite them. Worldwide, but mostly in the north temperate zone. About 24 genera and more than 1000 species.

PULSE or BEAN FAMILY (Leguminósae)

Herbs, shrubs, and trees with alternate compound leaves. The perfect flowers are commonly irregular (regular in the Mimosa subfamily). Calyx is united and the corolla is five-lobed; the five petals may be distinct or the two lateral ones united. Stamens mostly ten, combined in one or two rows. An enormous family, worldwide, with 400 genera and about 10,000 species.

PURSLANE FAMILY (Portulacaceae)

A family of small herbs (in our area) or sometimes shrubs with rather thick and fleshy, alternate to opposite leaves. The flowers regular and perfect, the calyx distinct or united at the base, corolla with four to six petals also distinct or united at the base, stamens four to many. Seed capsule usually opens by splitting horizontally through the middle; in others splits longitudinally. Worldwide, with centers in South Africa, South America, and western North America; 16 genera and about 500 species.

PYROLA FAMILY (Pyrolaceae)

Small, evergreen perennial herbs, usually growing in shady acid soil (or saprophytic, without chlorophyll). Leaves alternate or nearly opposite, scalelike, simple, or in false whorls. Perfect, regular flowers with five sepals, five petals, distinct and waxy, eight to ten stamens. A small family of the Northern Hemisphere often classified under the Heath Family as a subfamily. Mostly north temperate and arctic zones, but a few tropical; 10 genera and 40 species.

ROSE FAMILY (Rosaceae)

A very large family of trees, shrubs, or herbs with alternate, simple or compound leaves and stipules at the leaf axils. Perfect, regular flowers with five separate similar petals, five sepals joined at the base only, numerous stamens, and one or more pistils. Many of our fruits are in this family—apples, pears, peaches, plums, quince. It also includes blackberries, raspberries, and strawberries, as well as roses, and many other plants. Worldwide, but most plentiful in the north temperate zone. Nearly 100 genera and about 3000 species.

ST. JOHNSWORT FAMILY (Hypericaceae)

A small family of herbs and shrubs with opposite, entire leaves, usually sessile, and with punctate translucent dots. Perfect, regular flowers have four or five petals and, in genus *Hypericum*, numerous conspicuous stamens. By some authorities included with Guttiferae, a tropical family. A small family of the north temperate zone with about 300 species.

SAXIFRAGE FAMILY (Saxifragaceae)

A large family of herbs, shrubs, vines, and small trees. Leaves are alternate, sometimes opposite, simple or compound. The perfect, regular flowers, occasionally unisexual or irregular, may have four to five petals and the same number or twice as many stamens. Related to the Rose Family, a main difference is in the formation of the seed. Worldwide, but mostly in the temperate and arctic zones. Possibly 80 genera and about 1050 species.

SPIDERWORT or DAYFLOWER FAMILY (Commelinaceae)

Herbs with alternate, entire, parallel-veined leaves, sheathed by a basal membrane. Perfect, radially or bilaterally symmetrical flowers emerge from a sheathing pair of bracts, with mostly three sepals and a corolla of three petals and six stamens, only three of which have pollen. Flowers open only for a morning. Worldwide, but mostly tropical and subtropical; only a few in the temperate zone. About 25 genera and at least 600 species, all herbaceous.

SPURGE FAMILY (Euphorbiaceae)

A large tropical family of herbs (in our area) and some shrubs. Plants sometimes fleshy and cactuslike with an acrid, milky juice. Leave mostly alternate, sometimes opposite, mostly compound. Staminate and pistillate flowers may be borne on the same or different plants. Flowers mostly regular, varying from numerous petals to none. Flowers are arranged with a central, three-lobed, pistillate flower surrounded by a group of staminate flowers, each with one naked stamen. Worldwide, mainly tropical. About 280 genera and 7000 species. It includes *Hevea* (rubber).

SUNDEW FAMILY (Droseraceae)

Carnivorous herbs, rarely subshrubs of damp boggy soil, rarely aquatic, with sticky-hairy leaves that exude drops of clear sticky fluid, in which insects are trapped. In Venus's Flytrap, bristles also close around the victim. The tiny flowers are regular and perfect, with five petals distinct, convolute in bud, five to twenty stamens rarely united at the base. Only 4 genera and about 100 species. The Sundew (*Drosera*) is widespread in the Northern Hemisphere and Australia; others local.

TEASEL FAMILY (Dipsacaceae)

Herbs (in our area), rarely shrubs, with opposite or whorled leaves and tiny, perfect, irregular flowers, crowded in dense, bristly heads surrounded by two joined bracteoles. Flowers four- or five-parted, and corolla tubular. All 10 genera and 180 species are found in the Old World. None is native here, but the Teasel is the commonest member in this country.

VALERIAN FAMILY (Valerianaceae)

Herbs (in our area), rarely shrubs, with opposite leaves. Flowers tubular, often with a spur at the base, irregular, usually five-lobed, with one to three stamens. Flowers may be perfect or pistillate and staminate. Roots have a strong objectionable odor. About 14 genera and 400 species, mainly in the north temperate zone and mountains of South America.

VERVAIN FAMILY (Verbenaceae)

Shrubs or herbs (in our area), with opposite, mostly simple leaves and perfect, mostly irregular flowers, with a more or less two-lipped corolla, four- or five-lobed, four stamens, two long and two short, on the corolla tube. Worldwide, most abundant in the tropics; 90 genera and almost 3000 species. Our commonest example is Verbena.

VIOLET FAMILY (Violaceae)

Herbs (in our region), shrubs, rarely trees, with perfect, irregular flowers (bilaterally symmetrical), rarely regular; five petals, unequal, the lower one spurred at the base; and five stamens surrounding the pistil. Leaves alternate, rarely opposite, usually undivided. Worldwide; 16 genera and 850 species.

WATERLEAF FAMILY (Hydrophyllaceae)

Herbs (in our area), rarely shrubby, usually rough-hairy or bristly, with mostly alternate leaves, entire or pinnately divided. Flowers perfect and regular. Sepals, petals, and stamens in fives, tubular corolla united or rotate. A small family of plants, 18 genera and 275 species, nearly worldwide except Europe; best represented in the United States.

WATER-LILY FAMILY (Nymphaeaceae)

Aquatic perennial herbs, usually with floating, mostly simple, alternate leaves. Perfect, regular flowers, axillary and solitary, with three to five sepals, three to numerous petals, and few to many stamens. Worldwide, both tropical and temperate zones.

WATER-PLANTAIN FAMILY (Alismataceae)

Marshy or aquatic herbs with fibrous roots and scapelike stems sheathing long stalked leaves. Simple, regular, perfect flowers, or staminate and pistillate. Flower parts in threes, stamens six or more. Widely distributed in tropical and temperate regions, mainly Northern Hemisphere; 8 genera and 75 species.

WOOD-SORREL FAMILY (Oxalidaceae)

Herbs (in our area), some tropical species woody. Leaves are alternate, mostly compound. Flowers are perfect and regular, with five sepals, five petals, and usually ten stamens united at the base, in two rows. Flowers are convolute in bud. Worldwide but mostly tropical; 7 genera and about 900 species.

>>>->>>

The Parts of a Flower

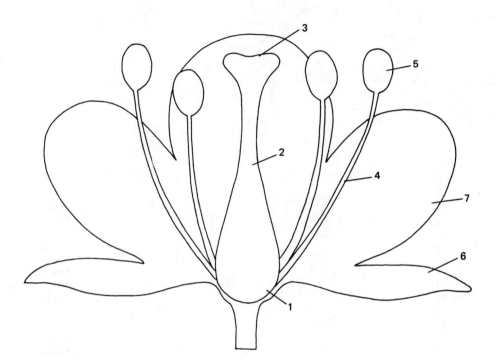

1. Ovary ⎫
2. Style ⎬ Pistil
3. Stigma ⎭
4. Filament ⎫
5. Anther ⎬ Stamen
6. Sepal ⎫
7. Petal ⎬ Perianths

Types of Flowers

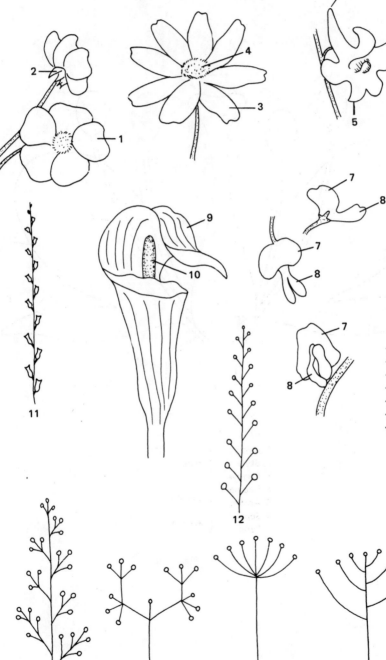

1. Petal
2. Sepal
3. Ray flower
4. Disk flowers
5. Corolla
6. Spur
7. Standard
8. Wing and keel
9. Spathe
10. Spadix
11. Spike
12. Raceme
13. Panicle
14. Cyme
15. Umbel
16. Corymb

Types of Leaves

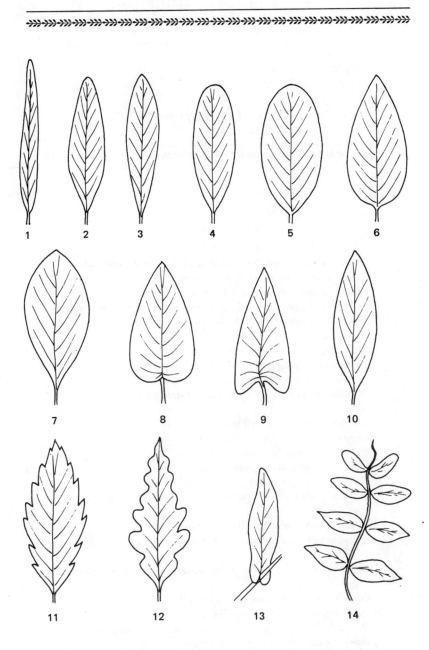

1. Linear
2. Lance-shaped
3. Oblance-shaped
4. Oblong
5. Elliptic
6. Ovate
7. Obovate
8. Cordate
9. Sagittate
10. Entire
11. Toothed
12. Lobed
13. Clasping
14. Compound pinnate

Glossary

>>>->>>

achene—a small, hard, dry, one-seeded fruit that does not split
alternate— (of leaves) not opposite each other
annual—a plant of one year's duration
anther—the upper, enlarged part of the stamen that carries the pollen
anthesis—the expansion of the flower as it matures
appressed—lying flat or close against
ascending—rising obliquely or curving upward
awl-shaped—tapering from the base to a point
awn—a stiff, bristlelike projection
axil—the upper angle at which the leaf stalk joins the stem

bearded—having long, stiff hairs
berry—a pulpy fruit containing seeds
biennial—a plant that lives two years and blooms the second year
bilateral—arranged or placed on opposite sides
blade—the flat, expanded part of the leaf
bract—a small leaflike structure usually under the flower or on the upper stem
bristle—a stiff hair or hairlike projection
bulb—an underground leaf bud with fleshy scales

calyx—the outer envelope of the flower, joined or in separate segments (sepals)
catkin—a dry, scaly, drooping flower spike
chaff—small, thin, dry scales or bracts
chlorophyll—the green coloring matter in the cells of plants
claw—the narrowed base of some petals
cleft—deeply cut
colonial—forming colonies, usually by underground stems
compound— (leaf) divided into separate leaflets

cordate—heart-shaped

corm—a solid, enlarged underground stem

corolla—the inner envelope of the flower, consisting of separate or united petals

corymb—a flat-topped flower cluster blooming from the margin inward

corymbose—corymblike

cuspidate—tipped with a firm, sharp point

cyme—a flattish cluster of flowers with the inner or terminal flowers blooming first

deciduous— (leaves) lasting but a single growing season, falling in autumn

decurrent—extending downward on the stem

deflexed—bent or turning abruptly downward

dioecious—having male and female flowers on different plants

disk—the central portion of the flower head in the Composite Family

distinct—not united, separate

divided—separated to the base; lobed

downy—covered with fine, soft hairs .

elliptical—equally rounded at each end, widest in the middle

entire— (leaf) without divisions or teeth

exserted—projecting beyond

filament—the threadlike lower part of the stamen that supports the anther

foliate—having leaves

fruit—the plant's seed-bearing product in whatever form

genus—a main subdivision of a family, including one or more species

herb—a nonwoody plant that dies back to the ground each winter

inflorescence—a branched structure with flowers

internode—the portion of the stem between two nodes

involucre—the leaflike bracts surrounding a single flower head or flower cluster

irregular— (flower) not symmetrical

lanceolate—lance-shaped

leaflet—a single division of a compound leaf

lip—the upper and lower divisions of an irregular flower, as in orchids

lobe—a division of a leaf or petal

margin—outer edge or border

monoecious—having separate male and female flowers on the same plant naturalized— (plant) completely established in a country to which it is not native

node—the point of attachment of a single leaf

oblanceolate—lance-shaped at the base, widest at the tip

obovate—egg-shaped, but broadest at the tip

opposite—across the stem at the same height, paired

ovary—the broader base of the pistil in which the seeds develop

palmate— (leaf) divided, as the fingers on the palm

panicle—a compound, elongated, branched flower cluster

pappus—the scales, bristles, or hairs attached to the seeds of the Composite Family

pedicel—the stalk of a single flower

perennial—living year after year

perfect— (flower) having both stamens and pistils in the same flower

perianth—the whole floral envelope, both calyx and corolla together

petal—a division of the corolla

petiole—the stalk of a leaf

pinnate— (leaf) compound, with leaflets arranged along the midrib, often in pairs

pinnatifid— (leaf) cleft in a pinnate manner

pistil—the stigma, style, and ovary, taken together

pollen—the powderlike yellow male sex cells on the anther of the stamen, for pollinating the flower

prostrate—lying flat on the ground, and spreading

pubescent—covered with short, soft hairs

raceme—few to numerous stalked flowers along an elongated axis

rays—the outer, petallike lobes surrounding the flower heads of the Composite Family

rhizome—an underground stem

rosette—a dense cluster, usually of basal leaves

rotate—having the parts flat and spreading or radiating

runner—a basal branch inclined to root, as in Strawberry

scape—a naked flowering stalk (without leaves)

sepal—a lobe of the calyx (usually green) under the petals

serrate—notched; toothed on the edge

sessile—without a stalk, as a leaf

sheath—a tubular envelope surrounding an organ

simple—undivided, as a leaf

spadix—a club-shaped stalk containing small, crowded flowers (Arum Family)

spathe—the leaflike sheath partly enveloping the spadix (Arum Family)

spatulate— (leaf) shaped like a spatula

species—a single distinct kind of plant; a subdivision of a genus

spike—few to many flowers sessile on an elongated stalk
spur—a hollow or saclike tubular projection on a flower
stamen—the pollen-bearing organ of the flower
standard—the outer large petal of a pea-shaped flower
stigma—the organ that receives the pollen at the top of the pistil
stipule—a small leaflike appendage at the base of a leaf stalk
style—the slender upper stalk of the pistil that bears the stigma
succulent—fleshy, juicy

tuber—a short, thickened underground stem having buds or eyes

umbel—a flattened flower cluster with the flower stalks radiating
    from the same point
united—joined together

verticil—a whorl
viscid—sticky

whorl— (leaf) radiating from the same level on the stem
wing—a thin expansion extending along a stem; also the midportion
    of a pealike flower

Suggested Reading

Courtney, B., and Zimmerman, J. H. *Wild Flowers and Weeds.* New York: Van Nostrand Reinhold Company, 1972.

Fernald, M. L. *Gray's Manual of Botany,* 8th ed. New York: American Book Company, 1950.

Gleason, H. A. *New Britton and Brown, Illustrated Flora of the Northeastern United States and Adjacent Canada,* 3 vols. New York: New York Botanical Garden, 1952.

Lawrence, George H. *Taxonomy of Vascular Plants.* New York: Macmillan, 1951.

Peterson, R. T., and McKenny, M. A. *A Field Guide to Wildflowers of the Northeastern and North-Central North America.* Boston: Houghton Mifflin Company, 1968.

Rickett, Harold W. *The New Field Book of American Wild Flowers.* New York: G. P. Putnam's Sons, 1963.

Rickett, Harold W. *Wild Flowers of the United States,* Vol. I, parts 1 & 2 (1966); Vol. II, parts 1 & 2 (1967). New York: McGraw-Hill Book Company.

Stupka, Arthur, and Eastern National Park & Monument Association. *Wildflowers in Color.* New York: Harper & Row, 1965.

Taylor, N., rev. ed. of F. S. Mathew's *Field Book of American Wild Flowers.* New York: G. P. Putnam's Sons, 1955.

Index

NEW: Page numbers in boldface refer to illustrations.

Index